How It Worked

How It Worked

**The Story of Clarence H. Snyder and the
Early Days of Alcoholics Anonymous
In Cleveland, Ohio**

Second Edition

by
Mitchell K.

Contents

Foreword

by William L. White

Interest in the history of Alcoholics Anonymous (A.A.) has grown exponentially since the 1979 publication of Ernest Kurtz's *Not-God: A History of Alcoholics Anonymous*. Such interest has been expressed through the formation of the AA History Lovers, innumerable academic conferences and papers on the history of A.A. and through the growing number of biographies on key figures within the early history of A.A. A notable contribution within these new resources is Mitchell K.'s *How It Worked: The Story of Clarence H. Snyder and the Early Days of Alcoholics Anonymous in Cleveland, Ohio*, first published in 1999. It is with deep pleasure that I welcome readers to this new edition of *How It Worked*.

Much of the attention paid to the early A.A. history has focused on A.A's two co-founders and the critical milestones in A.A. history that unfolded in Akron and New York City. Mitchell K retells the A.A. story through a Cleveland lens and through the personal biography of Clarence Snyder, a central figure in the history of A.A.

How It Worked will find appreciative readers among A.A. members and others interested in the history of A.A. and the broader arena of addiction recovery in the United States. With all that has been written on A.A. in recent decades from a distanced vantage point, it is good to have an insider's fresh account of A.A.'s early years and its coming of age.

When future texts are written on the history of A.A., *How It Worked* will provide important details not previously available to historians, but this book's greatest contribution will remain the engaging story of how one of A.A.'s most enigmatic characters found and maintained his sobriety within Alcoholics Anonymous and through that experience helped create a fellowship whose reach now encircles the globe.

William White
Author, *Slaying the Dragon: The History of Addiction Treatment and Recovery in America*
Punta Gorda, Florida   August 28, 2013

Foreword to First Edition

by Ernest Kurtz

Despite currently dominant academic fads, history really exists and we can find truth in its study. Where the self-styled "post-moderns" have it right is that the last word is never in. Our finite human minds are incapable of embracing "the whole truth." But we can get closer, we can know more, we can enrich our understanding of any reality, including historical reality.

Mitchell K., when some years ago he shared with me his treasure of mementoes and materials from Clarence Snyder, urged that I also write another book on the history of Alcoholics Anonymous, updating *Not-God* in light of recent discoveries. I declined, then and now, for it is up to another generation to produce the focused works that may lead another historian eventually to attempt a comprehensive new history of Alcoholics Anonymous, one incorporating the research of Mary Darrah, Robert Fitzgerald, Kathi Flynn, Mel B., Bill White, Maria Swora, and—in a prominent place—Mitchell K.

In this biographical study of Clarence Snyder and especially his role in and understandings of early Alcoholics Anonymous, Mitchell gives us both facts and interpretations—Clarence's, those of contemporaries and commentators, and of course his own. Some readers, both Mitchell and I hope, will be led by his work to check out some of those facts, in which process they may turn up still more information that will enrich us all.

Others will disagree with some of the interpretations—I know that I do. But that disagreement is a salutary invitation to think about the lifesaving and life-enhancing program and fellowship of Alcoholics Anonymous, which may be one of the best uses of our time available.

Mitchell K. has given us a gift very much like himself: a gem with some rough edges that can challenge our ability to evaluate, but a truly rich jewel well worth our notice and contemplation. This book will not get anyone either drunk or sober, but it will aid the progress toward sobriety of those fortunate enough to be on that wondrous journey.

Whatever leads us towards truth leads us towards its Author.

Ernie Kurtz
Ann Arbor, Michigan
February 22, 1998

Preface to the Second Edition

by the Author

Over three decades have gone by since Clarence went home to be with his God. It's been almost two decades since the first volume of this book began going to press and much has changed in both AA and in me.

I've become a grandfather to two boys and two girls, done a lot of traveling and been with my mother when she passed on at almost 99 years of age. My spiritual realities over the years have evolved, devolved and spun themselves around many times, always making every effort to improve my conscious contact with God. Things have been revealed to me during my quiet times throughout the day which have revolutionized my thinking and which have added more questions and seeking, leading me in different directions.

I've also begun to come to terms with my own mortality. Having experienced what I now call a "Control, Alt, Delete" moment (Mini stroke), and other deteriorating health issues, I look at each day in a different light. I see a need to record my memories so that maybe one day when they are gone and wiped clean, at least someone can remember them.

God will always be God to me. God is all things and can do anything God wants to do. My job is to be of maximum service to God and to my fellow inhabitants of this planet. I often fall short of that goal and then, there are those times when I am right on the mark and I can almost hear God chuckling and saying "See, I knew you could do it."

I have to remember those quiet times and what it says in Psalms 46:10—"Be still and know I AM God." Just as I look at AA's Basic Text as a guide to living, I also look at many religious and spiritual works as guides to spiritual living. I don't really believe that God subscribes to any particular sect or denomination. I do believe that the "hand" of God took part in the writing of all those guides.

Over the years, I have been led through guidance to search out the answers to some troubling and vexing thoughts. Certain inconsistencies had cropped up when I was writing the first edition of this work which didn't concern me as much as they did in later years.

The biggest of these was the differences between what Clarence shared with me and how he imparted AA's design for living in the early days, as compared to what he said during the latter part of his life. Since my original writing I revisited many recorded talks made by Clarence spanning several decades. What I found troubling was the differences I heard in how he presented things and his primary focus before 1971 and after 1971.

The man I knew as my sponsor loved Alcoholics Anonymous and looked at recovery through the design for living in AA's Basic Text as the way to get well. True, he believed in God and in Jesus all throughout his life in recovery but the man I knew always said our lives get saved in AA and not in a church. The retreats he and I put on in New York and those I attended with him in Florida had Alcoholics Anonymous as their primary focus. He took people through their steps individually and stressed to me, that after I had done the work with him, in the case of those who asked at the retreat to be taken through the steps, it would be done by me and those who came after me.

There was none of this wholesale group exercises or mixing religion, prayer and praise during the retreat. Clarence would announce that the so-called prayer and praise portion would take place after the official AA portion of the retreat had ended. After all, these were events geared to talk about and experience AA as Clarence had lived it in the early days and to experience what the 12 Steps meant to many of AA's early founding members.

Who Clarence was, what he said and what he stood for, and what he helped accomplish in Alcoholics Anonymous before 1971 was the person who had what I wanted. That story was the one he asked me to share in his biography and history of early AA in Cleveland. The influences that changed that early presentation and focus after

1971 were not what attracted me to Clarence, and was not the type of recovery I was seeking.

There are many people over recent years who have attacked Clarence and what they thought he stood for. I believe those resentments and attacks represent the Clarence after 1971 and those who continue to attack him are practicing what William Paley wrote those many years ago about "Contempt prior to investigation."

I miss the man and the sponsor I knew. I miss his chuckle and the sparkle in his eyes. I miss him reminding me that my focus in AA was always to be Alcoholics Anonymous and that religion and religious practices had no part of AA.

My prayer is that Alcoholics Anonymous never become relegated to the status of a footnote in some history book like the Oxford Group, the Washingtonians and all those movements which had preceded it. It won't be if AA members remember where we came from and remember that money, property, power and prestige will (and has) diverted AA from its primary purpose.

I remember where we came from and I pray that this small volume will keep that memory alive in some members who read it, so that the hand of AA will forever be there whenever anyone, anywhere reaches out for help. The reason I wrote this book was to fulfill a promise I made to my sponsor and to fulfill a pledge I believe in, which ends with the words "And For That, I Am Responsible."

Mitchell K. (August 2017)

"For we know when a nation goes down and never comes back, when a society or a civilization perishes, one condition may always be found. They forgot where they came from. They lost sight of what brought them along."

Carl Sandburg, *REMEMBRANCE ROCK* p. 19

Preface to the First Edition

by the Author

I staggered into the rooms of Alcoholics Anonymous on the evening of May 14, 1975 a broken man. I had been drinking on a daily basis.

I shook, I stank and I weighed almost 300 pounds. The little blue and silver sign with the Circle and Triangle drew me into that church as if it were a magnet.

Thus began my journey into the world of recovery. At 28 years old it appeared that I was the youngest person in the room. I sat down and was immediately surrounded by a couple of older gentlemen who placed their arms around me and held me throughout the meeting. I am not sure about what was said at the podium that night, but I remember the conversations after the meeting had closed.

They told me all I needed to do was "Don't Drink and Go To Meetings."

Each and every time I said, "BUT," they told me the only "but" I had was the one I sat on. They told me to make 90 meetings in 90 days, get a sponsor and that it will get better.

My sobriety date became May 15, 1975, the first full day without a drink. I followed directions, didn't drink, and went to meetings, got a sponsor who listened to my tales of woe and went to more meetings.

I was no longer drinking but nothing else in my life changed.

Life was still unmanageable for me; I still exhibited almost all the same behaviors as in the past, only this time without the benefit of beverage alcohol. I continued to lie, cheat, steal, lose my temper and worst of all, be unfaithful to my wife. The very same wife who had stood by me throughout my drinking the six years we had been married.

Most of that behavior continued until one evening in 1980. I was attending my then home group, a young people's meeting, when the walls came crashing in. The speaker that evening began his talk by stating: "I had a bad day at work, came home, slammed the door, yelled at the kids, kicked the dog and almost hit the wife." He continued with, "But I didn't take a drink!"

Everyone in the small room clapped and told him he was a winner.

"Just don't drink, no matter what." Tears rolled down my cheeks, he was describing my life and everyone affirmed the insanity of it as long as I didn't drink. There HAD to be more to recovery than that. If all I had to do was not drink and it would get better, why then was my whole life falling apart? I then decided that there were only three choices left: drink, die or find a better way. I wanted to drink every day. I didn't want to die and I knew of no other way to get better.

I picked up a copy of *Alcoholics Anonymous*, the Big Book, and began to read it.

I discovered the better way within the pages of A.A.'s Basic Text. I read about a program of recovery, much different from the one I had and different from the one I was hearing at the meetings. I wanted what those hundred men and women who had recovered from a seemingly hopeless state of mind and body had discovered. I wanted to be happy, joyous and free!

I then set out upon a spiritual search, reading everything I could on spirituality and religion. I spoke with long-term members of A.A. and members of the clergy from various religions and denominations; no one had the answer I was seeking.

At that time I was a member of A.A.'s Loners Program, meetings by mail. I was corresponding with a long-term member in Elyria, Ohio who was helping me to understand the history of A.A. and what it was that worked so many wonders for the original members. He told me that there was only one surviving member of the original 100 men and women. Roger gave me his address and suggested if I wanted to "get it from the horse's mouth," that I should write to this man.

I went one step further, I called this man and immediately knew, from the timbre of his voice and the serenity I felt over the phone that I wanted what he had. That man was Clarence H. Snyder, the Home Brewmeister of the Big Book.

Clarence and I spoke on the phone and corresponded throughout that year. I had not asked him to be my sponsor as yet but knew I was going to. How could he be my sponsor? He was living in the State of Florida and I was in New York. I arranged for him and his wife to come to New York to lead a spiritual retreat.

Upon his arrival in New York I immediately knew that this was going to be a turning point in my life. I wanted what he had and during the retreat, asked him to be my sponsor. He did not immediately accept my request. In fact, it took several requests before he felt I was ready.

That weekend, Clarence took me through the Steps, just as he had taken hundreds, if not thousands of others before me. He instructed me and introduced me into the program of Alcoholics Anonymous just as his sponsor, Dr. Bob, had done back in 1938. When I got up off of my knees in that hotel room on April 4, 1981, I was a new man.

The old had been washed away and I had been reborn. In 1983, Clarence asked me if I would write his biography and the history of A.A. in Cleveland, Ohio. The book *Dr. Bob and the Good Oldtimers* had been out for three years but Clarence felt that there was more to the story that needed to be told. He instructed me as to how he wanted the book to be written. He wanted a book that could be read by the average A.A. member, not a tedious scholarly work.

He wanted to impart the flavor of the Big Book. He told me that this was to be a book written about an A.A. member, for A.A. members.

He told me never to apologize for God, the personal God we both had shared together—the God he had introduced me to that evening at the retreat. The God Dr. Bob had introduced him to that day in February 1938 in Akron City Hospital.

Clarence reminded me, and told me never to forget, that I was saved not in a church, but in Alcoholics Anonymous and never to mix the two together. He told me that my ministry was to "fix rummies." I was told that if a rummy wanted what I had, I was to tell them about, and introduce them to, that Power greater than myself.

The same Power Dr. Bob had introduced him to. The same Great Physician, Dr. Silkworth had told those alcoholics who were declared hopeless could "cure" them. That Power, that Great Physician, was the Christ—Jesus.

Clarence told me that if someone wanted what I had, I could only give away what I had. He told me that I should never force Jesus down someone's throat and that if they wanted Him, they would have to come willingly of their own accord. He told me that this was to be a book about Alcoholics Anonymous.

I was asked by my sponsor to write this book as a testimony to the hundreds of "founders" of Alcoholics Anonymous. I was told that if the readers of this book wanted the program of recovery that those early members had, they would come willingly, of their own accord.

I promised my sponsor that I would write this book.

I wrote this book not as an author, but as a drunk who made his sponsor a promise to allow the Fellowship of Alcoholics Anonymous the opportunity to understand what it was like during the early years of A.A., the struggles and the triumphs. To give the reader a better understanding of:

HOW IT WORKED

Mitchell K. (1999 edition)

Acknowledgments

To my parents, Frances and Louis, thank you both for everything.

Both of you are no longer with us, you will live forever in my thoughts. To my children, Marissa and Micah, I love you both with all my heart. May you never have to go through what I went through until I finally got the message of recovery in 1975. To the late Ernest Kurtz, Ph.D., for all your help and guidance as "mentor" on this journey into the world of writing. To William L. White for your friendship, assistance and your contributions to our knowledge of the history of recovery. To Carol Anstey who did most of the typing from my original scribbling and notes, tape transcripts and without whose help, this book may not have happened. I lost track of Carol for many years and once again, God placed her in my path to make sure the thanks she deserves gets recognized. Thank you again Carol.

To Bill H., without whose patience and technical help, this updated 2nd Edition would not have been possible. To "Shakey Mike" and Anne Marie G., whose love, support, help and showing me to "get the message" that a new edition should come out was of utmost importance. Their part of this project made it all possible. Mike calls me his sponsor but more often than not, who is sponsoring who?

Thank you to Les and Jess who love my children and a super special thanks to Lila Bea, Noah Louis, Carter Leslie and Reagan Madeline, four of the most beautiful and intelligent grandchildren in the entire universe. (Of course, I'm not in the least prejudiced).

To Roger Wetz who introduced me to Clarence, that debt cannot ever be repaid.

To the dozens of other "special" people I have met as I "trudged the road," and who have helped me along the way. Some are "civilians," and some are members of A.A. You are all my friends. It would take another book to thank you all and if I have left anyone out please forgive me.

Edward R. A., Liz B., Alan Beder, Charlie Bishop, Jr., Earl H., Kevin Hanlon, Marjorie H., Matthew M., Frank Mauser, Merton M.

III, Bill Pittman, Royal F. Shepard, Jr., Grace Snyder (Clarence's widow went home to be with her beloved Clarence on March 9,1998), Joan Soveroski, Harry "The Wino" V., Al W., Bill White, Lois Wilson, Sue Smith Windows and Nell Wing.

A further debt of gratitude is owed to all of the archivists, historians, researchers, collectors and members of the Fellowship of Alcoholics Anonymous who hold A.A.'s history dear to their hearts. No acknowledgement would be complete without mentioning some of the other "friends" and "founders" of Alcoholics Anonymous: Frank N.D. Buchman, Ruth Hock, Henry G. Parkhurst, Henrietta Seiberling, Samuel M. Shoemaker, Dr. William D. Silkworth, Dr. Robert Holbrook Smith, T. Henry and Clarace Williams and William G. Wilson.

Unless otherwise noted, quotes by Clarence H. Snyder were taken from a series of interviews conducted by the author with Clarence in Casselberry, Florida, and New York between April 1982 through February 1984. Other quotes by Clarence H. Snyder are taken from archival documents, audio and/or video recorded talks or transcripts of aforementioned talks made by Clarence H. Snyder from 1962-1983.

Other quotes attributed to Clarence H. Snyder are likewise noted as such.

Any quotes by Lois W. were taken from audio taped interviews conducted by the author at her home in Bedford Hills, New York on August 21, 1988. Any quotes by Nell Wing (non-alcoholic) who was Bill W.'s secretary from 1947 until his death in 1971 and A.A.'s first Archivist were taken from a series of taped and telephone interviews conducted from 1988-1992 at her home in New York City or in the A.A. Archives Office in New York City. Quotes by Sue Smith-Windows (Dr. Bob's daughter) were taken from an interview conducted in October 1988 at her home in Akron, Ohio. Any quotes by Mary C. Darrah were taken from conversations either on the telephone or in person in Ohio, West Virginia, or Providence, Rhode Island. Other quotes were taken from various audio taped talks and/or transcripts of talks by long-term A.A. members or from original archival materials given to the author by Clarence H. Snyder or as noted below.

The author is indebted to the following archival repositories for their assistance and for allowing him to view archival materials relating to the history of Alcoholics Anonymous:

> The Archives at the New York A.A. World Services Office
> The Archives at the Stepping Stones Foundation in Bedford Hills, N.Y.
> The Rockefeller Archives in Tarrytown, N.Y.
> The Archives at the Cleveland, Ohio A.A. Central Service Office
> The Chester H. Kirk Collection on Alcoholism and Alcoholics Anonymous housed at the Brown University Center for Alcoholism and Addiction Studies in Providence, Rhode Island
> The Providence Rhode Island Historical Society
> A.A. Archival repositories located in Arizona, Arkansas, Ohio, Oklahoma and West Virginia
> Private collections of A.A. memorabilia owned by several A.A. members throughout the United States and Canada

This book is dedicated to God* who reigns over us all and to the thousands of alcoholics who have recovered, and will recover through mercy, grace and doing the work necessary to achieve and maintain that recovery. (*As each of us understand a Power greater than ourselves)

Chapter 1

I Was Born At A Very Early Age

"An individual becomes an alcoholic for three main reasons:

1. As a result of inheritance. He possesses a nervous system which is non-resistant to alcohol. (In no sense is a direct craving transmitted from parent to offspring.)

2. By reason of his early environment. Through the ignorance of his parents or from their own nervous constitution, the alcoholic was either spoiled or neglected. He was not brought up to face the world courageously. He is lacking in self-reliance, no matter how physically brave he may be or how bold he may appear on the surface. Psychologically, he is unable to stand on his own two feet. As a result of this, he unconsciously craves a stimulant-narcotic.

3. Because of the effects of his later environment. That is to say, school, college, economic and social competition, marriage, and, for one generation at least, the World War."

—from Richard R. Peabody,
The Common Sense of Drinking[1]

Cleveland, Ohio, December 26, 1902

It was a cold, gray, winter morning. The forecast had called for snow with brisk west to southwest winds. Christmas had just passed Clarence's parents without much incident. The Salvation Army had just had their annual Christmas dinner at the Grays Armory the day earlier.

Grays Armory

More than 2,500 of the city's homeless and destitute were fed what may have been their only hot meal in weeks. The morning paper said there were "Pathetic Scenes Witnessed About Big Tables." The *Cleveland Plain Dealer* was full of articles concerning suicides, hangings, and deaths. Page one told of a saloon fight that ended when the proprietor had shot a man to restore order in his establishment. Page Five spoke of "forty cripples at a dance."

Clarence's Parents

Jenny Patterson Snyder, who had been born in St. Clairsville, Ohio, took much pleasure in reading and hearing about other people's misfortunes.

On this particular day she had plenty to read about as she awaited the birth of her first daughter. Charles Henry and Jenny Snyder had already been blessed with two fine boys—Richard Harvey and Charles William. Jenny was a determined woman. She had made up her mind to have a girl this time. When she made up her mind that something was going to be done, it had better be done, and her way—or else!

As was the custom in those days, much time and money was being spent getting the layette in readiness for the soon-to-be coming arrival. About six weeks prior to this particular day, Jenny had fallen down some stairs in her home and had broken her leg. The fall left her bedridden and in a cumbersome plaster cast.

She was left with plenty of time left on her hands. With those hands she had knitted pink booties, pink dresses, pink hats … everything was a beautiful shade of pink. All to be presented upon the arrival of her new baby daughter.

Clarence on bottom step, parents in background

The doctor was hurriedly summoned to 64 Breck Avenue (later

called 1280 East 89th Street in Cleveland), the house that Charles had built only a few years earlier. Charles had been born in an old farm house on Route 113 in Amherst Township, four miles west of Elyria, Ohio. He had come from a large family. He had three brothers and four sisters. A couple of years earlier, Charles' parents had celebrated their sixty-first wedding anniversary which was written up in the society column of the local Elyria newspaper. It appeared that "Mr. and Mrs. Conrad Snyder of South Ridge" really did it up big. Five of their eight children were there with their spouses. Also present were sixteen grandchildren and five great grandchildren. The Newspaper article said, "The table where a seven course dinner was served was beautifully decorated with carnations and ferns. Several musical numbers were rendered. "When Jenny gave birth at the Breck Avenue house, it wasn't too difficult a birth. But when the doctor congratulated the proud parents upon the birth of yet another son, the matter was of great concern to Jenny. As Clarence later stated, "I don't think that she ever forgave me for that. She never fully recovered." It was on this note that Clarence Henry Snyder was born, the day after Christmas, in the year 1902.

He was the ugly duckling, the scapegoat, the black sheep of the

family for the rest of his time at home. His mother had sustained massive disappointment when he was born. He was, however, very close with his brother Richard, who was one and a half years older than Clarence. Clarence and Richard, whom everyone called Dick, were so inseparable that later on, as they were growing up, if someone picked a fight with one

brother, they had to contend with the other. The two brothers were a formidable duo. Since they belonged to one of the families of German descent in an all Irish
neighborhood, the brothers stuck up for each other quite often.

Clarence in the middle

Just before Clarence's second birthday, his mother had left him downstairs in front of the Christmas tree as she went about her daily household chores in the upstairs bedrooms. While she cleaned, she would walk over to the top of the staircase and call down to Clarence to see if he was okay and out of trouble. The two older boys had gone out shopping with their father, leaving Clarence and his mother at home as they shopped for their Christmas dinner.

Each time Jenny called out to him, Clarence would laugh and call out to her in baby talk, "boken, boken." This routine went on for quite some time until Jenny had finished with her cleaning and started back down the stairs to the living room to join her son. When she had reached the bottom steps, she abruptly stopped.

Her mouth dropped open, and she released whatever she was holding in her hands. The load cascaded down the steps with a loud crash, startling Clarence. She appeared to him as if she were frozen, unable to speak or even move. One of the older boys had received as a Christmas gift, a tool box, complete with tools. Clarence had somehow figured out not only how to unwrap this gift, but how to open it as well. He had taken a hammer out of the box and proceeded to demolish every Christmas ornament within his reach. He did this with a glee and purpose that only a two year old could possess.

There was chaos and debris all over the living room. Bits of colored glass, unrecognizable pieces of wood. Many had been parts of family heirlooms. Most of the broken items were irreplaceable, having been passed on from generation to generation. Then, in a blind rage, his mother flew down the stairs, wrenched the hammer from his little hands and, as Clarence recalled with a laugh, "I guess I got boken for that also."

Clarence's mother had a hairbrush, which consisted of a stone back piece which was covered with carvings of images of little fish. Clarence recalled "I had imprints of fish all over my bottom and every place else that she whaled me with that thing. I can still remember that hairbrush. It's etched into my memory like the fish were etched onto my body." Clarence said that much later, when he grew older, "I stole that damn thing and threw it away. It was a means of torture."

Clarence's father was self-employed in the carnival and park entertainment field. He ran concessions and rides at Luna Park in Cleveland. Clarence and his brothers were never at a loss for a place to go for fun and entertainment. Best of all, as Clarence remembered, they never had to pay either an entrance fee to the park or for any of the rides.

Luna Park operated as an amusement

park from 1905 to 1929

Clarence attended a local kindergarten and first grade. For some unknown reason ("I still can't remember why," he related) he skipped the second grade and went directly into the third. He got along with everyone in the school. He made many childhood friends and ran around after school with his brothers playing popular games of the day.

With his extremely bright and logical mind, Clarence did well with all of his studies and in all classroom activities. He was an outgoing, happy, and well adjusted child. Until something happened

that changed his whole school career and life around. Something so devastating to him that it had a profound effect upon the rest of his childhood, adolescent years, and well into young manhood.

Clarence at age 10

The event occurred in September of 1913. Clarence was in the fifth grade. His favorite brother, Dick, contracted a childhood disease, the nature of which Clarence didn't remember. This particular childhood disease, occurring in an era of inadequate medical care and knowledge, proved fatal. Clarence fell apart. He was devastated and fell into a tailspin of depression.

He and his inseparable brother were, by a cruel twist of fate, separated. They were separated forever. The funeral on November 3, 1913, was a day of disaster for Clarence. He did not want to attend it. He cried. He screamed. He was depressed, and he refused to say good-bye to the only person in the world with whom he had felt the most comfortable and best. In one month Clarence would be eleven years old. A time that was supposed to be special in his young life. His brother, his friend, and his confidant would not be there to celebrate or share it with him. He felt that life was almost not even worth living.

Clarence in front row, center

His studies went downhill in a rapid and steady spiral. He became withdrawn, extremely depressed, and lost most of his former self-image and confidence. A confidence that had been so often bolstered by the closeness and friendship of his older brother.

Clarence's father tried to comfort and help guide him through this trying time in his young life. But his mother had not overcome her disappointment at Clarence's not being a daughter. Her not yet being resolved over the death of her son Dick made things worse. Jenny was not supportive at all. She was lost in her own grief and, as ever, distant towards her unwanted son, Clarence.

The two brothers, Clarence on the left

As fate would have it, a couple of years after Dick's death, Clarence's father was called to go with his concessions. He traveled constantly around the country. After that, the only contact that Clarence had with his father was by mail.

In a letter dated June 17, 1915, and postmarked from Lansing, Michigan, Clarence's father described what was going on, and spoke of the new additions to the amusement park: "We have a lot of shows, an Eli Ferris Wheel, and a 3 abreast merry-go-round."

He also wrote, complaining of something amusement parks always dreaded: "We also have plenty of bad weather. We could not show Monday night here on account of rain, and is raining here now, and don't think we can show tonight." He continued to write in the letter that he expected to be in Flint, Michigan the following week.

He wrote Clarence: "... Tell your Ma, that I do not want any laundry sent me till next week." Included with the letter to Clarence was a book of passes to the *Aikes Amusement Co*. This little booklet had been issued by Chas. H. Snyder and signed over to "Clarence & Strand Theatre." The rides that were listed inside carried such names as, "Carry-us-all," "Fifteen-in-one," "Motordome" and "Musical Comedy."

In another letter, this one dated Saturday, September 14, 1918, 4:00 PM, and postmarked Weston, West Virginia, Clarence's father chastised him for not writing. He wrote, "I sure expected a letter in

Clarksburg, but got none. If you want to make a good business man of yourself, you must answer letters promptly."

His father always stressed that Clarence should be a good business person and always be the best at whatever he did in life. In

another letter dated September 9, 1918, and postmarked Wheeling, West Virginia, Clarence's father wrote, giving Clarence business directions.

The letter started off, "Well Hello, Mgr. Clarence." It continued, "You can give Ma $26.50, and pay the charges on the canvas and the small register when it comes."

Clarence's father

At the age of sixteen Clarence was managing his father's concessions at Luna Park. This was a formidable responsibility for one so young. His father wrote on the back of the envelope that along with managing the business, Clarence should "pay good attention to school." His father, being a consummate business person, always signed his letters to Clarence, "C.H. Snyder" or, "C.H.S." He never concluded his correspondence with "Your father," or even, "Dad."

There was never any love either expressed or implied, only business and a request for a "report of what you done etc." But Clarence acquired a drive for pleasing his father and being a "good business man" which lasted throughout his life in all of his dealings. Despite his later drinking, Clarence always drove himself towards perfection in business, a perfection that his father had always demanded of him.

Eventually, even in recovery, perfection permeated Clarence's thoughts and actions. Clarence had very little tolerance for failure, in himself and in others.

The Cleveland school system had at that time instituted "Junior High School." Clarence however after graduating from public school by the "skin of my teeth," went directly from eighth grade into High School. He hadn't had the opportunity or advantage of taking preparatory courses in advanced math or English. Nor had he been able to learn at the pace of his peers in school. When he did transfer over to Cleveland's East Side High School, he felt not only at a loss, but very much out of place. He felt as if he didn't belong there. His self image and confidence had not yet fully recovered enough for him to inform his teachers that he had not gone through Junior High School, had not taken any preparatory courses and felt that he couldn't keep up with any of the other students in his classes. All this seemed overwhelming to Clarence at the time, and he began to withdraw even further into his own little world. Withdraw so that he could at least begin to feel a little bit comfortable with life itself, no less with school or with those around him.

This withdrawal was interpreted by his teachers as a sign of ignorance. Some took it as rebellion. Many branded him and ridiculed him as a "first class dummy." Some teachers placed a chair in front of the classroom in a conspicuous position and demanded that Clarence sit there. This was done to show other students the results of being rebellious, and it set Clarence up to ridicule. He related, "I wasn't any great shakes of a student in High School, so I failed almost all of my classes." After three years as a freshman, another devastating event began to develop which, once again, had a profound impact and altered the course of Clarence's young life.

He was about seventeen years old when his father contracted tuberculosis. This forced his father to quit his traveling and remain at home, something that, for a long time, Clarence had secretly been wishing for. However, not in this way, and not with the fatal results.

Once more in Clarence's life, due to the lack of knowledge by the medical profession, Clarence watched his father suffer, just as he had done years earlier with his brother. He watched for many months as his father's health declined. He watched until his father eventually succumbed.

When his father did pass on, Clarence was afforded the opportunity to quit school and venture out into the world of full time employment. Clarence saw no promising future in continuing on with his education. With the urgent and overwhelming need to support himself and help with the family expenses, he decided to leave school. He dropped out and started on his journey into the world of life and adulthood—a journey that fate had assigned to him, not one of his own making or choosing.

Looking back, Clarence remembered that one of the most important events in his High School days was his meeting a young woman and embarking on his first real romance. Clarence was no stranger to the members of the opposite sex. Years later, he remarked, "For some unknown reason I always took a liking to the girls."

He remembered that once, when he was about five years old, he had "eloped" with the little girl from across the street. Clarence and his brothers, Charles and Dick, were going to Luna Park one Sunday evening to go on the rides and play the games at the concessions which their father ran.

In accordance with his mother's custom on Sundays, Clarence was all dressed up in white: a white peanut hat, knee socks, knickers, shirt, and patent leather shoes. On Sundays, he was allowed out in the morning to play in his regular clothing, but by the afternoon he had to return home to bathe and get dressed up in his all white outfit. Then was ordered by his mother to stay spotless and clean until it was time for him to retire to bed for the night. "God forbid that I got one spot on my uniform of the day," he remembered. If this happened he would have to answer to his mother and her stone-backed hair brush, and he dreaded that.

Clarence remembered that on this one particular evening, Florence Drew, his sweetheart from across the street, was going along with the Snyder family to Luna Park. Florence was the daughter of the family butcher. The Drews were long time friends of the Snyders.

After Florence Drew and the Snyders had arrived at the park, gone on some of the rides, played games at the concessions, and eaten lots of cotton candy, Clarence and Florence had disappeared. They vanished from both parental and sibling supervision. They had strolled over to Rockefeller Park to play with a "cute little dog." Until well after dark, they played with and "tormented" this dog, oblivious to the passage of time. Then, they realized it was late and began to make what must have seemed to them the long and scary trek homeward, home being many blocks away.

By this time Clarence's parents had sent out search parties. Florence's parents had called the police. Both sets of parents had scoured the neighborhood and park. All to no avail. Both families were fraught with terror, fearing the fate that their respective children might have suffered.

They were also very angry and discussed among themselves the fate that their wayward children would suffer if and when they finally did arrive home.

Clarence's white, spotless Sunday outfit had been through the sand and dirt of the park. It was covered with muddy little paw prints and it was, of course, no longer white and spotless.

Clarence managed to find his way home and walked Florence to just outside of her door. However, out of fear for himself, he ran away before Florence knocked. He himself stayed out even later, knowing the state of disarray that his clothing was in, a state that he said, "was no means in comparison to the mess my mother made of me when I got home." Florence got her spanking from her parents across the street, but it was nowhere like near the beating Clarence suffered that night. The beating was administered by his mother with her stone-backed hair brush—that same brush that, once again, as it had so many times before, and had so many times after, etched its impressions of little fish all over Clarence's body.

Clarence was not at all unfamiliar with work. When he was five, he had a paper route. A few years later, he delivered orders for a local butcher shop—not the one owned by Florence's parents—on his bicycle (a bicycle that he had purchased with his own money). Clarence was very industrious and continuously looked for ways to earn money.

Always looking for an angle, he was willing to try anything. He even worked for a period of time as an usher at the Metropolitan Theatre in downtown Cleveland. This was in the days of the five and ten cent movies: cliffhangers and daily newsreels. Clarence recalled that "the Metropolitan was a high-class joint. They had the nerve to charge thirty cents when everybody else was charging a nickel." He had gotten his friend a job there and they both worked for Bill Friedman, the manager at the theater. On many occasions they would sneak their girlfriends in for nothing and then would "schmooze" in the box seats after everyone was seated and the movie had started.

Being industrious, Clarence found out that the Board of Education was paying twenty cents an hour for tutors. Clarence got a job reading school work to a blind boy named Larry. Much of what Clarence had missed in High School, he later learned through this job. He also began taking violin lessons, paying for them with some of the money he had earned on his various and sundry jobs. Clarence became very close to Larry and his family, and they all remained close for many years to come.

Clarence enjoyed driving cars and did so at every available opportunity. Larry's family would let Clarence drive them all over Cleveland and the surrounding areas and it was on one of those outings that another profound event occurred in Clarence's life which once and forever altered the course of his very existence. On this particular outing, Clarence had his first introduction to "*John Barleycorn*." It was at this first introduction that Clarence experienced his first of many, for-years-to-come, drunken episodes.

In his youth, Clarence was to have only three such episodes, but each ended with his getting both drunk and into trouble.

On this first occasion, Clarence had driven Larry's parents and Larry to their family reunion in Toledo, Ohio. There he was offered a drink. He didn't like the taste so much, but he did like the effect the drink was having upon him. He then proceeded to get quite drunk rather quickly on all the free-flowing booze that was made available. By the time that the party was over, Clarence was unable to find the car that they had arrived in, and was unable to negotiate the long drive back to Cleveland.

This did not at all please Larry's parents, nor Larry for that matter. From that day forward, they wouldn't let Clarence drive them around any longer. Despite the disastrous events of that day, they and Clarence remained close friends. Much later on, they were even able to laugh about it.

The second time that Clarence became involved with alcohol, it was again at a family reunion, this one in Alliance, Ohio. The parents of a young woman Clarence was dating offered to take him to their family reunion. This was as long as he did all the driving. They were a friendly and outgoing family. Clarence enjoyed the company not only of the young woman, but of her parents as well.

When the group arrived at this reunion, there was dancing, party games, home-cooked foods, friendly people, and much to Clarence's delight, plenty of homemade dandelion wine. In fact, an unlimited supply.

Clarence loved to dance and despite the disastrous effects that alcohol had caused him on the previous outing, he tasted the sweet wine. He recognized it seemed to make the dancing more enjoyable. The more he consumed, the faster he drank, and the more he liked the effect the liquor was having upon his personality. It made him feel more at ease, less self-conscious, and eventually invincible.

He became a totally different and, he felt, better person. So much so, that he made a play for his girlfriend's mother. The mother was flattered and enjoyed the attention being lavished upon her by this young man. However, the attentions didn't sit too well with the girlfriend, or with her irate father. Needless to say, the ride back to Cleveland was tense and very long. Clarence recalled, "I guess that episode contributed to the ending of that relationship real quick." Clarence chuckled as he related that story. He thought that many of the events of his past, despite some of the pathos, had their humorous side.

Ever since his young childhood, Clarence went to Sunday school—not because his parents were religious people—it was a way they kept him out of the house, occupied, and out of trouble. He said he never felt comfortable with any of the other children who attended this school with him. He stated he felt everyone looked at him as different. He himself felt inferior to, and different from them. He was sure that the way that his mother had treated him while he was growing up had a great deal to do with his distorted perceptions at Sunday school.

Clarence decided that since he wasn't a good student, the other children would still have to look at him differently if he could excel in something—anything. He felt he then wouldn't feel so different and so inferior.

He began to develop a strong and growing interest in sports. He was slow at first, but he began to excel. He rapidly acquired an expertise at the sports he did try, especially those he liked. At first, it was baseball. Then, as the seasons changed, he was on to master basketball. Later on, he got the opportunity to play semi-professional sports. That is until his professional career as full-time alcoholic interfered. Earlier, however, he used sports, and his obvious innate ability at them, to improve his flagging self-image and his low self-esteem.

He also sought to improve upon his dancing. He felt he was such a "natural dancer," that he took only two lessons at the Zimmermans' Dancing School. But he then decided he was wasting both his precious time and hard-earned money—money he felt could be better spent on women and other "fun" activities.

One early winter day, while practicing basketball for a YMCA Church league, Clarence noticed a very attractive young blond woman on the sidelines. She appeared to be watching him intently. Never one to miss an obvious opportunity, especially when it came to women, Clarence rushed over to the woman to inquire when he could go out with her on a date. He knew that if he could take her to a dance, he could impress her with his dancing abilities. He was sure he would then be on "home ground." He would feel comfortable and would very much be in charge of the situation. After only five minutes of conversation, the young woman told him that she lived on the south side of Cleveland and she would love to go to a dance with him.

Clarence picked her up to go to the dance and they took the streetcar. They talked all the way to the dance. Clarence charmed his way into her heart. Always the salesman, he sold himself to this new person.

The two had a lovely evening, dancing, talking, and holding each other tight as they whirled about the dance floor. All was lovely until it was time for Clarence to take the young lady home. Then it turned out to be an exceptional evening.

When they arrived at the girl's home, she invited Clarence in to spend some more time with her and to talk. In the ensuing conversation, Clarence discovered she was a preacher's daughter and that she had a genuine interest in sports. This was wonderful. So Clarence had found out how much she loved to dance, that she loved sports, that she enjoyed being held close, and that she laughed at his jokes.

However, when she produced a gallon jug of wine from the cellar, he decided he had found a match made in heaven. Both drank until way after midnight, finishing off the entire jug. Unfortunately for Clarence, the relationship had to end.

In fact, it ended before it really had a chance to take blossom. The girl's father discovered them: both were extremely drunk, and all the father's wine was missing, wine he used in Holy Communion. The father was perturbed, to say the least, and asked Clarence to leave, never to darken the man's doorstep again and never to speak with his daughter.

The taste of alcohol wasn't as important to Clarence as how it made him feel inside. It produced in him a profound personality change that transformed him and made him no longer feel inferior. He no longer felt different. He had used sports to assert himself and to become an equal—equal to his peers and to others, often playing to the point of exhaustion. But he found that alcohol made him feel more than equal. And he readily asserted himself while under its influence, without the strenuous physical labor. He had discovered the easier softer way. This was the beginning of his descent into the spiraling abyss of active alcoholism.

It was at another dance—this one in the month of January—that he met someone who was to become very special in his life. Her name was Dorothy. Clarence swept her off of her feet and danced his way into her heart, and she into his. Clarence married Dorothy on April 1, 1926.

Clarence had always been reluctant to discuss his first two marriages. This writer continues to search out pertinent information relating to the marriages and related events. However, with this, his first marriage—the marriage to Dorothy—does our saga begin.

Chapter 2

What We Used to Be Like

"Our stories disclose in a general way **WHAT WE USED TO BE LIKE**..."

—from the Big Book of *Alcoholics Anonymous*

"Who hath woe? Who hath sorrow? Who hath contentions? Who hath babbling? Who hath wounds without cause? Who hath redness of eyes? They that tarry long at the wine; they that go seek mixed wine. Look not then upon the wine when it is red, when it giveth his colour in the cup, when it moveth itself aright. At the last it biteth like a serpent, and stingeth like an adder. Thine eyes shall behold strange women, and thine heart shall utter perverse things. Yea thou shalt be as he that liveth down in the midst of the sea, or as he that liveth

upon the top of a mast. They have stricken me, shalt thou say and I was not sick; they have beaten me, and I felt it not; When shall I awake? I will seek it yet again." [2]

—Proverbs 23:29-35

Clarence's marriage to Dorothy cannot be described as idyllic. Even though Clarence had swept her off of her feet, Dorothy, with her close family ties, had "swept" Clarence off on their honeymoon to her sister Virginia's house in the City of Yonkers, in Westchester County, New York.

Clarence's first wife Dorothy

Dorothy and her sisters were, to say the least, very close. Clarence complained that they did everything together. He said he didn't just marry Dorothy. He also had married her entire family. In spite of the fact he constantly complained about them, Clarence recognized that Dorothy and her family had been instrumental in his recovery, and Clarence was always grateful to Dorothy's "clan."

Clarence became and remained a periodic drunk for a number of years. He and Dorothy moved to 1552 Baltimore Road, in Lindhurst, Ohio, and began to settle down.

They had friends, mostly Dorothy's. They had a home. Clarence had a good job, working for the Mutual Loan and Guaranty Company in the Discount Department. What happened next seemed to be the next logical move. They decided that it was about time to start a family.

Dorothy became pregnant, and everyone concerned was overjoyed. The proud father-to-be strutted around, pontificating about his "common sense, sane, domestic life." He strutted around, that is, until Dorothy began complaining of problems associated with early pregnancy. His "sane, domestic life" started taking on a different, if not ominous, complexion. Dorothy stayed in bed for days on end. She changed her diet, her sleeping patterns, and her room. All to no avail. Dorothy's sanity was fading rapidly.

They consulted a local doctor who recommended the use of "Porter Ale." They tried this "cure," borrowing some of that ale from one of their neighbors, an amateur brewmeister. It worked! Clarence consulted with other local brewmeisters as to how he could go about manufacturing this "cure" himself. He bought a six-gallon crock, dozens of bottles, and various and sundry pipes, wires and other apparatus necessary for his construction of his home brewery. He began to put everything together and hoped his life would return to some semblance of sanity.

Sanity was, however, not the end result. He not only manufactured the beer for his wife, he also *drank* most of it for her as well. He recalled, admiringly, "I made some of the best ale that anyone ever had the pleasure to drink. After about two bottles of that stuff, you would go home and rob your own trunk."

Dorothy, remaining uncomfortable, continued to complain. Clarence increased his production capability. He went out and purchased a few ten-gallon crocks and cases of bottles. These, he felt, would surely return his life to sanity.

All of Dorothy's problems in early pregnancy, as well as her continuing complaining, eventually stopped. But the beer production, and the massive consumption of it, did not. They increased.

The excuses to continue drinking became more prevalent. Parties, card games and friends were constantly invited over for coffee and cake, but the events all became beer feasts. Soon Clarence ran out of excuses for drinking, and he just drank. He then discovered that "a little shot of liquor now and then between the beers had the tendency to put me in a wacky mood much quicker than having to down several quarts of beer to obtain the same results." So, now whiskey became the mainstay, and the beer just helped to wash it all down.

Clarence then became the primary topic of discussion in Dorothy's family gatherings. There was not much else to talk about concerning the pregnancy. Besides, Clarence's drinking was a much juicier topic.

Rather than listen to these "busybodies," Clarence began to frequent the local beer joints. This, he said, was "to quench my ever increasing thirst, and to complain to all who would listen, about my wife and her meddlesome family." Clarence's increased consumption did not help him to lose his resentments towards those who he perceived were trying to run his life. He did, however, manage to lose his job instead.

It was also about this time that Dorothy gave birth to their son, Charles Richard Snyder. The son was named not only after Clarence's father, but also for Clarence's brother, who had died as a child. Their son was rarely called by his first name, but rather, was referred to as "Dick," the name that everyone had used for Clarence's brother.

Clarence got another job, this one at the Morris Plan Bank in the Collection Department. The bank was closer to his home than the previous bank; and Clarence now felt he could spend more time with his wife and newborn son.

In actuality, however, he began spending more time patronizing the local saloons which dotted the streets on his route home. Four or five shots of whiskey, followed by a few beer chasers at one establishment, were but a beginning. If Dorothy happened to meet him at work, and walked him home, he only stopped at one or two bars, rather than the customary four or five. His lunches became the liquid variety, and the dinners (that he would invariably be late for), became non-existent, as Clarence lost his appetite for real food. Dorothy even came to give up cooking, other than for herself and for their son.

By this point Clarence had become a daily drunk. He appeared drunk at his initial interview at the Morris Plan Bank. He remained on that job for three and a half years, all the while in a state of constant intoxication.

Clarence remembered that the only reason he had gotten the Morris Plan job was because of the help of a close friend. This friend had worked with Clarence for seven years at Clarence's previous bank job and was now managing the Finance Department at Morris Plan. In addition to managing the Finance Department, the friend was also on the Board of Directors. Clarence related, "Joe knew that I was the best man for the job despite my being a drunk." Joe had also conveniently left out of his recommendation to the Morris Plan that hired Clarence, that Clarence had been terminated from his previous bank position for being drunk on the job on a consistent basis. Clarence figured the Morris Plan had never seen him sober and wouldn't know the difference. He was, in his own sick way, proud of this kind of alcoholism, even though he did not, at that time, have a name for it.

Clarence opined that he was a "chronic alcoholic, a daily drunk." This was a diagnosis of dubious value to Clarence. But it was a characteristic that he insisted upon and even took to his grave.

Clarence had disdain for the periodic drunk even though at one time in his drinking career, he was one. "Periodics," he said, "are the people that give us drunks a bad name." Periodics, he felt, are the type of people who "get a job, get a family, get a nice home, get a couple of nice cars, belong to a couple of clubs, and have a few kids. They also have some bills [dollars] in the bank. And, for no apparent reason, all of a sudden, this turkey gets drunk and down goes everything. Out go the wife and the family, the house, the bank account, the two cars and the furniture.

"Everything is gone and he's flat. Well, what does this monkey do? He goes and gets himself another job; and what kills me with these fellows, is that they usually get a better one than they had before. This is rather a jealousy on my part. Then they get a new house, two new cars, a new wife, a new family, new bank account, new club, more exclusive this time, and away they go again. The next thing you know, BOOM!

"The whole thing goes up. Now, no wonder alcoholics are looked down upon. These kinds of people, you can't depend upon 'em." Clarence felt that chronics were dependable daily drunks like himself. He said, "You always knew how they were going to be— *DRUNK!*"

At Morris Plan, Clarence—in a short period of time—had developed a full-time department, with the best finance people and collectors that he could find and train. He was able, with his own system, to recoup thousands upon thousands of dollars for the bank. Eventually, he was promoted and made an officer of the bank.

He often came to work in the morning wearing the same clothing he had worn the day before. He vividly remembered that he was "stinking the office up." He would check his paperwork, touch base with his "boys," and then he was off and running. This routine lasted for about three and a half years.

During this time, his drinking had become progressively worse, and it was having a profound physical and emotional effect upon him. He lost a lot of weight and began to forget even the simplest things. At first, he forgot only minor thoughts, but later major ones. Appointments began to be missed, and opportunities to recoup the bank's money, and business in general began to slip. Clarence's "boys" began to take advantage of his loss of memory.

Clarence was forgetting things he had said or done only moments before. He began to have temporary blackouts. Often he would be sitting at his desk and just staring into space. He would be talking with a customer, stop in mid-sentence, and start doing something else, completely unaware of what had previously transpired.

The people in his department talked with him and attempted to cajole him into quitting or at least cutting back on his liquor consumption. All of this failed. He continued to get worse. Morris Plan didn't want to lose him—he was the best manager they had ever had—but nothing they tried worked. Soon not even Clarence worked.

The bank's Vice President—whom Clarence described as "a strict Lutheran, a fine gentleman, who wouldn't cause or do anything out of the way"—just blew up at Clarence one morning. The bank officer had become so frustrated with trying to help Clarence with his drinking problem, that he just gave up. He started jumping up and down and screaming. He told Clarence that he, Clarence, was the best in the business, if only he could stop destroying himself. The Vice President pleaded for Clarence to look at what he was doing to his job, his family, his friends, and all those who loved and cared about and for him. But all of this was to no avail. Clarence was unwilling—in fact unable—to listen to the voice of reason. He had a bad case of tunnel vision, and all that was in the tunnel was his alcohol.

The Vice President told Clarence that he was being terminated, and gave him two weeks' notice. Clarence was even told he didn't have to report in to work for those two weeks and that the bank would pay him anyway. Clarence still didn't listen. He kept coming in to work each and every morning. He was drunk and unable to stop. He was afraid to stay at home, and had avoided telling Dorothy he had been dismissed—afraid to tell her that this was yet another position that had been taken away from him for being a drunk.

The two weeks quickly passed, and the fateful day finally arrived. The Executive Vice President called Clarence into his office. Clarence related, "He gave me my last hurrah. He told me all that crap that they tell you when you get fired. What a talent you have, how much you wasted it. What you could have done in this bank …. my future was shot and I'll never have any now." He gave Clarence his final pay check and told him to go upstairs and clean out his desks.

Clarence slowly walked out of the office, his head bowed, once again a failure. He walked up the flight of stairs to what had been his own office—walked there for the last time, feeling dejected and ashamed. The only thought that ran through his mind concerned how much he wanted—no, needed—a drink.

As he arrived at his office, Clarence opened the door. SURPRISE! His whole department was there, and so were many of the other bank employees. The office was decorated for a party, and party they did.

Both of his desks were filled with presents and the other desks were covered with bottles of alcohol. Clarence told the author, "Now who gets fired for being drunk and has a going away party with presents *and* booze? Nobody but some bloody drunk. That doesn't happen to regular people."

After Clarence left Morris Plan, he had several jobs that scarcely lasted for more than a few weeks each. His last one was for a finance company. He recalled, "I was supposed to dig up new business." He would sneak in every morning before the other employees got there. Only the switchboard operator would be on duty that early in the morning. He would check his desk for messages and quickly and quietly run out before any of the other workers had a chance to arrive. The switchboard operator reported to her employers that Clarence had indeed checked in each and every morning. However, after spending three weeks on that job and not producing a single bit of new business, or even servicing any of the old accounts, Clarence was once again fired: dismissed for drunken behavior and non-productivity.

Clarence was "between jobs" after that for several years.

In 1933, he and an old acquaintance discussed going into business together. Stan Zeimnick wrote Clarence on September 18, 1933, suggesting their going into the brewing business on a professional level. Stan said his main concern was that, "some, or rather most, beer-place proprietors say that naturally they expect a decided slump in beer sales soon, but that they don't know much about small towns; they may drink beer in the winter nearly as much. Of course, that's our gamble." This business venture never materialized, and Clarence continued to retain his amateur standing as a home brewmeister and, of course, beer consumer.

He went on interviews, answered advertisements in the help wanted columns, and walked into store fronts to inquire about jobs. He begged his former friends and business associates for jobs. He did everything he could—everything, that is, except stop drinking. Even Dorothy, who was at that time the manager of the men's department of a local employment agency, couldn't do anything for her husband.

He would show up for job interviews drunk, reeking of alcohol, and his appearance was, to say the least, disheveled. Quite often, his reputation as a drunk had preceded him. He had no luck acquiring a position doing anything.

Clarence was often the main topic of discussion at numerous family conclaves. These occurred on a weekly basis, and he was discussed daily over the telephone. Everybody agreed that he was a "great guy" when he was sober. However, he was no longer ever sober.

After one of these weekly meetings, Dorothy's family finally came up with a last-ditch opportunity for Clarence. It was time, he was told, to sink or swim. Either he worked for Dorothy's brother, or he would be thrown out on to the street.

Dorothy's brother owned a tractor-trailer rig. He hauled merchandise over-the-road between Cleveland and New York City with various stops in between. Clarence was to learn how to drive this tractor-trailer and go into business with his brother-in-law.

The very prospect of this frightened Clarence—the thought of learning how to drive one of those large trucks, with all of that freight looming behind you, was unappealing. What was even less appealing, and was the second-most but more important consideration, was the thought of hard work "which this job reeked of." It didn't sit right with him. But the thought that frightened Clarence the most, paramount over all of the others—was the thought that his brother-in-law would never allow him to have a drink. Not even a single beer on the hottest of summer days after driving a thousand miles.

This was spelled out in no uncertain terms and in so many different ways, that Clarence could not find any excuse or loophole to get around it or out of it—swim or sink. It was the truck and the open road or the street.

The thought of being on the bum, with winter rapidly approaching, was less appealing than the dismal prospect which now faced him. Clarence agreed to take the truck job, though rather reluctantly. He did, however, retain a silent reservation that, at the first opportunity that was afforded to him, he would pick up just one drink. Maybe two. Just enough to enable him to feel better but not enough to be noticed by his brother-in-law as being drunk. Clarence thought, in so doing, he wouldn't risk everything, and being left on the streets, in a strange place, with no money, and in the cold of winter.

A couple of nights later, Clarence and his brother-in-law had begun their trip to New York City via Albany and Buffalo. Clarence didn't have any clothing to speak of, not even an overcoat. He had sold most of it to purchase alcohol for his last hurrah. Out of necessity, he had packed light. In fact, he had packed all that was left of his clothing in a little duffel bag. He was to sleep, it was decided, in the top back sleeping compartment, the perch of the cab. His brother-in-law was to sleep on the seat itself so that Clarence couldn't leave the truck without being noticed, even if the brother-in-law was asleep.

Over the preceding few days, Clarence had managed to save a small amount of change in nickels and dimes. This small hoard, he decided, was to be used in case of emergency. He had surmised that an emergency would indeed eventually arise. He carefully wrapped these few coins in a handkerchief and placed the handkerchief snugly in the bottom of his trouser pocket. He made sure it wouldn't move at all so the coins wouldn't make any noise, be noticed and be confiscated.

Clarence had not been able to get away from his brother-in-law for even a single moment. He had not had a drink all day. Before they started the trip, Clarence had consumed all of the alcohol that was hidden in the house, and his bags had been thoroughly searched by Dorothy just prior to his departure. All the bottles that had been stashed were summarily removed and dumped down the kitchen sink in full view of Clarence and Dorothy's gathered family.

Clarence was in a bad way, sick, shivering, coughing, and throwing up out of the window of the truck. He was not allowed to leave his brother-in-law's sight. When they stopped for breakfast, Clarence had no appetite, but had to go into the diner anyway. He sat with his arms folded across his shaking body.

At one point, Clarence became nauseous and bolted for the bathroom, probably due to Clarence's watching everyone eating and smelling the aroma of the food. His brother-in-law quickly followed him into the bathroom. Clarence was followed everywhere he went and was watched at all times. His brother-in-law was under very strict and specific orders and knew he would have to answer to the family if anything went wrong.

Early in the evening they stopped for the night in Albany, New York. Clarence's brother-in-law was exhausted from all the driving and from having to watch each and every move that Clarence made. He decided to pull over to the side of the street and catch a few hours of much needed sleep. Clarence saw his awaited opportunity and seized it.

He convinced his brother-in-law that he had never been to Albany and that he wanted to see the Capitol building. He told the brother-in-law that this was something he had always wanted to see. He even offered to take him with him for security. He begged and he pleaded. He pointed to the building, which was all lit up in the darkened night sky. His brother-in-law was so exhausted he couldn't and didn't have the strength to argue any more with Clarence. He eventually just gave up. He assumed Clarence had no money and therefore couldn't get into any trouble. He mumbled, "Good-bye and don't come back too late." He then immediately drifted off into a sound sleep.

Clarence did not have any intention of seeing the Capitol. He did however, have what he thought, was a "capital idea." That idea was that, as soon he got out of the view of the truck, he would run as fast as he could to the nearest bar. And this he did.

The first place Clarence came across was a little too rich for his blood. He then ran a few more blocks to a seedier neighborhood. He quickly located something more to his stature and position in society—a dump. He carefully pulled out his handkerchief and untied it slowly, with his now trembling hands, so that none of his "bank" would fall out. He walked into the bar. He said he "plopped all the change on to the bar in one loud clatter and ordered a drink." He quickly downed that drink and, without waiting, ordered another.

As was Clarence's good fortune, he met a benefactor. He recalled "I met an angel, I think he was a fairy, but I'll call him an angel. Because he started to ply me with drinks and he was putting them up as fast as I could drink 'em. This was great. But then things started getting a little stuffy, and I thought it was about time I take my leave. So I went to the men's room, locked the door, went out the window, and headed back for the truck. I imagine this guy is still waiting for me there." Clarence did not run back to the truck. He was unable to. He walked as best he could. By the time he returned to the place where the truck was parked, all of the alcohol he had consumed began to take its effect. He was not in the best control of his body.

While trying to climb back into the truck and into his sleeping perch, he stepped on his brother-in-law's face. Awakened with a start, smelling the stench that emanated from Clarence's body, and observing him weaving back and forth, the brother-in-law put two and two together. After much loud arguing and having to restrain himself from beating Clarence to a pulp, the brother-in-law explained this was to have been Clarence's last chance. He told Clarence that as soon as they arrived in New York City, he would have to put Clarence out and leave him there.

"Dumped." Never to return home to Dorothy, or Cleveland for that matter, ever again. Regardless of how much Clarence begged and pleaded, New York City was to be his last stop. Dejected and devoid of all hope, Clarence crawled up into his perch to sleep, wishing that this was all an alcohol-induced nightmare or hallucination.

When they had arrived at the New York waterfront, true to his promise, the brother-in-law dumped Clarence on the docks and warned, "Never dare come back to Cleveland!" Clarence got down on his knees and begged, crying with all of the earnestness at his command.

The words "good riddance" were heard and echoed throughout his head as the big truck released its air brakes. It lumbered away and faded off into the distant, unknown and foreign streets. Clarence was left there, on his knees, tears streaming down his cheeks on to the cold and dirty concrete.

There he was, no other clothing than that which was on his back and in the little duffel bag. Winter was rapidly approaching, and he had no money. The only person Clarence knew was his sister-in-law Virginia.

Clarence felt that "She owed me plenty." According to Clarence, due to an indiscretion that her husband had come home early to witness, Virginia had been forced to flee Westchester County and to come and live with Clarence and Dorothy. Clarence, who at that time was still working, paid for all of Virginia's bills, including one for an operation when she had taken ill. He fed, clothed, and sheltered her. "She owed me plenty, you better believe that," he related.

Clarence began to make his way up to Yonkers, a suburb of New York City. By the time he had gotten there, he remembered that Virginia lived way up on top of a long hill. By this time Clarence was very thirsty—so much so after his long ordeal, that he decided he couldn't make it up the hill.

He went instead down another hill, down into what he remembered as an Italian neighborhood. He recalled, "This being bootleg days, all Italians had wine. A lot of them made it. Some of 'em sold it. They all drank it. Some of them shared it with their friends. So I went down there and made friends."

A few days later, exactly how many he didn't remember, he finally managed to make it up the hill to Virginia's home. One of the few things that he remembered about that visit was that he was drunk. He was drunk (as usual), dirty, and probably smelled bad, he thought. He also vaguely remembered that he was rolling around on the floor with Virginia's two little girls. Records show that Virginia (age 37) and her husband Myron (age 40) lived at 15 North Broadway in Yonkers (Westchester County) New York, which is a couple of blocks from Getty Square. The records also show that in 1939, Mary Lon (age 17) and Carol (age 7) weren't as young as Clarence recollected in later years.

When Virginia came home, she did not take too kindly to this sight. She told Clarence, in no uncertain terms, that he had to leave. To insure this, she placed him in the back seat of her car and drove him down to the same waterfront area in New York City from which he had started. Virginia threw him out of the car—rather, dragged him out, just as her brother had done previously. Clarence once again begged and pleaded. He got down on his knees and cried. He reminded Virginia that he had taken her in and that she owed him, at least just this once. But this was all to no avail.

Virginia admonished Clarence not to return either to her home or back to Cleveland to her sister, Dorothy. This time he was threatened with being arrested if he dared to return. Virginia got back into her car without looking back, slammed the door and drove off.

Once again Clarence was left on the cold concrete street, tears running down his cheeks. He had never felt so all alone in his life. He had no money, no real clothing to speak of, no friends, no family and no hope. "No nothing." He swore that he would never pick up another drop of alcohol in any way, shape or form ever again. This he swore to the heavens above at the top of his lungs. He had to exist, so exist he did as best he knew how. As was the case in the mid 1930's, many of the truckers left their rigs on the waterfront beneath the elevated roadway. They spent their nights in cheap rooming houses or hotels, to shower and to get some needed sleep. Some of those who parked their trucks were also looking for entertainment, the kind of entertainment that a cab of a tractor-trailer could not accommodate. At least not comfortably.

These men needed someone to watch their trucks. And Clarence used all his best sales techniques to convince them he was indeed their perfect watchman. He did manage to convince quite a few. He was paid fifty cents a night to watch over their trucks. In some, he slept snugly, insulated from the damp and bone-chilling cold.

Back in those days, Clarence bought his booze in a wallpaper store for seven cents a pint. He recalled that his "special mix" was comprised of "denatured alcohol, mixed with water and anything else that I could get a hold of to mix it with. It wasn't the best, but it did the trick. It knocked ya out." For the most part he always had at least two or three pints of that "mix" with him. So much for Clarence's swearing to the heavens that he would never pick up another drink.

Here he was, dumped on to the docks of New York City, not once but twice. But he had a warm place to sleep and plenty of booze. He was earning fifty cents a day, and at seven cents a pint, he was saving money.

Being a survivor, he also found clever and devious ways to get clothing to ward off the winter chill and thereby stay "healthy." He also found ways of getting something to eat when he was hungry, which wasn't very often.

He attended services at the various missions around the city in order to obtain the bare necessities of existence. This being the time of the great depression, there was never any shortage of missions. All he had to do was get there, go inside, get up, and sing.

He couldn't, however, stand their food. No matter how hungry he had gotten, mission food was something that he detested. The food was usually overstocks, leftovers, or spoiled goods that were donated by various establishments.

Because of its usually deteriorated condition, the food was always sprayed with and saturated by "bug juice." Clarence said of this insecticide, "Everything is bug juice. You go in there. They spray you with it, your clothing—they spray everything. Bugs are running every place you look, all over, in and around everything. They seemed to eat that spray. They got fat on it. They thrived off of it, I think."

So, rather than eat mission food, Clarence devised another way to eat for free: Clarence discovered the automat. He related, "The automat was a place with lots of little square windows, walls of 'em with different foods behind each window. You put in your nickel or dime through this little slot and turned the knob. The window popped open, and you took out your food. One window for soup, one for sandwiches, one for beans, etc."

He had observed that almost everyone in New York City was always "on the run." He found out from experience that, if you stood outside of one of the large office buildings at noon, "you took your life in your hands." Everyone, it seemed, would run out as if in one big swarm in order to rush off to lunch. He said, "Some of 'em had as much as a half hour." They would then gulp down their food and run back to work again.

Clarence watched these, as he called them, "idiots," for hours and even days at a time. He found them very amusing to watch. Probably some of those same "idiots" didn't find *his* antics so amusing.

He watched as they would run into the automat. They wouldn't even sit down. They stood at a counter or small table. He related, "A little round thing there, there's three or four of 'em at a counter."

Clarence watched them eating and talking. Some were reading the newspaper and eating. Sometimes they were doing all of these things at once. "They didn't even know what they were eating," he said.

He then came upon what he thought was an ingenious and foolproof plan—a scheme. He devised a plan to get some of this food to himself for free.

He said this of his plan: "I went out to the curbstone and took out one of my paws, and I rubbed it into the dirt and filth out in this gutter and dirtied this hand up. I came in and stood beside one of these guys and put this hand up in some guy's food. Now this takes a little crust to do this, but if you know human nature, you can get away with it. This guy turns around and sees this, and he wants to belt me. So, I look at him. I'm starving. I have this look on my face. He can't hit me. He can't do it. It's just too much for him. He gets so frustrated that he walks out and leaves that whole damn thing."

Clarence would then gather the food and take it back to the truck in which he was staying at the time. Sometimes this "foolproof" plan didn't work out so well. Sometimes he would get punched. Sometimes he would get thrown out. More often than not, though, he did get food, enough to satisfy whatever appetite he did have left.

This went on for some time. He had a place to sleep, food to eat, clothing on his back, and booze to drink. He was still saving money, earning fifty cents a day, and spending seven cents a pint for his "mix."

This all was happening around October or November 1937. Clarence had spent the better part of a year living as a homeless person in New York City, a place that several months earlier had been both foreign and frightening. This was just another indication to him of his resourcefulness and his instinct for survival in the face of adversity and absolute hopelessness.

However, as all good things must come to an end, Clarence began to develop a homing instinct. He felt that something, he wasn't sure of what it was, was calling him, drawing him back to Cleveland, Ohio.

He gathered up his meager belongings, counted the money that he had saved, packed four or five pints of his "mix," and set out for home. He was unsure of what, if anything, awaited him. He did know that he had to go home.

He convinced one of the truckers to give him a lift which took him in the general direction of Ohio. One trucker took him as far as Erie, Pennsylvania, and another took him to the outskirts of Cleveland.

He was back in the area where he had been thrown out of his home almost one year earlier.

Back to someone who he thought was still his wife, back to his son, and back to Dorothy's family. He was still unsure why he felt that he had to return, but he did know that he was glad to be back.

He knew his life seemed to be lost and hopeless, and he was unsure about how to regain it. He couldn't stop drinking. He had tried on numerous occasions with little or no success. He wanted some semblance of sanity back in his life. Yet he didn't know quite how to go about getting it or even who to ask how to get it.

He was truly lost and he was sure that "home" was where he would find what it was that he so desperately sought. He was in Ohio, home at last.

Chapter 3

What Happened

"Our stories disclose in a general way what we used to be like, **WHAT HAPPENED....**"

— from the Big Book of *Alcoholics Anonymous*

"There have been millions and millions of alcoholics stagger across the face of the earth. They've lived and died in alcoholism. They have died, and they have carried down in disgrace, families, friends and associates with them. They have caused carnage in this world, and they have died hopelessly. It's been a tragedy.

Out of all these millions of people, therefore, why? You tell me why just a few thousand of us have this opportunity. Why are you chosen for this? Why am I chosen for this? Why do I get this chance? Why do you get this chance and thousands and thousands and millions and millions of other people never had this chance and there are probably millions around who never will or never shall? Ask yourself this, sometime. It might put a new value on your membership here. These are things we ought to check ourselves with once and a while. I think it's a miracle that any of us are here. 'Cause no one ever gets here until he's hopelessly lost."

— Clarence H. Snyder, at Roanoke, Virginia, 1963

Chapter 3.1

HOME ... for just a brief moment

"The crowning experience of all, for the homecoming man, is the wonderful feeling that, after all he has suffered, there is nothing he need fear any more—except his God." [3]

UNLESS YOU HAPPEN TO BE AN ACTIVE ALCOHOLIC. AN ACTIVE ALCOHOLIC FEARS EVERYTHING!

With an act of sheer determination, Clarence managed to make it back to his home. He was cold and numb, knee-deep in snow. He charged up to the front porch and looked around. A puzzled expression began to form on his face.

The screen door was still up, as were all of the screens on the windows. This, he surmised to himself, was the reason that he had been called, summoned in on his homing instinct. His wife needed him. She couldn't get along without his help and knowledge. The screens were all the proof that he needed. Everybody, he thought, knew that you don't keep the summer screens up all winter.

He pounded on the screen door which, much to his dismay, was locked with a hook on the inside. He shouted and continued to pound. He demanded to be let in. How dare she lock him out of his own home! He had forgotten he was told, in no uncertain terms, that he was forbidden to return there.

Eventually, Dorothy came to see who it was who was making all of this commotion. Upon seeing Clarence, she did not unlock the door. Rather, she spoke to him through the door. She kept the security chain on and opened the door as much as the chain allowed.

Clarence stood straight as he could and endeavored not to show her how cold he actually was. He pointed out to her that people didn't leave screen doors and windows up all winter long. He told her she needed a man around the house to take care of all these little details. He tried to utilize all his best sales techniques and ploys, plus good old-fashioned guilt, to convince her to let him inside. After all, he was freezing out there on the front porch. He also thought that if he were able to convince her at least to let him into the house, at least to let him warm up, he could then charm and talk her into letting him stay.

Dorothy was having none of this and would not budge an inch. She did, however, concede that she needed a man around the house. Clarence's hopes began to rise as his chest puffed out and his shoulders drew back. But this hope was deflated instantly when she told him she really didn't need one that badly. She also said that, even if she did, it certainly wasn't going to be him.

She did say, however, that she had a counter-offer to make to him. His hopes once again began to rise. Unbeknown to Clarence, many months earlier—after he had romped on the floor with Virginia's children—Virginia had found the need to call the family doctor. Her children had become very ill and since the doctors of that day still made house calls, the doctor came to her house.

After the doctor had examined the children, he and Virginia began talking. The conversation included her fears about Clarence. She told this doctor that Clarence was the best brother-in-law possible when he was sober. She related that, when she had had to go to Ohio to live with her sister, Clarence paid for all of her bills. These bills included an operation, there when she had taken ill. She told the doctor she felt that she owed not only Dorothy, but Clarence as well.

The two continued on, discussing the evils of drinking at great length and also "cures" that were available. Virginia's doctor did mention one very likely possibility. If Clarence was really willing to quit drinking for good, he knew of another doctor—this one in Ohio—who had had a great deal of success in working with alcoholics of Clarence's sort. Virginia's doctor related to her the sad story of his own brother-in-law, who had also been a seemingly hopeless alcoholic. He told her that this very same brother-in-law had not had a single drink of alcohol in almost three years. The doctor's brother-in-law had relied upon this same treatment that the doctor in Ohio had used so successfully.

As it turned out, Virginia's doctor was Leonard V. Strong.

Dr. Strong's alcoholic brother-in-law was William Griffith "Bill" Wilson. The doctor in Ohio was Dr. Robert Holbrook Smith.

Virginia had written to Dorothy regarding this conversation and had given her sister Dorothy Snyder the name and address of the doctor in Akron. Virginia's doctor had given them to her on the off chance that Clarence might some day show up in Cleveland.

Dorothy remembered Dr. Robert Smith's name and asked Clarence through the slit in the door if he was now ready to stop drinking. "Yes, yes," Clarence yelled, willing to say anything that might get him inside the house and into the warmth before he froze to death. His hopes were once again dashed to the floor, however. Dorothy still refused to open the door, and would not let him inside. She told Clarence that Virginia had written her about this doctor in Akron who "fixes drunks," and that if he really wanted to quit, she would make sure he got to Akron to meet this wonderful man.

Clarence's mind was working on overtime. He was in desperate need of a drink. He was also in desperate need of getting warm. He figured that if he could just get into Dorothy's car for the long ride to Akron, he could then convince her to stop at a bar or liquor store and get him just one little drink. After that had been accomplished, he knew, his mind would be working better. Then, with the right fuel, he could convince her to turn the car around. She would then take him back home where they both belonged. After all, didn't he once sweep her off of her feet? He was sure that, with the right words, he could do it again.

Dorothy responded to the idea of getting her car. She brought their son to a neighbor's house, and she and Clarence proceeded towards what he thought was going to be Akron. During the ride, he could not convince her to stop anywhere, nor could he convince her to turn around. He became crestfallen when she pulled her car into the bus depot in Cleveland. She took her car keys and asked him to accompany her as she went inside. She purchased a one-way ticket to Akron. With that ticket, Dorothy handed him a small slip of paper. On it was the doctor's name, address and phone numbers: "Dr. Robert Holbrook Smith, 810 Second National Building, Akron, Ohio. Office phone: HEmlock 8523, Residence phone: UNiversity 2436. Hours 2 to 4 PM."

She made sure that Clarence was on the bus when it left so that he could not cash in the ticket for money to buy alcohol. When the bus left the terminal, Clarence noticed that Dorothy also left. She followed the bus a few blocks to make sure that Clarence didn't convince the bus driver to let him off.

On the way to Akron, to while away the time, Clarence read a couple of newspapers he had found on the bus. The bus was warm, which to Clarence was a little bit of heaven. Dorothy had given him a sandwich to eat. He was warm and fed, and the news in the paper was certainly exciting reading.

Chapter 3.2

"The Mad Butcher of Kingsbury Run"

"Yet suicide, quick or slow, a sudden spill or a gradual oozing away through the years, is the price John Barleycorn exacts. No friend of his ever escapes making the just, due payment." [4]

"But to the imaginative man, John Barleycorn sends the pitiless, spectral syllogisms of the white logic. He looks upon life and all its affairs with the jaundiced eye of a pessimistic German philosopher. He sees through all illusions. He trans-values all values. God is bad, truth is a cheat, and life is a joke. From his calm-mad heights, with the certitude of a god, he beholds all life as evil." [5]

Clarence had been away from his home for almost a year and had quite a lot of catching up to do with current events. The headlines in the newspapers told of a series of indictments concerning "Cleveland's Bad Boys," Donald A. Campbell and John E. McGee. These two men were the most feared and powerful union bosses in the city. The indictments were the culmination of months of investigation by the office of the Safety Director of Cleveland.

The Safety Director's name was Elliot Ness—the same Elliot Ness of "Chicago Untouchable" fame, Elliot Ness the crime fighter who helped destroy Al Capone's criminal empire, helped put away the Purple Gang, and cleaned up Chicago. The newspapers also reported another of Elliot Ness' famous cases, a case that fascinated Clarence more than all of the political hoopla.

This was the case of the "Mad Butcher of Kingsbury Run." Clarence had taken an interest in this case long before he had been "asked" to leave Cleveland. He remembered that this case, in particular, involved a series of murders which had taken place in the Kingsbury Run area of Cleveland. The area was a vast stretch of land around what was known as the "Roaring Third Precinct," near the Cuyahoga River. The river divided East and West Cleveland.

These gruesome murders, which began to surface around September 1935, involved the murders and dismemberment of several people, most of whose identities were never determined. The police surmised that the killer would pick up a hobo or prostitute, befriend them, and take them to some unknown place. Police assumed the victims were taken to the killer's home, fed and then murdered.

These murders, it was also reported, began with decapitation. This while the helpless victim was still alive. The killer then would cut the body up into smaller pieces, and these pieces, often minus the head, would turn up in Kingsbury Run, cleaned and drained of all of their blood. The neatness of the amputations and the precision of the cuts led the police to believe that the murderer was probably a doctor, or at the very least a person with trained surgical skills. The coroner of Cleveland stated that the logical suspect would be a physician "who performs the crime in the fury of a long drinking bout or derangement following the use of drugs." These bodies would turn up approximately every five months.

As Clarence read these accounts on the bus, he saw that the latest body, "Victim #9," had been found sometime in July of that year, 1937. It was now December, and Cleveland was about due for another grisly murder.

Clarence was familiar with the "Roaring Third," due to its notorious drinking establishments. He had often frequented these establishments. He remembered that when he had seen the hobos and down-and-outers who were forced to live in the shanty towns hidden deep within the run, he had often said to himself, "Before I get as bad as them, I'll stop drinking."

Clarence drifted off to sleep briefly, remembering the glaring headlines of almost a year earlier. In February 1937, a body had been found washed up on Euclid Beach. It was found by a man from East Cleveland. He had told police he just happened to be walking by at that time.

Clarence woke up with a start. What had awakened him so abruptly was that the name of the passerby at Euclid Beach had disturbed him greatly. Not just disturbed him, but sent shivers of terror up and down his spine and throughout his whole body. He sat up, jumped with a start, and was in a cold sweat. But no matter how hard he tried, he could not recall the name of the man who had just sent such utter terror into him.

Clarence finally arrived in Akron. Slowly he got off of the bus. He had convinced the driver that he was on his way to a doctor and needed some money to get there. The driver loaned Clarence some money, and Clarence quickly proceeded to the nearest bar to quench his thirst from the long bus ride and to calm his now jittery nerves.

Chapter 3.3

"Meeting the Doctor"

"Some of these human relationships and fallacies that we have been mentioning may seem formidable hurdles to you at the moment. But you will be surprised at how quickly they become insignificant if you stop drinking. IF you stop drinking .... Do you want to stop? Are you completely sincere in your desire to stop once and for all? Put it another way. Do you finally realize that you have no choice but to stop? Are you convinced that you would rather quit drinking than go on the way you are?" [6]

When Clarence had run out of the money he borrowed from the bus driver, and when there were no free drinks, he left the bar. He felt somewhat bolstered by the effects of the alcohol. He slowly unfolded the piece of paper that Dorothy had given him. Straining to read in the unfamiliar sunlight, he read the address, 810 Second National Building. Looking at a clock in a store window, he saw that it was almost twelve noon. Plenty of time to reach the office by the hours of two to four P.M. He proceeded on to another bar down the street for, maybe, "just one more, or two."

Clarence reached the Second National Building a little before two. He went upstairs and walked directly to the doctor's office. He read the name on the door. It was painted in black and gold on the glass window: "Dr. Robert Holbrook Smith, Rectal Surgeon."

Clarence laughed as he thought to himself, "My, that's a new approach to cure drinking." He paced the hallway. He hesitated, trying to decide whether to go or stay. He knew that his problem was most probably located in his head, but he thought that this particular doctor worked on this "cure" a bit lower than that. He paced for what seemed like hours; but in all actuality, it was probably just minutes.

Doctor Smith arrived just after the stroke of two P.M. He shook Clarence's hand with a firm grip. That shook Clarence all over. Dr.

Smith said, in a loud, strong, booming voice with a distinct Vermont accent, "Young feller, you must be Clarence. You can call me Doc."

Clarence was taken aback. He thought to himself, "How did he know my name?" He didn't stop to think that Dorothy probably had called earlier. Which in fact, she had. She had called to tell the doctor that her wayward husband might be showing up at his office that day. She had warned the doctor that, if Clarence did indeed show up, he would probably be in a state of intoxication.

The doctor took Clarence through his waiting room and office into another and smaller room. This room had a table and a couple of chairs in it. Doctor Smith — "Doc"— asked for him to sit down.

When they were both seated, Doc proceeded to tell Clarence about the doctor's own personal story of recovery from alcoholism.

Clarence, still suffering from the lingering effects of his last "just one more," heard something totally different.

It seemed, to Clarence's alcohol-fogged mind, that the good doctor was telling him all of the events surrounding Clarence's own sordid existence. "How does this man know all about me?" he thought to himself. "He must have been following me."

Then Clarence remembered the articles about the Mad Butcher. Panic set in. The sweat began to soak through his pores, and he thought he was about to become the Butcher's next victim.

At just about that time, the doctor told Clarence that he wanted to put him away in a hospital so no one could get at him. The doctor had probably said that to him because he had sensed Clarence's panic, agitation, and paranoia. This was, however, at that very time, exactly the wrong thing to say to Clarence.

For at that very moment, the name of the man in Clarence's dream became very clear. Clarence suddenly remembered the name of the man in his dream on the bus—the name that had frightened Clarence so much that it sent waves of terror throughout his whole body.

That man's name was Robert Smith! What Clarence couldn't remember, in his alcohol-induced fog, was that Robert Smith was the name of the person who had found a body and was not himself a suspect. And he certainly was not the same Robert Smith who was sitting directly in front of him.

Robert Smith (not Dr. Bob) points to the place where he found the murdered body at Euclid Beach
— a photo from the Cleveland Plain Dealer

The Robert Smith, the Doctor Robert Smith who sat in front of Clarence, sensed that this particular drunk sitting in the chair opposite him was about to jump out of his own skin. Dr. Smith sensed that Clarence was filled with unspeakable and unknown terror.

"No one could get at me," Dr. Smith had said. That was the problem: Clarence wanted, at that very moment, to be where everyone could get at him. Everyone except for the Mad Butcher.

Clarence bolted out of his chair, nearly knocking the doctor over. He ran through the office, bumping into patients who were waiting in the outer office. He pushed open the door and ran down the stairs and out into what he thought for sure was the safety of the streets.

He didn't stop until he was far away and hidden in the confines of a darkened tavern. His thoughts raced through his brain. They ranged from relief to rage, and everything in between. Relief that he had gotten away with his very life, and rage over his wife, his loving wife, who he now thought was in cahoots with the Mad Doctor—the same doctor who, he thought, had been about to set him up for a painful and gruesome death. The rage intensified, as Clarence plied himself with alcohol; and then it subsided, as he drifted off into another alcoholic stupor.

Chapter 3.4

Back To Cleveland

"… the theoretical importance of the instincts of self-preservation, of self-assertion and of mastery greatly diminishes. They are component instincts whose function is to assure that the organism shall follow its own path to death, and to ward off any possible ways of returning to inorganic existence other than those which are imminent in the organism itself. We have no longer to reckon with the organism's puzzling determination (so hard to fit into any context) to maintain its own existence in the face of every obstacle. What we are left with is the fact that the organism wishes to die only in its own fashion. Thus these guardians of life, too, were originally the myrmidons of death. Hence arises the paradoxical situation that the living organism struggles most energetically against events (dangers, in fact) which might help it to attain its life's aim rapidly—by a kind of short-circuit." [7]

Somehow Clarence found his way back to Cleveland. Not back to his home, but to the East Side. He was an explorer. He would go anyplace, a barroom, an abandoned building, a deserted alley. He would explore and, quite often, discover things that were beneficial to his very existence, his survival.

At this particular point in time he was exploring the basements of bars. "I got a lot of free booze doing that," he recalled. There was one bar in particular that was located in East Cleveland that he chose to visit at least twice per week, sometimes more often when other pickings became slim.

It was one of the larger establishments, which contained a nice restaurant as well as a bar. Sometimes food was the focus of his quest, but more often than not, it was beverage alcohol.

He had found his way into the basement of this particular East Side building through a delivery ramp that was never locked. Much to his delight, he had discovered a wide array of empty bottles: beer bottles, wine bottles, Champagne bottles, whiskey bottles. Every kind of bottle, in all shapes, sizes and colors imaginable, even some that he had never imagined existed.

If they contained at least a drop of their former contents, Clarence didn't care what the alcohol was, or what it looked like or tasted like. All the bottles had one thing in common, according to Clarence: they all contained at least a couple of drops of that precious elixir that he needed in order to live.

Sometimes he got lucky, and the bottle contained more than a few drops. Sometimes the bottles were almost full. The full bottles contained alcohol that had somehow spoiled, and a customer returned it. Clarence didn't care. Mixed with the rest of the contents of the other bottles, it all tasted the same.

In the 1930's, bars were required to dispose of the empty bottles by destroying them. This bar in particular, and many others, got away with leaving the empties intact, probably by paying authorities to leave the establishment alone.

Clarence developed a twice-weekly ritual of dealing with the bottles. He had found a large, flat metal pan with a protective lip, and when he had finished his ritual, he would hide the pan in the dark recesses of an unused corner. Into this pan he would pour the last remaining drops from the bottles. He patiently let each bottle drip slowly into the pan, making sure that he didn't lose one precious drop. If only he could have squeezed these bottles to speed up the process, he would have done so.

His pan would fill up with a murky colored liquid as he drained the bottles. When the pan was full, he would rapidly drink the mixture and begin the process all over again. "Boy, what a buzz you can get on that stuff," he once commented.

Clarence was "on the bum" for about a month and a half in East Cleveland, ever wary of the Mad Butcher, and of what were known as the Nickel Plate Railroad Police. These police were, in reality, just a group of "paid goons," as Clarence called them.

Clarence was about six feet tall. He weighed one hundred and thirty pounds soaking wet, in his clothing. And this time in his life, he was relegated to living in hobo shanty towns, under bridges like the Kinsman Road Bridge, which was about two thirds of a mile up from Jackass Hill. Anywhere he could "flop," he would do so.

He could not remember any time in his life that he had felt so alone, so desolate, so afraid and so lost—not only lost as to where he was at this particular time, but lost as to where he was going in his life, lost even as to where he had come from. He had lost his wife, his home, his son, a lucrative banking career, his health, his clothing, his self-respect, and (he often feared) even his sanity. Or whatever there was left of it.

Everything that had ever meant anything to Clarence was gone, gone except for the ever-present urgent need and overwhelming burning desire for beverage alcohol. There he was, just thirty-five years old, cold, wet, sick, and—most devastating of all—hopeless.

Two events occurred in the latter part of January, in the year 1937, that would eventually have a profound impact on the remainder of Clarence Snyder's life—a life that, unbeknown to him, had already been touched by Divine Providence.

The first event occurred during one of Clarence's exploratory sojourns. Clarence came across a discarded issue of a recent national magazine. While he was glancing through this issue, an article immediately caught his eye. The article appeared to spell out graphically what Clarence felt that he had become, all that he was.

Richard Rogers Peabody

The magazine was *The Saturday Evening Post*, the issue was January 15, 1938, and the article was titled, "The Unhappy Drinker." It was written by Frances T. Chambers, Jr., as told to Gretta Palmer.

Chambers was a self-professed alcoholic who had been "cured" by Richard R. Peabody, of 224 Commonwealth Avenue, Boston, Massachusetts. Richard R. Peabody was the author of a book (extremely popular during the early 1930's) titled *The Common Sense Of Drinking*, a book that many of the founding members of what was to become Alcoholics Anonymous had read with great interest.

The Peabody book was an outgrowth of an earlier study titled, "Psychotherapeutic Procedure in the Treatment of Chronic Alcoholism." This study had been read before the Harvard Psychological Society and the Boston Society of Psychiatry and Neurology.

Courtenay Baylor (Peabody had adapted methods used in Boston by Courtenay Baylor and Dr. Elwood Worcester of the Emmanuel Movement)

Peabody's study was later published as the book *The Common Sense of Drinking*. Coincidentally, after his book was published in 1931, he moved from Boston, Massachusetts, to New York City, to 24 Gramercy Park. Peabody's new home was located in the same New York neighborhood as Calvary Episcopal Church, where the rector, the Rev. Samuel M. Shoemaker, was active in the Oxford Group. This was the same neighborhood as the Olive Tree Inn (25 cents a night for lodging) where Ebby T. had gone to, right next door to the Calvary Mission. This mission, on East 23rd Street, was where Bill Wilson had "taken the pledge."

In any event, Chambers—the author of the *Post* article—had worked with alcoholics in his private practice in very much the same manner that Richard R. Peabody had previously worked with Chambers. According to the article, Chambers took treatment with alcoholics. "Are you ready to stop drinking," he would ask. "No," the patient often answered, with a dare-to-make-me air.

Chambers related this example: "'All right,' I told him. 'Call me up when you are.' As I hung up the telephone receiver, I fancied I could hear him pouring himself another drink, but within twenty-four hours he telephoned me to announce that he wanted to stop. Until that had happened, I could do nothing for him; It is my strong belief that no man was ever helped by being hoisted onto the water wagon by his friends or advisors. He must climb up of his own free will."

Clarence knew he was indeed unhappy. He also knew he desperately needed to stop drinking. He knew that the doctor in Akron was probably his only hope. This in spite of his overwhelming fear that the very same doctor might be the feared Mad Butcher.

Clarence ripped out the *Post* article and kept it with him at all times. Whenever he experienced doubts, he re-read it. Many years later, he mounted the article on pieces of colored paper and wrote beneath it: "My first intimation that alcoholism was a disease—my first ray of hope."

Thinking back on this, he once stated that he felt that the article was a message directly from God to him, Clarence Snyder. "James Snyder" was the name of the photographer from the *New York Times* who had taken the photograph at the heading of the *Saturday Evening Post* article. Clarence had thought at the time that this was proof that the article in the *Saturday Evening Post* did solidify Clarence's start towards sobriety.

Interestingly, this very same magazine would publish an article about Alcoholics Anonymous just over four years later, on March 1, 1941. That article would be the start for many more thousands of alcoholics to begin their journey on the road to sobriety. That national publicity would catapult Alcoholics Anonymous toward what it has become today.

However, there were still some reservations about sobriety that were left in Clarence's alcohol-clouded mind. Fears and doubts—fears about the doctor and who he possibly might be, and doubts concerning the possibility of success—the kind of success that had eluded him so often in the past and, with each failure, had become even a more remote possibility. So it took one more event to solidify Clarence's resolve to quit drinking for good.

That other significant event occurred deep within the woods of Kingsbury Run. Clarence, after reading the article about the "Unhappy Drinker," had been in constant turmoil over the sorry state of affairs his life had taken.

As he lay on the cold damp ground, in the midst of his so-called peers—"a bunch of bums" he called them—he glanced around. He looked at the squalor, the ravaged faces, and the disheveled clothing. Fear and desolation sank in. That picture surrounded him on all sides and was even evident within his own body, mind, and spirit.

All the homeless people in Kingsbury Run were in constant fear and terror of the Mad Butcher, the Railroad Police, and even of each other. All were mere shadows of their former selves, suffering from a loss of the spark of life, the spark that kept them alive, or at least managing an existence.

They were indeed the walking dead, the great unwashed and the great unshaved.

This is what Clarence's life had become. Unless he did something soon, and something drastic, this is where his life, such as it was, would anonymously end. He would cease to exist with no one to know and no one to care. His clothing would be removed from his emaciated body, and his remains would be rolled into a ditch or shallow grave for the vermin to feast upon. Such was to be his legacy.

Clarence vaguely remembered the doctor in Akron somewhere deep within the recesses of his foggy brain. He remembered that the doctor had talked to him about "fixing drunks" so that they never drank again. He remembered the glow, and the radiance that the doctor had about him.

He wanted that in and for his life. He somehow knew the doctor was probably the one man, no matter how afraid of him that he was, who could put some meaning and purpose back into his meager and now meaningless life.

He attempted to stand up. He had a difficult time with this, but after considerable effort, he did manage to stand erect. Well, as erect as a man in his weakened condition could get, or even hope to get. All it took, he felt, was determination. He made an attempt to dust off his clothing—the clothing that was so imbedded with dirt and filth that his dusting simply caused a small cloud around himself, a cloud that, like a magnet, was drawn back to the very same clothing he was trying to clean. Discouraged, he shortly gave that up and tried to brush back whatever hair was left on his head. He then made a loud and bold announcement to those of his peers who happened to have been gathered in the vicinity.

"I'm through with this foolishness, I'm going to quit drinking," he said. After the laughter subsided somewhat, no one responded or even looked up at him. After all, he was just like them, a hopeless drunk. He repeated his statement to the gathered masses—even louder this time, and with more conviction: "I'm through with this foolishness, I'm going to quit drinking!" The laughter and derision continued. Shouts of "sit down and shut up" were heard from the group.

One of the other drunks made an effort to stand. Clarence remembered him only as a "flannel mouthed Irishman," one of the leaders and a spokesperson of the group. This man placed his hands on his hips and laughed. His head was thrown back, mouth wide open, exhibiting a large, almost toothless grin.

"You quit drinking," the Irishman said. "You'll never quit drinking. Look at you. You don't have the guts to quit drinking." Clarence took a couple of unsteady steps forward, but not enough to be in direct swinging range of this other person. He put his hands on his own hips and yelled, "I'm gonna quit drinking!" The Irishman took a few more steps closer and pushed his face into Clarence's. "You'll NEVER quit drinking!" Spit was flying out of the Irishman's mouth. "You know that to quit takes determination. To have determination you have to have a chin. Look at you," he roared. He continued to laugh and then said, "You've got a chin like Andy Gump. You're no damned good!"

The Irishman was no doubt sharing from his own experiences. He too, had probably quit drinking, with determination and with his large and chiseled chin, many times in the past—times too numerous to remember, with little or no success.

Clarence then got even closer, and yelled even louder. He threw caution was thrown to the wind. "I'm gonna quit drinking, I know a doctor in Akron that can fix me," he shouted. The Irishman yelled back, moving right into Clarence's face: "No one can fix you!" Clarence replied, "I'll show you." The Irishman laughed into his face, and said, "Show me."

The shouting continued for about a half hour. A small group of the drunks was egging Clarence on and the rest egged on the other man. Though it probably looked quite pathetic, the scene was probably also quite funny as well. Two drunken bums, face-to-face, hands on their respective hips in the midst of a cadre of other bums. Dregs of society, surrounded by the squalor that exemplified Kingsbury Run. With the last little bit of pride he was able to muster, Clarence utilized almost all of the strength that was left in his emaciated body. He wheeled around, luckily without falling, and staggered away.

The sharp and stinging sounds of laughter, jeers of derision, and even some scattered applause were ringing in his ears. The sounds faded as he picked up his pace. His head was now held high as he picked up speed, proud of what he thought was his final decision. Proud, and deathly afraid of the unknown prospect that lay ahead— the prospect of possibly finding out who Clarence Snyder was without the aid of beverage alcohol—the prospect, frightening as it was, of living life without a drink.

When he got out of the sight of his erstwhile comrades, Clarence started to run. He ran as fast as he could in his present and weakened condition. It had taken a lot out of him to stand up to that Irishman. He began to stumble over debris, running as if his life were at stake. Running, thinking if he stopped, he might change his mind. Running *to* something for what seemed the first and only time in his life rather than running away *from* something. Somewhere in his consciousness he knew that it felt better to run *to*, rather than to run *from*.

The next couple of days were a blur for him. He continued drinking and running, running and drinking. The drinking was not having the same effect on him that it had in the past. He continued drinking only because he felt that if he stopped, he would surely die. For this was the only way he knew how to stay alive—to stay alive, he had to drink.

He somehow managed to call the doctor seven or eight times during the next few days. He didn't remember when or how. He didn't even remember speaking with the doctor once. Doc Smith told him later on that it was at least seven or eight times.

He had gone to a phone and made all of those toll calls while on the run. He had probably had to break into someone's home to do this since whatever money he was able to panhandle and find, he had used for alcohol.

During one of the calls, the doctor had told Clarence to meet him at Akron City Hospital the next morning. Scared as Clarence was, this time there was no turning back. It was a matter of life and death this time—his own!

He managed to scrape together enough money to make the bus fare back to Akron. He walked to the bus depot. It took hours, it was night time, it was cold and dark, but he had to get there. He bought his ticket for the bus which was leaving just after dawn. And he tried not only to stay awake, but also not to cash in the ticket for a drink. He stood vigilant, awaiting the departure to the unknown, scared and alone.

When he arrived in Akron, it was in the middle of a blizzard. The temperature was sub-zero, and he didn't have an overcoat. All that he had was just the mismatched old clothing that had been picked up in various missions and from those poor unfortunates in the "Run" who had succumbed to the cold and the ravages of their drinking. He didn't even have the money for the trolley, and since he couldn't find anyone in the midst of a blizzard to beg the money from, he "decided" to walk. He *HAD* to get "fixed."

"Akron," Clarence once said, "is the city of seven hills, and all of their hills are up. They don't have any down hills." But his sense of determination was tremendous.

He put his head down, buttoned up his jacket as best he could, and put up his frayed collar. There were many times, more often than not, that he felt utterly discouraged. The hills seemed steeper and longer than he had ever remembered. The cold bitter wind was cutting through him like a knife. The blinding snowstorm battered at his body, often driving him backwards. Yet he walked on. His mind was set. His feet, numb from the cold and the frozen snow, were reluctantly placed one in front of the other. One step at a time.

He often fought the little voice that told him that the warmth of a local bar would bring him relief and that he could continue his journey after one little drink, maybe two. All he had to do was warm up on the outside as well as on the inside, the voice said, and he could then continue.

His "Andy Gump" chin pressed close to his sunken chest, he was determined to make it to the hospital—the hospital where an unknown fate awaited him, a "cure" for this devastating, debilitating drunkenness that had consumed his every thought and every fiber of his being. No matter what, "I was gonna get fixed," Clarence recalled.

He finally made it to the hospital, numb, exhausted, frozen to the bone. His clothing was, by now, stuck to his body. He walked into the lobby of Akron City Hospital, strode up to the reception desk, pounded his fist on the counter, and—while demanding to see Doctor Smith—he passed out.

Chapter 3.5

"In the Hospital"

"No person ever really lives until he has found something worth dying for." [8]

Clarence awakened with a start. He was disoriented to say the least. He was in a strange room with a group of people, all dressed in white uniforms, who were milling around him. "And for some strange reason, they're giving me a bath," he quipped in telling the story.

He was then wrapped in a shorty hospital nightgown, a little bit of a thing, with no back to speak of, and just a couple of strings to hold it together. He slowly reached up to his face, unable to make any sudden movements, and discovered that he was clean shaven. His hair, the little that he still had left, was cut short; and he even smelled clean.

His mouth felt as if someone evil had packed it full of old, musty cotton balls. His tongue felt three inches thick, and he noticed that his head was throbbing. And the throbbing was getting worse as the seconds went by.

The muscles in his body felt as if they were contracting in a rapid succession and in no particular order. Some muscles he didn't even know he had were also acting in this manner. His stomach fluttered as if it were filled with a flock of Canadian geese who were migrating south for the winter. At times, the geese all changed direction and began to migrate north. It was at these times that Clarence began to vomit.

IIis eyes had a difficult time focusing on anything in the room as did his brain. As he surveyed the terrain, however, there was one thing that his eyes did manage to focus upon.

A bottle of "rub" on the window sill: rubbing alcohol. "My ace in the hole," he had thought. He made a mental note. This note was out of necessity, a mental note of where the alcohol was, and how to get there. How many steps were necessary to get there if he were going to need it.

Recalling the experience, Clarence said: "I was always scared of the D.T.s (Delirium Tremens). I never had 'em, but I saw some of my buddies who had 'em. And I saw people who died with 'em. I figured if I started seeing a circus and there is no tent, I hear music and there is no band, there's my answer right there: the bottle of rub. People get the D.T.s when they quit drinking. I was scared to death of 'em, that's why I never gave 'em a chance to set in." He was probably never sober enough to get the chance.

The knowledge of where the bottle was, how to get there, and how long it probably would take, gave him strength. It "gave me guts, my ace in the hole, that bottle of rub," he said. He knew that he could conquer the world knowing that he was only a few short steps from salvation. Bolstered by his newfound strength, he wasn't too concerned when the nurse walked into the room.

Clarence remembered her as a very large woman. He remembered that her starched, bleached white uniform seemed to be bursting at the seams. Her hair, kind of salt-and-pepper, was plastered back into a bun that stood out of the back of her skull as if it were a permanent growth.

Her white nurse's cap was adorned with a couple of medical looking pins, and it looked as if it were tacked to her head. Steel-rimmed bifocal glasses, at least a half dozen chins, on some of which were situated little, dark brown moles with long strands of black hair growing out of them.

She wore no make-up that he could see. She had short (probably bitten-off) nails, white orthopedic shoes, and stockings with leg hair clearly visible through them. This vision was Clarence's angel of mercy as he remembered her. He at first thought that this was the beginnings of the D.T.s, and was ready to bolt from the bed to the rub on the shelf. He was ready to bolt, that is, until he saw what she carried in her hands.

In her short stubby fingers, she held a small, white, metal tray. This tray was the kind you found in older hospitals with the edges chipped off and the black metal underneath showing through. Spider-web like veins of black and rust existed throughout its surface.

Two glasses sat on top of this tray, one large and one small. The small glass was filled with what looked like about 30-50 mg of some sort of white liquid, similar to watered-down milk. The other glass, an eight-ounce drinking glass, he was sure contained booze.

She walked over to his bed, ever careful not to spill her precious cargo. With a low, raspy voice, she said, "Mister Snyder." This was the first time in a long time that anyone had called him by his name.

"Mr. Snyder," she said, "I have some medicine here for you. You drink down this nice medicine here with the milk, and you can follow it up right after with this whisky." He looked at the two glasses and then back at the nurse.

Clarence had heard a lot about that "nice medicine" from his drinking buddies. It was probably paraldehyde. Paraldehyde is a synthetic, non-barbiturate, sedative-hypnotic, which is now considered to be potentially dangerous. It has a bitter taste, therefore the need for the milk. It also causes burning in the mucus membranes. In hypnotic doses, such as the one they attempted to give to Clarence, it can induce sleep in as little as ten minutes, and its effects would usually last from four to ten hours.

Clarence knew what that little glass held. "That stuff will knock you flatter than a rug, real quick," he thought. No way was he going to fall for that "nice medicine" line that the nurse was trying to hand him. He wasn't born yesterday.

He sat up in the bed, put on his most sincere face, looked the nurse right in her eyes, and said, "Lady, I come down here to quit drinking, not to drink. I'll thank you to take that stuff away from me."

He later stated that it was probably one of the worst and stupidest moves he had ever made in his life until then. This was because the nurse did indeed take the tray away. He remembered that he "suffered the agonies of the damned." He began to sweat profusely. He felt as if spiders and other small insects were crawling all over his body and his insides, in large numbers. He shook and convulsed, screamed and cursed. He threw up until there was nothing left in his system to throw up anymore, and then he continued with the dry heaves. He held on to the bed railings for dear life, but not once did he make an attempt to get to that "bottle of rub" on the window sill.

He thought about the rub, obsessed on it, wondered if it would take away this agony. But he knew, despite the pain that he was feeling, that if he took even one little sip, his agony would be prolonged. He knew that his life would probably be over. This, he knew, was his last chance at redemption.

The date he entered Akron City Hospital and refused that one last drink was the tenth of February, 1938. The next day, his first full day free from beverage alcohol, became Clarence Henry Snyder's sobriety date, the date that he celebrated for the next forty-six years: February 11, 1938.

Chapter 3.6

WHAT HAPPENED

"On Our Knees"

"'What we want to do is get in touch with Him and turn our lives over to Him. Where should we go to do it?' At once the lad replied: 'There is only one place—on our knees.' The lad prayed—one of those powerful, simple prayers which are so quickly heard by Him who made the eye and the ear:

'OH LORD, MANAGE ME, FOR I CANNOT MANAGE MYSELF.'" [9]

It was Valentine's Day in 1938. Clarence was feeling well enough to receive visitors. He had, as he put it, "gotten over a lot of my shakes, gotten them a little under control. I didn't get over 'em by a long shot."

He recalled that, beginning with that day, each day, a couple of "the men who preceded me in Akron" came to visit, and each afternoon, Doctor Smith checked in on him. All of these men, about fifteen in number, who came while Clarence was in the hospital, were in their forties to late fifties. Clarence was only thirty-five at the time. These men would sit at his bedside, tell him the sad and sordid stories of their lives, and the depths to which alcohol had taken them. They told him of their lives as they were living them today, and then told him that they had the answer to his problem. They stood up, shook his hand, and wished him well. They all said they would pray for him. At that point, they would turn and leave the room.

This went on for almost a week. Never in Clarence's life did he have this much attention. These were people who genuinely seemed to care for him. They wanted nothing in return, other than his continued success and physical well-being.

After these visits, each and every afternoon, he would question Doctor Smith, who kept insisting that he just wanted to be called Doc, about what was going on.

Doc was known to have very long and bony fingers, which—Clarence quipped — "probably served him well in his profession." He would often poke Clarence hard in the chest with them as he spoke to Clarence.

During one of these visits Doc said to Clarence, "Young feller"—Doc had a nick name for everyone, Clarence's happened to be young feller — "young feller, you just listen." Doc said nothing further about Clarence's questions until the last day Clarence was to be in the hospital.

It was a Wednesday, and there was a definite chill in the air as Doc sat on the edge of Clarence's bed. Clarence was still a little wary of Doc—still not sure whether or not he was the Mad Butcher. Doc stood well over six feet tall; and even though he was seated, he still presented an imposing figure.

Doc was known for his very loud neckties and argyle socks. Clarence remembered that he also wore a stick pin which had a lion's head on it. Clarence also remembered that this particular stick pin had a diamond in it, a diamond of which Clarence was envious for it spelled success.

After many minutes of strained silence, Doc finally spoke. "Well young feller, what do you think of all this by now?" Clarence replied, "Well Doc, I think that this is wonderful. All these fellows coming in to see me. They don't know me from a load of hay, and they tell me the story of their lives. They tell me what booze did to them. But I'm puzzled about something." Doc asked, "What are you puzzled about?" Clarence replied, "Every one of these men tells me the same thing. They tell me that they have the answer to my drinking problem—and on that note, they leave. They don't actually tell me anything. Now, I'm laying around here for about a week, I'm ready to get out of here. What are you going to do to me? What's next? What's the answer? What arc these fellows holding from me? What is this?"

He was not at all ready for the reply that Doc gave him. Doc looked at Clarence seriously, pondering his next few words. He folded his massive arms in his lap and said, "Well young feller, we don't know about you. You're pretty young, and we haven't had any luck with these young fellows. They're all screwballs."

Clarence was not about to comment that he wasn't a screwball. All of the men who had spoken to him were much older. All seemed pretty responsible and sane. He looked at Doc imploringly and said, "What do I have to do to be ready? I weigh one hundred and thirty pounds, I've been on the bum for several years, and I'm unemployable. I have no more home than a rabbit, I have no clothes, I have no money, and I have no prospects. I have nothing. It's the middle of winter, and I'm in a strange town and you people say that I'm not ready yet? What more do I have to go through? How many more years of living hell?"

Doc looked at Clarence and shook his head up and down. "Okay young feller," he said, "I'll give you the answer to this." Doc turned his body on the bed to get closer to Clarence, pointed a long bony finger at him, and asked, "Young feller, do you believe in God? Not *a* God, but God!"

Clarence was ready for a medical cure. He was ready for surgery, any kind of surgery. Even rectal. After all, he was in a hospital, wasn't he? He was ready to sign a pledge, swear off booze, sing for his supper, and stand on his head if need be. He was, however, definitely not ready for God!

He had already been to the missions when he needed clothing or shelter. He even sang a little bit. He had listened to all they had to say about God. He had "agreed" with them and they gave him what he had needed. How many times had he turned his life over to Jesus Christ for just a pair of pants, on old and worn overcoat, a pair of shoes? Most of these items he had sold for alcohol anyway. He sold them when the need arose, as it always did.

Doc repeated himself, louder this time and with a trace of annoyance: "Do you believe in God?" Clarence tried as hard as he could to evade this question, but one did not evade Doc—especially when Doc believed in something this strongly. Clarence asked, "Well, what does that have to do with it?" Doc answered, "Young feller, this has everything to do with it. Do you or do you not believe in God?"

By this time, Doc appeared to Clarence to be getting ready to get up off of the bed and leave the room. Clarence was afraid that Doc wouldn't "fix" him unless he went along with this line of questioning. Yet there were still the vestiges of resistance. Clarence tried to evade the question once more. He tried to answer on a more positive, but non-committal note. He said, "Well, I guess I do."

Doc abruptly stood up, pointed his finger at Clarence, and yelled. "There's no guessing about it. Either you do or you don't!" Clarence became increasingly frightened. He thought that Doc was about to walk out and never tell him the answer to his problem—the answer which in fact Doc had already given to him, but which Clarence was unable or unwilling to hear.

"Yeah," Clarence replied, resigned to the fact that he really wanted to get well and that Doc wouldn't help him unless he responded in the affirmative. "I do believe in God," he said.

Doc didn't sit right back down as Clarence had expected him to do. Instead he just stood there and stared at him. This time Clarence really was frightened. This time he thought that he had "blown my opportunity," as he put it, to rid himself of his drinking problem; and he began to think that he was relegated to a life of misery and despair. Both the fear and the desire must have shown all over his face because Doc eventually said, "That's fine. Now we can get someplace." Clarence breathed a sigh of relief. Once again, however, he was not at all prepared for what was to happen next.

Doc said, "Get down out of that bed." Clarence was shocked. He asked, "For what?" Doc replied, "You're gonna pray." Clarence pleaded with him, for enough was enough. "I don't know anything about praying," Clarence said. Doc, still as stern as before and not willing to compromise his beliefs, said, "I don't suppose that you do; but you get down there, and I will pray. You can repeat it after me, and that will do for this time."

Doc then took Clarence by the hand and "hauled" him off of that "nice warm nest," as Clarence put it, and down to the cold, hard, concrete floor—Clarence in his shorty hospital nightshirt tied together in the back by a couple of strings; Doc in a suit with a loud colored tie, argyle socks, and a diamond stick pin with a lion's head.

What a sight to behold! Both men on their knees, by the side of the hospital bed, in an attitude of prayer. Doc uttered some sort of a prayer, pausing every few words so that Clarence had the time to repeat them. Clarence didn't quite remember the words of the prayer exactly, but he did remember its being something like this: "Jesus! This is Clarence Snyder. He's a drunk. Clarence! This is Jesus. Ask Him to come into your life. Ask Him to remove your drinking problem, and pray that He manage your life because you are unable to manage it yourself."

After they had concluded this simple prayer, they rose from the side of the bed. Doc shook Clarence's hand and said to him, "Young feller, you're gonna be all right."

Clarence sat back down on the side of the bed. He was sweating profusely. But he was feeling something strange, something he had probably never felt before in his entire life. He felt absolutely clean.

He also felt relieved of a great burden that had weighed heavily upon him for what had seemed forever. He had just prayed that prayer—not like he had done so many times in the past, not like he had prayed in Sunday School, in churches and in the missions—he had prayed this particular prayer like he really meant it, meant every word that had come out of his mouth. He prayed the prayer directly from the center of his heart and not from a brain befogged from alcohol. He had prayed that way because he had felt his very life had depended upon each and every word that came out of his mouth.

In all actuality—**IT DID!**

Chapter 3.7

"At T. Henry and Clarace Williams' Home"

"You cannot belong to the Oxford Group. It has no membership list, subscriptions, badge, rules, or definite location. It is a name for a group of people who, from every rank, profession, and trade, in many countries, have surrendered their lives to God and who are endeavoring to lead a spiritual quality of life under the guidance of the Holy Spirit."[10]

That same evening, Doc took Clarence out of the hospital. Clarence was a new man, dressed in old clothing. All the clothing he owned was the clothing he wore on his back, his old mission clothes—no overcoat to protect him from the elements, a mismatched suit that was way too large for him and that had patches on it of different colored material where it had worn out, a shirt with a frayed collar and ripped pocket, with a tie that Doc had given him that didn't seem to match anything except the loudness of its colors. He wore one black shoe and one brown one with socks that had no toes or heels.

He felt, at the very least, self-conscious. Doc said it really didn't matter because where they were going, no one was going to look upon the outside of him. They wouldn't be interested in his worldly appearance. All they would be interested in, Doc continued, was what was on the inside, in his spirit.

They walked outside, not as doctor and patient, but as two drunks. They got into Doc's car for the short ride to what Doc had promised him would be a rewarding evening. Clarence had, through experience, learned not to question Doc, but just to go along.

They drove to 676 Palisades Drive, in Akron. It looked like a millionaire's home to Clarence. It was, in fact, the home of T. Henry and Clarace Williams, who were prominent members of the Oxford Group in Akron. (See Appendix A, "What was the Oxford Group?")

When the Oxford Group people had been required, by the high rent, to move from the Mayflower Hotel in Akron, the Williams's had opened up their home to the group.

The Williams' home on Palisades Drive

T. Henry and Clarace Williams

The first regular Oxford Group meetings in Akron had been held at the same Mayflower Hotel in which Bill Wilson was staying in May 1935 when he supposedly made his phone calls, seeking to help himself by helping another drunk. One of those calls was to the Reverend Dr. Walter Tunks, an Oxford Group adherent who put him in touch with Henrietta Seiberling, another Oxford Group adherent. Wilson's conversations with Henrietta had led him to an introduction to Dr. Robert H. Smith. The ensuing meeting of the two—Bill W. and Dr. Bob—at Henrietta's home at the Gate House of the Seiberling Estate on May 12, 1935, was to lead to the founding of what was, four years later, to become known as Alcoholics Anonymous. [11]

Clarence was still very self-conscious. But with Doc's gentle guidance and insistence, he walked inside. He had not been inside a home like this in many years. There were oriental rugs on the parquet wood floors. Beautiful oil paintings from both European masters and contemporary American artists adorned the walls. There were shelves on the walls which were lined with miniature figurines and bric-a-brac.

The expensive porcelain figurines and bric-a-brac caught Clarence's rapt attention. Still relying on his survival mode thinking patterns, Clarence thought that if things got too uncomfortable, he could pocket a "few of these trinkets," and sell them for bottles of alcohol. He stored the location of the most expensive looking figurines in his mind for future reference. He continued walking further into the house, directly behind Doc, noticing and storing the location of many more valuables in his mind. These included, for some unknown reason, a Grand Piano in the corner. It probably wasn't the piano that he was after, but the silver picture frames and more expensive bric-a-brac that were on it.

He then started noticing something else. He noticed all of the women sitting around the house in comfortable chairs. These, he surmised, were "high class" women. All were dressed in fancy, expensive *haute couture*. At least, that is what it looked like to Clarence, who had "been on the bum" and was used to mission clothing.

These women were sitting and chatting among themselves, and with the well-dressed gentlemen who also abounded. These men, he surmised, were definitely not "rummies." They were "earth people," "civilians."

His mind was reeling. He felt, for a moment, that Doc had taken him to a fancy brothel, a rich people's house of prostitution. But there, sitting in one of those large, overstuffed, Victorian wing-backed chairs, apart from all the others, talking to a woman that he later found out was Doc's wife, Anne Smith, was Dorothy. His own wife! His heart almost stopped there and then in shock. He had to hold on to something to steady himself. What he held on to was Doc.

It seemed that Doc had telephoned Dorothy to come to Akron for this meeting.

Doc later told Clarence that she was reluctant at first, and had refused to come. Doc also told him later that he had then invited her to come to his home so that Doc and his wife could talk with her about this new "cure," a cure that Doc himself had taken, and about this new way of life that was so successful with him and the others to whom he had passed it on—men just like Clarence.

Dorothy had still not been convinced. Not until Doc put Anne on the telephone to talk with her. Clarence remembered that Anne Smith had a way about her that could charm a troubled spirit like nothing else could. Later on, after the alcoholics' membership began to flourish, Anne Smith would meet with the wives at her home and they would have their own sort of fellowship. Dorothy gave in to Anne and stated that the only reason that she was coming to visit was because of Anne. Not Clarence.

Dorothy drove down to Akron to meet with Doc and Anne. She found them to be two of the nicest, most down-to-earth people she had ever met. They instilled in her a hope that this new "cure" would work on her husband. Though she still held on to numerous reservations as far as Clarence was concerned, Dorothy had listened. She told Anne and Doc about Clarence's drinking history, about his promises to stop, and about all the fruitless "cures" he had tried over the years.

Doc promised Dorothy he would bring Clarence to a meeting attended by Dorothy, only when he felt that Clarence was ready. She agreed to come when, and if, this event actually occurred. When Doc told her that Clarence would probably be ready the following Wednesday evening. Dorothy didn't believe that this would happen but she was curious and wanted to "check out" these other people. She was also curious to see with her own eyes this "new Clarence" that Doc had told her about.

Dorothy was neither asked to, nor did she make any guarantees that she would take Clarence home with her. She did, however, agree to be there at the meeting the next Wednesday night. Dorothy and Anne had hit it off quite well; and in spite of her reservations about Clarence, Dorothy knew that she did want to continue the dialogue with Anne.

Doc had arranged for the mother of one of the other "rummies" to drive Dorothy to Akron that Wednesday.

This woman was Mrs. T., and she was a lot like Anne Smith—friendly and with a spirit of serenity and genuine goodness that Dorothy hadn't seen for years.

Her son Lloyd T. was an early member who had gotten sober in 1937 with Doc's help, and was himself a frequent visitor to the meetings in Akron. When the book *Alcoholics Anonymous* was being written, Lloyd was asked to submit his story for inclusion in the book. His story, *"The Rolling Stone,"* appeared in all sixteen printings of the First Edition.

On the appointed Wednesday night meeting at the Williams' home, Clarence just stood there. Dorothy just sat in her chair. Both of them with their mouths dropped open. They were staring at each other in complete shock and disbelief.

Dorothy had been told that Clarence would be there, but he was in fact the last person she ever expected to see. She thought that Doc would never feel that Clarence was ready for this meeting. But there Clarence was, and Dorothy did see something very different in Clarence.

Despite Clarence's obviously disheveled appearance, there seemed to be a newness about him. He stood straight. His blue eyes were clear and sparkling. True, he looked quite emaciated, but at the same time he also looked healthier than Dorothy had seen him in many years. He seemed as healthy as he had been when he first swept Dorothy off of her feet at that dance, that now seemed so many years ago—not so much healthy on the outside as he appeared to be healthy on the inside.

Clarence still felt self-conscious—his clothing, his physical demeanor—what would Dorothy think? Now that he really felt he was on the road to recovery, would Dorothy be willing, after all that they had been through, to travel it with him? Would it be travel or just travail?

Clarence was about as prepared for this encounter as he had been prepared to get down off of that hospital bed on to the cold concrete floor dressed in his shorty nightshirt—about as prepared for this as he had to ask God to manage his life. He had trusted Doc before. Why not again? But still ….

Just at that moment, Doc grabbed Clarence's hand and began to introduce him to the other people in the room. "Doc saved me again," Clarence recalled. Clarence met Anne Smith, Henrietta Seiberling (who had been instrumental in bringing Bill and Doc together), Henrietta D. (the wife of Bill D., whose story, "Alcoholics Anonymous Number 3," is in the second and third editions of the A.A. Big Book), and T. Henry and Clarace Williams, whose magnificent house this was.

Bill D., Alcoholics Anonymous Number 3

Clarence then began to notice some of the men who had visited him in the hospital, who had given so freely of their time and who had shared their lives with a complete stranger. There was Jim S. (whose story, "Traveler, Editor, Scholar," was in the first edition of the Big Book), Bill V. H., (whose story, "A Ward of the Probate Court," was in the first edition), the S. brothers, Paul (whose story, "Truth Freed Me," was in the first edition), and Dick (whose story, "The Car Smasher," was in the first edition), Lloyd T. (whose mother had driven Dorothy to Akron), Bill D. himself, and quite a few others.

All welcomed him, shaking his hand, and saying that they all genuinely meant what they said. Clarence rapidly began to feel less ill at ease. Even Dorothy came up to him, took his hand in hers, and smiled. It was a smile that Clarence had not seen in years and had thought, prior to this night, he would never see again.

Bill V. H. wanted to speak with Clarence privately. Clarence reluctantly excused himself, exacting a promise from Dorothy that she would be there when he returned. He followed Bill into a side room.

Bill took out his wallet—a worn leather billfold, stuffed to overflowing with papers and cards. All of this was held together with a rubber band. Clarence thanked Bill in advance for what he thought was to be money, and waited for a couple of dollars to pass into his hands. Instead, to Clarence's dismay, Bill dumped the billfold's contents on to a small marble table, atop which was a Tiffany lamp. Bill began laboriously to sift through all of these papers, stopping once and a while to take a closer look and examine what was written on them.

At last he found what he was looking for. He held it up to Clarence as if it were made of a precious material. He slowly placed the item into Clarence's outstretched palm. He placed his other hand over Clarence's and looked seriously into his eyes.

He then uttered only three words. Clarence always remembered that scene as if it had happened just the day before. The three words were, "Read and remember." Bill turned, picked up the contents of his billfold and slowly walked away, leaving Clarence with this piece of paper in his hand.

Clarence held the card up to read this very important message. The message contained on this small piece of paper had a great impact on the rest of Clarence's recovered life, a recovered life that lasted over forty-six years.

Clarence learned the message. He memorized it. He believed in it. He taught it to everyone who would listen to him. And most important of all to Clarence, he *lived* it. It was a quote from the *King James Version of the Bible*, a passage from the book of Second Corinthians, Chapter Five, verse seventeen:

"Therefore if any man be in Christ, he is a new creature: old things are passed away; behold, all things are become new."

Clarence began to cry. He really felt that the old indeed had just passed away, and that all things had become new.

Chapter 3.8

"The Meeting at T. Henry's"

"Guests at these House-parties are treated as guests; they meet on an equal social footing, whatever may be their social status elsewhere; gloom is conspicuous by its absence, and there is more laughter at an Oxford Group House-party than at many ordinary social gatherings." [12]

"Moved by the spirit of anonymity, we try to give up our natural desires for personal distinction as A.A. members both among fellow alcoholics and before the general public." [13]

"But why shouldn't we laugh? We had recovered and have been given the power to help others. // Everybody knows that those in bad health, and those who seldom play, do not laugh much. So let each family play together or separately, as much as their circumstances warrant. We are sure God wants us to be happy, joyous, and free." [14]

The meeting was about to begin. Everyone began to take his seat. Clarence and Dorothy sat next to Lloyd T. and his mother, as was suggested by Doc. There were about fifty people at the meeting: alcoholics from Akron, a few from Cleveland, and the balance "just plain old sinners who didn't drink," as Clarence put it.

The chosen leader for that night was, as Clarence remembered, Paul S. ("Truth Freed Me" in the first edition).

Paul opened the meeting with a prayer for all of those in attendance and for those unfortunates who were still living in sin on the outside. Paul then read a verse or two out of the King James Version of the Bible. Clarence remembered that the particular verses, as well as everything at the meeting, had been "gotten from guidance" before the meeting.

In the Oxford Group, guidance was by the Holy Spirit and was received through "two-way" prayer. There was a prayer to God for guidance and then listening for leading thoughts from God. The person who through guidance was chosen to lead the meeting would pray for God to "guide" him or her as to what to read and say at the meeting. Then there would be "quiet time" spent silently waiting for, and then listening to God's response. The Group would then read from a Bible devotional—usually *The Upper Room*. This was a publication of the Methodist Church South out of Nashville, Tennessee.

"When thou prayest, enter into thy closet, and when thou hast shut thy door, pray to thy Father which is in secret; and thy Father which seeth in secret shall reward thee openly"

April May June

The Upper Room

The Upper Room was, and is, a daily devotional, published as a quarterly every three months, and in the 1930's it cost five cents per issue. For each day of the month, there was an inspirational Bible quote, then a verse from the Bible to study, then two or three paragraphs pertaining to this particular Bible verse as it related to what was then the modern world. Then there was a prayer and a thought for the day. *The Upper Room* is still published today, and except for the price per issue, contains essentially the same type of material that it contained from its inception in 1935.

After the group at the Williams' home completed its prayer, Bible reading, quiet time, and reading from the Bible devotional, the leader would "give witness" (tell about his or her past life and what God had done for him or her). This witness lasted about twenty to thirty minutes. Then the leader "giving witness" would open the floor to those in attendance at the meeting. Those present would raise their hands; the leader would call upon them, and then they too would "give witness."

The
UPPER ROOM
Daily Devotions for Family and Individual Use

EDITED BY
GROVER CARLTON EMMONS

APRIL, MAY, JUNE
1935
Five Cents per Copy

ISSUED QUARTERLY BY THE
GENERAL COMMITTEE ON EVANGELISM
THROUGH THE
DEPARTMENT OF HOME MISSIONS, EVANGELISM, HOSPITALS
BOARD OF MISSIONS
METHODIST EPISCOPAL CHURCH, SOUTH
656 DOCTORS' BUILDING
NASHVILLE, TENN.

But for a shorter period of time as Clarence described it, "They went on and on with all kinds of things. People jumping up and down and witnessing and one thing or another. Some of 'em would get pretty emotional and carried away. Crying and all kinds of business going on." Clarence went on to say, "It sure was a sight to see, especially for this rummy. After all, just being on the bum like I was, and a total stranger to all of this mumbo-jumbo stuff."

On Monday nights there was a preparatory meeting, called for all of those who were, according to Clarence, considered "most surrendered." These were people, Clarence said, who had already made their full surrender according to the "tenets" of the Oxford Group. This preparatory meeting involved, among other things, sitting in T. Henry's living room and praying for "guidance" from God as to who should be the leader for the regular Wednesday night meeting. There was a "quiet time" of complete silence. Those assembled would then write down, on a piece of paper, the name of a person God had revealed to them in answer to their prayers.

Clarence said he had been absolutely amazed to see that, on most of these occasions, a majority of these people, and sometimes all of them, ended up with the same name on their respective papers.

Clarence said that when a new person was invited to the regular Wednesday meeting, each man or woman, one at a time, was taken aside, and had the tenets of the Oxford Group explained to him or her. A major Oxford Group practice involved "guidance," and as stated, guidance at meetings took place during mandatory "quiet time."

Clarence told how when Doc explained to him about guidance that, "The good Lord gave me two ears and one mouth. That should give me an indication that I should listen twice as much as I should pray."

New people were told they had to read the Bible—the KING JAMES VERSION of the Bible. They were instructed to do this on a daily basis. Clarence said that newcomers were also told to read THE UPPER ROOM daily and to read THE SERMON ON THE MOUNT by Emmet Fox.

Clarence said the new people were then instructed on the Four Standards. These were Biblical principles the Oxford Group people had taken from the teachings of Jesus Christ found in the Bible. These Four Standards were also called the Four Absolutes— Absolute Honesty, Unselfishness, Love and Purity. In an early A.A. pamphlet which is still in print and used in Cleveland, Ohio, the Four Absolutes are described as follows:

"…The Twelve Steps represent our philosophy. The Absolutes represent our objectives in self-help, and the means to attain them. **HONESTY**, being the ceaseless search for truth, is our most difficult and yet most challenging objective. It is a long road for anyone, but a longer road for us to find the truth. **PURITY** is easy to determine. We know what is right and wrong. Our problem here is the unrelenting desire to do that which is right. **UNSELFISHNESS** is the stream in which our sober life must flow, the boulevard down which we march triumphantly by the grace of God, ever alert against being side tracked into a dark obscure alley along the way. Our unselfishness must penetrate our whole life, not just as our deeds for others, for the greatest gift we bestow on others is the example of our own life as a whole. **LOVE** is the medium, the blood of the good life, which circulates and keeps alive its worth and beauty. It is not only our circulatory system within ourselves, but it is our medium of communication to others." [15]

Clarence said the early Oxford Group people were told to live by these Absolutes to the best of their ability. They were told to judge their actions and thoughts by first asking themselves four questions:

> *1) Is it true or false?*
> *2) Is it right or wrong?*
> *3) How will it affect the other fellow?*
> *4) Is it ugly or beautiful?*

These questions can also be found in the pamphlet, which is still available from the Cleveland Central Committee, called ***The Four Absolutes***.

The early meetings ended with "fellowship time," a period of time which was set aside for socializing, exchanging telephone numbers, speaking with newcomers, and making plans. These plans were for social events, in which all participated, in the regular meeting for the next week.

**"Young feller, it's about time you
make your full surrender."**

It was the custom for the older Oxford Group people to participate in the "surrender" of the newer members. When Clarence had attended weekly meetings for a couple of months, he was taken upstairs to make his surrender.

Doc told him, "Young feller, it's about time you make your full surrender." Clarence was still unsure what this meant, but he knew that Doc never steered him wrong and that he had to listen to Doc in order to continue in his new life. A life now free from alcohol and the resulting misery that had always accompanied his drinking.

At Clarence's surrender, T. Henry, Doc, and a couple of the other Oxford Group members went into T. Henry's bedroom. They all, including Clarence—who by now was used to this kneeling—got down on their knees in an attitude of prayer. They all placed their hands on Clarence, and then proceeded to pray.

These people introduced Clarence to Jesus as his Lord and Savior. They explained to Clarence that this was First Century Christianity. Then they prayed for a healing and removal of Clarence's sins (according to the Oxford Group, sin was anything that separated us from God and from others), especially his alcoholism. When he arose, said Clarence, he once again felt like a new man.

After Clarence's first Oxford Group meeting upon leaving the hospital, Doc told Clarence to go back to Cleveland and "fix rummies" as an avocation for the rest of his life. Doc also told Clarence to make amends to all those he had harmed. Doc told him the most important things in life were to "Trust God, clean house and help others."

At first, Clarence didn't have much luck attracting anybody to this new "cure." However he himself stayed sober. He continued to attend the weekly meetings at T. Henry's in Akron. Soon after his later full surrender, Clarence had his first "baby." He now really had a message to carry.

Chapter 3.9

"The Message Is Brought To Cleveland"

A traveler once saw an old man planting a carob tree. 'When will the tree bear fruit?' asked the traveler. 'Oh, perhaps in seventy years,' the old man answered. 'Do you expect to live to eat the fruit of that tree?'
'No,' said the old man.
'But I didn't find the world desolate when I entered it, and as my fathers planted for me before I was born, so do I plant for those who come after me.'" [16]

After Clarence's first meeting, Dorothy invited Clarence to come home with her. She was so impressed not only with the meeting, and with Doc and Anne and the other Oxford Group members, but also with Clarence. She felt within him a new spirit, a new man.

Clarence went back to Cleveland, as he put it, to "fix rummies as an avocation—for free." That was his assignment, his ministry. This way of life had been strongly suggested to him by his Oxford Group sponsor, Doc Smith. It wasn't so much a suggestion—it was an order!

Clarence recalled of these early days: "Now picture this, kids. There was no A.A.'s Big Book, there was no A.A. groups. There was no nuthin! I'm alone in Cleveland, Ohio. Out of a country of a million and a quarter people ... there was no shortage of rummies ... I felt that I'd never really be a good member of this bunch of rummies in Akron until I'd sponsored somebody."

Euclid Avenue, Cleveland

Sponsorship then was nothing like sponsorship as it is known as in A.A. today. Clarence said that in the 1930's, no one could just walk into the Ohio Oxford Group meeting from off of the streets. Nor were the meetings advertised in the newspapers for the most part, except for the large house-parties and team meeting rallies. A person had to be "sponsored" into the meetings, just as was the case for the more select country clubs, and what were known as the "father and son" labor unions. A person would have to be brought in by another Oxford Group adherent. You couldn't just walk in.

Public Square

Clarence had little to show anyone other than himself. There was no A.A. Big Book. There were no A.A. pamphlets, no A.A. history,

nor A.A. groups. There was, of course, the Oxford Group's lecture, but it was not tailored for the alcoholic. Clarence therefore started out by walking the streets of Cleveland. He went into places where "rummies" hung out. He certainly knew many personally.

Clarence wasn't afraid he would pick up a drink himself because his—as he put it—his "purpose was right." He said he could go "into the depths of Hell if my purpose was right." He went every place that he could think of—every place where, a few short months before, he himself had been. "I went into the joints and tackled 'em!" he said. "I walked right in and tackled some rummy and told him he ought to quit drinking. He ought to be like me."

Somehow, each and every time he did that, he met with resistance. Some of it was verbal. Some of it was physical. That, however, in no way deterred him from trying to fulfill the directions given to him by his sponsor. "I talked to hundreds and hundreds and hundreds of assorted rummies," he said, "dipsomaniacs, drunks and what have you. Alcoholics."

Clarence went into saloons, alleys, and abandoned buildings. He went even so far as to go back to Kingsbury Run and the "Roaring Third." He went to speak to, and with, the Associated Charities, the police, doctors, and the clergy. At first to no avail.

No avail, that is, until soon after he had made his "full surrender" in T. Henry's bedroom, on his knees.

Almost seven months after he had left the hospital, said Clarence, "I trapped my first one. I got my first baby into the hospital. I will never forget that experience if I live to be a thousand years old. Because it did something to me, and for me. I never figured I'd be a real Indian and win my feathers until I'd sponsored somebody successfully."

The Depression was in full swing. Many people had lost their homes. They just vacated them and left the area. Either that, or they had doubled up with relatives or friends.

There were scores of homeless people, a lot of them "rummies," as Clarence called the people who were just wandering around. Many of these homeless people moved into the abandoned buildings, just as they do today. They went into these buildings to live and to gain some shelter from the elements. They went to these abandoned places to avoid the eyes and stares of others and the shame associated with their situation in life. Most of these people were men, but there were also many women who were placed in the same predicament. They however somehow didn't seem so visible. Many of the women had relatives or social organizations that took them in, more so than the men.

Clarence recalled, *"I was way over on Fleet Avenue, in the Polish section over there. Bohemian section. I went into one of these houses, and there was probably fifteen or twenty rummies lying around in various conditions. Some of 'em were up, and some of 'em were down. Some of 'em were passed out. Some of 'em were walking around."*

He noticed, as he carefully surveyed the area, a very large man lying on the floor. The man hadn't passed out, but he also wasn't moving. This man was in a condition known as "alcohol paralysis." He was able to see and hear everything, yet he just couldn't move.

"Here was the perfect man for me to speak with," Clarence thought. He couldn't get up and leave. He couldn't take a swing at Clarence, and he couldn't really argue back or make too many excuses. He was the perfect prospect: a captive audience.

Clarence got down on the floor beside this man and proceeded with his sales pitch. Through this encounter, Clarence learned that this man's name was Bill H., and that Bill H. had been an auditor for the Sherwin Williams Paint Company. Bill told Clarence that he had been employed by Sherwin Williams for many years until the depression came on, and that they had then fired him. He also told Clarence he hadn't seen or spoken to his family in years. This, he said, was because he'd been "on the bum."

Clarence then asked him if he wanted to quit drinking for good. Tears were coming into Bill's eyes as he said, "Yes." This was the first prospect, out of the hundreds with whom Clarence had spoken, who had given him even the least bit of encouragement. Clarence was elated.

Clarence said, "So I asked him the next silly question." This man had been unemployed for years. He hadn't seen or spoken to his family for an equal amount of time. He was paralyzed, and he was living in an abandoned building during the depression. I asked him 'Could you get a hold of any dough? Fifty bucks? I'll get you into a drying out place and get you sobered up.'"

Clarence didn't have to wait too long for an answer. From the dejected look on Bill's face, Clarence knew that he might just as well have asked Bill for fifty thousand dollars. Clarence too began to feel dejected. He had finally come across someone who wanted help and was willing to do anything to get it. Yet Clarence couldn't do anything to help him.

Just when Clarence was ready to give up and get up off of the floor, a broad smile slowly crept across Bill's face. He told Clarence that his elderly, widowed mother, who lived in Madison, Ohio, which was about fifty-five miles east of Cleveland, probably had the money. Bill said that if Clarence were to go out there and tell the mother that he had found her son, she would give him anything. "Anything," said Bill, "if she knows that you're gonna help me."

Clarence jumped up, told the man, who lay paralyzed on the floor, to "stay right there," and ran out. He borrowed a car from one of the other "rummies" in the Oxford Group, and headed out to Madison, Ohio.

The trip took over an hour and a half. The house where Bill's mother was supposed to have lived was a farm house about a half mile distant at the end of a dirt road that branched off from the main road. Since Clarence had borrowed the car and the road was quite muddy and full of rocks and depressions, he decided to walk. He thought that it wouldn't be such a good idea if he got stuck and couldn't get out. Off he went down this muddy dirt road, on foot.

In the not too far distance he heard the distinct sound of gunfire. "Boom, boom, boom, all over the place," said Clarence. In all probability, it was the hunting season, and the people with the guns, he surmised, were "probably some of Bill's pals or relatives. They're probably all jug heads, and they're running around there shooting at everything that moves."

Clarence had to decide quickly whether or not to continue up this road and risk his life and limb, or go back to the safe car and "let the whole thing go down the drain." He decided to continue on up to the house, ever mindful that the next step he took might be his last. He prayed, with each and every step that he took, for God to protect him. After all, wasn't he on a mission for God? Wasn't he doing God's work? The least that God could do was allow him to complete the task at hand.

He knocked on the door and waited. He knocked on the door again. Eventually, this little white-haired old lady appeared at the door, looking at him as if to say, "Who are you, and what are you doing here?"

She looked around behind him and, seeing no car, looked him over from head to toe. She looked down at his muddy shoes and pants legs and then back up to his sweaty face. She had an expression on her face which seemed to say, "You've got to be crazy walking in the woods. Don't you know that it's hunting season?"

All of this ran through Clarence's mind as he started telling her that he had found her long lost son. He told her he was going to put her son into a hospital to dry him out. Clarence told her that he himself was cured of this very same terrible disease, and that all he needed from her was fifty dollars to cover the expenses at the hospital.

He told her that her son Bill told him she would be willing to give him the money. He then asked her what she thought of all this? She stared at him with a totally blank expression on her face. Oh, no, Clarence thought. She too was a drunk, and was also in a stupor.

But this, as it turned out was not the case. If only it had been that simple. In fact, Bill had neglected to tell Clarence one very tiny, minute detail. Bill had forgotten to tell Clarence his mother was Polish, and that she neither spoke nor understood a single word of English. Somehow, Clarence learned the truth.

Clarence was dumbfounded. He knew what he thought were two things in Polish — "*Jak się masz?*" and "*Dziękuję.*" Roughly translated, they were "How are you?" and "Thank you." Clarence knew, sadly, that he could "thank you" and "How are You?" for just so long, and then he would run out of conversation.

But then along came a seven or eight-year-old child, who Clarence presumed was the lady's grandson. The child spoke broken English that he had learned from going to public school for a couple of years. He also spoke fluent Polish. Out of necessity, this child became the interpreter. Very slowly, the whole story was retold.

The old lady started to cry and began to thank Clarence profusely. She kissed him, shook his hands, and hugged him. She chattered away endlessly in her native tongue, leaving Clarence unaware of the meaning of her words.

These were the depression years, and many people didn't trust the banks too much. This because many banks had closed and gone out of business. Many people kept their money at home, close to where they could get to it. They buried it in their back yards, in tin cans and in mattresses—anywhere they thought it would be safe. Many felt that "no interest" was a lot better than "no money."

The mother excused herself and left the room. Clarence quipped that she had probably "cut a lump out of the mattress." When she came back into the kitchen where she had left Clarence with her grandson, the mother extended her trembling hand to Clarence. In it was a large stack of dollar bills that were tied together with a string. These were the old-style bills, larger than the ones in use today. She started counting these dollars, in Polish. She was placing them into Clarence's hands, one-by-one.

She tried to insist that Clarence take more than the fifty that he had asked for. This she explained to him, was to cover any other expenses that he might have had to incur and for all of his troubles.

Clarence refused to take any more than the amount that he had originally requested. "Fifty is all I need to get your son into the hospital," he said. She kept insisting, pleading at times. She said that he was insulting her and her family honor. Clarence held steadfast.

He ran down that long road oblivious to the continued sounds of gunfire. He got into the car and started back to Cleveland. This trip that had taken him an hour and a half to get there, only took about an hour to get back. Clarence was flying, in more ways than one.

When he returned to Cleveland, Bill was still lying there, just where Clarence had left him just a few hours earlier. After telling Bill he had seen his mother and that she had given him the money, Clarence went outside to call Doc.

Reaching Doc at his office, he told him that he had gotten his first "baby." He said he was going to drive him down to Akron and asked if Doc would meet them at the hospital. He had to repeat the message a few times. He was talking so fast that Doc had constantly to tell him either to repeat it or to slow down.

When he got off the phone with Doc, Clarence asked some of the other "jug-heads" to help him lift Bill up, and to put him into the back seat of the car. Away Clarence and Bill went. Clarence had "arrived." He was a sponsor. He had now gotten his "feathers."

Looking back, Clarence remembered that Bill finally came out of the paralysis in the hospital and that they had a very difficult time with him.

Bill found it difficult to "swallow" the spiritual program that was being outlined to him. Clarence remembered that he and Doc had numerous verbal bouts with Bill. There was even a point in the treatment where Doc had almost given up on Bill and suggested that Clarence do the same.

But because Bill was Clarence's first "success," Clarence refused to give up. He tried even harder. He eventually convinced Bill to "accept that he needed new management in his life." He added, "Bill *did* get on his knees." Later on in Clarence's sobriety he didn't force anyone to accept anything. He merely told them that they were the ones who had come to him because their lives were "messed up." He told them that if they "didn't want what I had, they could go on their merry way and come back, if and when they were ready to go to any lengths to get well. To recover."

Bill managed to stay dry, as Clarence remembered it, for about two years. But as Clarence put it, due to Bill's continued stubbornness, he began to manage his own life once again. Each time he did this, it ended in disastrous results.

According to archival material relating to the A.A. Association, Bill had to be hospitalized on at least two more occasions. These records showed that on March 12, 1940, William J. H. owed a hospital balance of $34.07. In the records for November, 1940, Bill's balance was "Paid by the A.A. Association."

The A.A. Association was a committee that was set up for the purpose of recording hospital bills owed by prospects and members. "Prospects" were people who were prospective members, but who had not as yet "taken their Steps." The A.A. Association committee was comprised of members of the Fellowship who collected money from prospective members, their families, and other members, and turned the money over to the "Approved Hospitals."

The Association often paid the bills of those less fortunate who were unable to do so themselves. The Association kept an ongoing monthly record of who owed what. These records often showed that the patient—the "prospect"—was "still in house." What this meant was that the newcomer was still in the hospital when the monthly report came out.

There were places in some of these reports where Clarence had penciled a notation of the amount still owed. An example of this would be an item listed as "Charles R ... 3/10/40 ... still in house." After that was written in pencil an entry of "$61.28." Some of the other notations contain the name of the sponsor and/or the group into which the prospect went.

This committee was eventually disbanded in the early 1940's as the A.A. membership increased. In part this increase was due to a series of articles published in the *Cleveland Plain Dealer* in October and November of 1939. The membership increased even more when A.A. received its first national publicity some sixteen months later. This publicity came from an article in *The Saturday Evening Post* by its staff writer, Jack Alexander, in the March 1, 1941 issue. Due to

Cleveland's phenomenal success, a large part of the article covered the experiences of Cleveland members.

After the A.A. Association committee was disbanded, it became the responsibility of A.A. groups and of the newcomer's sponsor to see that his hospital bill was paid. The prospect was constantly "encouraged" until the bill was paid in full. (See archival section for "Hospital Rules.")

Bill H. eventually "got" the program, and as Clarence remembered, "stayed sober for the rest of his life."

THE CLEVELAND PLAIN DEALER, SATURDAY, OCTOBER 21, 1939

Alcoholics Anonymous Makes Its Stand Here

By ELRICK B. DAVIS

Much has been written about Alcoholics Anonymous, an organization doing major work in reclaiming the habitual drinker. This is the first of a series describing the work the group is doing in Cleveland.

Success

By now it is a rare Clevelander who does not know, or know of, at least one man or woman of high talent whose drinking had become a public scandal, and who suddenly has straightened out "over night," as the saying goes—the liquor habit licked. Men who have lost $15,000-a-year jobs have them back again. Drunks who have taken every "cure" available to the most lavish purse, only to take them over again with equally spectacular lack of success, suddenly have become total abstainers, apparently without anything to account for their reform. Yet something must account for the seeming miracle. Something does.

Alcoholics Anonymous has reached the town.

Fellowship

Every Thursday evening at the home of some ex-drunk in Cleveland, 40 or 50 former hopeless rummies meet for a social evening during which they buck each other up. Nearly every Saturday evening they and their families have a party—just as gay as any other party held that evening despite the fact that there is nothing alcoholic to drink. From time to time they have a picnic, where everyone has a roaring good time without the aid of even one bottle of beer. Yet these are men and women who, until recently, had scarcely been sober a day for years, and members

of their families who all that time had been emotionally distraught, social and economic victims of another's addiction.

These ex-rummies, as they call themselves, suddenly salvaged from the most socially noisome of fates, are the members of the Cleveland Fellowship of an informal society called "Alcoholics Anonymous." Who they are cannot be told, because the name means exactly what it says. But any incurable alcoholic who really wants to be cured will find the members of the Cleveland chapter eager to help.

The society maintains a "blind" address: The Alcoholic Foundation, Box 658, Church Street Annex Postoffice, New York City. Inquiries made there are forwarded to a Cleveland banker, who is head of the local Fellowship, or to a former big league ball player who is recruiting officer of the Akron Fellowship, which meets Wednesday evenings in a mansion loaned for that purpose by a non-alcoholic supporter of the movement.

Cured!

The basic point about Alcoholics Anonymous is that it is a fellowship of "cured" alcoholics. And that both old-line medicine and modern psychiatry had agreed on the one point that no alcoholic could be cured. Repeat the astounding fact:

These are cured.

They have cured each other.

They have done it by adopting, with each other's aid, what they call "a spiritual way of life."

"Incurable" alcoholism is not a moral vice. It is a disease. No dipsomaniac drinks because he wants

to. He drinks because he can't help drinking.

He will drink when he had rather die than take a drink. That is why so many alcoholics die as suicides. He will get drunk on the way home from the hospital or sanitarium that has just discharged him as "cured." He will get drunk at the wake of a friend who died of drink. He will swear off for a year, and suddenly find himself half-seas over, well into another "bust." He will get drunk at the gates of an insane asylum where he has just visited an old friend, hopeless victim of "wet brain."

Prayer

These are the alcoholics that "Alcoholics Anonymous" cures. Cure is impossible until the victim is convinced that nothing that he or a "cure" hospital can do, can help. He must know that his disease is fatal. He must be convinced that he is hopelessly sick of body, and of mind—and of soul. He must be eager to accept help from any source—even God.

Alcoholics Anonymous has a simple explanation for an alcoholic's physical disease. It was provided them by the head of one of New York City's oldest and most famous "cure" sanitariums. The alcoholic is allergic to alcohol. One drink sets up a poisonous craving that only more of the poison can assuage. That is why after the first drink the alcoholic cannot stop.

They have a psychiatric theory equally simple and convincing. Only an alcoholic can understand another alcoholic's mental processes and state. And they have an equally simple, if unorthodox, conception of God.

Chapter 3.10

"Cleveland Begins to Come of Age"

"Ideas do have legs, and they travel fast and far, for 'they need no ships to cross the seas!' Indeed they move with such speed that 'the idea conceived and born by the passion of one heart can shape and change the lives of millions, leading great nations on to destruction or destiny.'" [17]

Soon after Bill H. came into the Oxford Group, Clarence began to experience some success in his life—success not only in carrying the message of recovery as an avocation, but success in something equally as important—finding employment.

Years back, when Clarence was still in the finance business, he had worked with numerous automobile dealerships, many of which he had helped to stay in business through some the worst years of the Depression. One of these car dealerships was E. D. Latimer & Company. Mr. Latimer had surmised that Clarence had all of the innate qualities for sales and had what it took to be a super salesperson.

When Clarence approached him about a position, Latimer hired him on the spot. He didn't ask about where Clarence had been working prior to that time, where he had been, or what he had been doing the previous couple of years.

In an amazingly short period of time, and much to Mr. Latimer's delight, Clarence began bringing in customers faster and with more success than any of the other salespeople, past or present, regardless of experience. Clarence had taken all of the old sales and service records from his predecessors and organized a massive list of all of the people who hadn't brought their cars in for service on the scheduled date, or had never brought them in at all. He also compiled a list of all of the customers, past and present, who were due to purchase a new car.

Utilizing these lists, Clarence routed out his course. He arranged his schedule around the locations where they lived. He got into his new demonstrator car and visited each and every one of them personally. He did this mostly in the evenings, to help insure that not only the customer but his entire family would be present.

He kept only one evening free: Wednesday evening was set aside for Clarence's Oxford Group meetings in Akron. In the fifteen months during which he attended Wednesday night meetings at T. Henry and Clarace Williams' home, Clarence may have missed only one or two.

Clarence was very shrewd in his sales practices. He showed a lot of concern. Yet he also often berated his potential customers. He usually did this in front of their families, where this practice had the most impact. He scolded these customers, often telling them, "You are not taking care of your investment."

He developed a reputation throughout the greater Cleveland area for really caring for his customers and taking a personal interest in them. "He cared so much," they would say, "that he went personally to visit with them at their homes." This practice was something unheard of for an automobile salesperson.

E.D. LATIMER was touted as being "Ohio's Largest Ford and Mercury Dealer," and advertised, "You can always do business with Latimer." But personal care had never been Latimer's strongest selling point. Never, that is, until Clarence began working there. People came in droves to see Clarence at the dealership—car owners, families, friends, even "rummies." For Clarence not only sold Fords and Mercuries, he "sold" sobriety and the Oxford Group. And Mr. Latimer didn't care what else Clarence sold, as long as Clarence was selling cars in the volume that he did.

He had not one, but two, demonstrator cars at his disposal and in his possession: one Ford and one Mercury. This special treatment was unheard of in those days. Usually even the best salesperson got just one demonstrator car for his personal use.

Clarence often said, "Now kids, think about this. Think about Divine Providence." After being on the bum, with no home, no money to speak of, no job, and his marriage down the tubes, Clarence had been introduced to a doctor who later turned out to be one of the founders of A.A. He had been introduced to this doctor indirectly through another doctor, who not only lived over four hundred miles away, but who "just happened" to be the brother-in-law of the other co-founder-to-be of A.A. The doctor in Akron got him "fixed." Clarence got his relationship with his wife back and was living back in his home. He was earning a good salary (twenty dollars a week draw on commission). Even more important, he had two cars that were always at his disposal. These cars were used every Wednesday night to ferry alcoholics back and forth to the meetings of the Oxford Group in Akron, Ohio.

"This just doesn't happen to ordinary people," as Clarence stated, shaking his head as he thought of the incredible events that had happened in his life.

Both of Clarence's cars began rapidly to fill up with "rummies": Clarence himself (and his wife Dorothy), George McD., John D., Lee L., Charlie J., Vaughn P., Clarence W., Bill H., Kay H., Sylvia K., Ed M., Lloyd T., and assorted wives, husbands, and other family members. All drove to Akron on a weekly basis. The "Cleveland Contingent," as they were called, hardly ever missed a Wednesday night meeting.

When they did miss a meeting, it was due to extremely hazardous driving conditions which had been produced by inclement weather. And the Cleveland Contingent stayed home *only* after praying and receiving "guidance" against traveling that particular night.

Sylvia K. was one of Clarence and Dorothy's "babies." After living with them for a while, Sylvia returned to her native Chicago, and helped start A.A. there. Her story, "The Keys Of The Kingdom," is in the second, third and fourth editions of the Big Book.

**Sylvia K. eventually returned to her native
Chicago and helped start A.A. there**

Clarence was one of the small handful of early A.A. leaders who were instrumental in helping to bring women into A.A. He argued strongly for their inclusion in the fellowship at a time when they were often unwelcome. Many of the older male members of A.A. felt that women "were nothing but trouble," Clarence said. "Even Bill and Bob were scared of 'em and the trouble they often caused with the old bucks."

A letter to Clarence from Bill V. H., written on January 7, 1951, shows the attitude some of the A.A. men had toward women, even their own wives. Bill wrote and said, "You remember Roland and his good-looking wife at King School don't you? Don't get too excited …."

King School was the location of the first meeting in Akron that was set up after the alcoholics broke off from the Oxford Group. The break occurred after the first edition of the book *Alcoholics Anonymous* had been published in April of 1939 (according to the United States Copyright Office, the actual publication date was April 10, 1939).

In the late 1930's, most of the members of the Cleveland Contingent were Irish and belonged to the Roman Catholic Church. Clarence remembered that they were "getting a hard time of things with the Church." The problem, as Clarence remembered, was the Church's concern with the tenets and teachings of the Oxford Group, which was essentially a Protestant evangelical fellowship.

At the early A.A. meetings, leaders read aloud from the King James Version of the Bible. They "witnessed" and confessed their sins openly, one to another. Clarence said this did not "sit too well with the Catholic Church." On numerous occasions, Clarence had to sit down and meet with Roman Catholic alcoholics and the hierarchy of their Church to explain to them that the alcoholics were not intentionally violating the Church's teachings.

He remembered telling Roman Catholic alcoholics and the Church hierarchy that the groups were instead helping these members of the Church who, due to their excessive drinking, had become non-productive members of society—outcasts as it were. He remembered explaining that they, the "alcoholic squad" of the Oxford Group, were working with these drunkards and, through this life-changing program, their "First Century Christian Fellowship," were turning them into "good Catholics." Good Roman Catholic, productive, income-earning citizens. He also pointed out that many a marriage was being salvaged, thereby keeping members of the Church from getting divorced and undergoing excommunication. "The Church didn't buy this line, not one bit," said Clarence.

He noted that the problems with the Church grew in direct proportion to the ever-growing numbers of people from the Cleveland Contingent who had started attending the weekly meeting in Akron, which was an Oxford Group meeting. Clarence often spoke with his sponsor Doc about this increasing dilemma.

According to Clarence, the Roman Catholic members were being warned by their Church not to attend the Oxford Group meetings. No matter how hard Clarence begged, pleaded, and cajoled church leaders, he could not dissuade them. The Church officials, as Clarence remembered, were threatening the newly "fixed rummies" with excommunication. The "rummies" felt this was putting in jeopardy not only their spiritual lives, but also their continued physical well-being.

The overwhelming problem as Clarence saw it, was that if the alcoholics left the Oxford Group, they stood a strong chance of returning to their alcoholic drinking, and then to eventual insanity or death. On the other hand, if they stayed with the Oxford Group and maintained their new-found sobriety, they would surely be excommunicated from their Church. Then, they assumed— according to their beliefs—they would lose all hope of ever going to heaven when they died, or even of having a personal contact with God—a personal contact which, the Oxford Group stressed, was their only means of maintaining their sobriety.

The Roman Catholic alcoholics were thus in a double bind. Stay with the Oxford Group and be denied the Kingdom of Heaven, or leave the group and be denied their new-found sobriety—the sobriety which, in fact, had returned them to their God after years of an alcoholic Hell. No matter which way they turned, Clarence felt, they were lost. And they turned to Clarence for help. This placed him in an equally confusing dilemma.

Doc was very stringent and outspoken in his loyalty to the Oxford Group, mostly because the Oxford Group had saved his life, Clarence's life and the lives of all the other "rummies," not to mention the restoration of all of them to their families, homes, and jobs, and to new lives made out of old discards. Doc felt that since there was nothing else to offer these alcoholics that differed in any way from what they now had in the Oxford Group, he could offer Clarence no solution—no solution other than to keep talking with the Church officials in an effort to change their minds and hearts. "Otherwise," Doc told Clarence, "if the Church leaders did not change their minds, the men had but two choices: remain with the Oxford Group and probably risk excommunication, or very simply, leave the Church."

Neither of those choices was acceptable to Clarence or to the Roman Catholic members. But Clarence could not offer any alternative choice to them. He was, himself, in a major bind. He felt he had to listen to his "sponsor," the man who had saved his life. He also felt that he needed to pray daily, incessantly, for "guidance" concerning what should be done about this problem.

Events in the following months produced what was eventually to be another choice—a choice that Clarence and the Cleveland contingent had been praying for, a series of events, Divine Providence, that none of them had any idea existed.

The resulting choice produced the beginnings of a program of recovery—a program that was similar to that of the Oxford Group, yet very different—an option that would be open to all who still suffered from alcoholism, a choice that would eventually become known around the world as Alcoholics Anonymous, a fellowship for, and by, those who had an honest desire to quit drinking.

Chapter 4

The Book

"To show other alcoholics PRECISELY HOW WE HAVE RECOVERED is the main purpose of this book." [18]

Chapter 4.1

Its Beginnings, and the Writing Of

"In the early days of A.A., the entire fellowship was bound together by a chain of personal relationships—all created on the basis of a common program, a common spirit and a common tradition." [19]

In 1937, William Griffith "Bill" Wilson traveled throughout the Midwest looking for job prospects. He stopped off in Akron, Ohio, to visit with Doctor Bob and Anne Smith. Both he and Doc discussed their successes and their many failures. They reminisced about their first meeting and about trying to find some means to help change their lives.

Two years earlier, in a handwritten letter, dated May '35, Bill had written his wife, Lois, "I am writing this in the office of one of my new friends, Dr. Smith. He had my trouble and is getting to be an ardent Grouper. I have been to his house for meals, and the rest of his family is as nice as he is." This letter, which was written on Dr. Bob's office stationary, went on to say: "I have witnessed at a number of meetings and have been taken to a number of people. Dr. Smith is helping me to change a Dr. McK., once the most prominent surgeon in town, who developed into a terrific rake and drunk. He was rich, lost everything, wife committed suicide, he was ostracized and on the point of suicide himself. His change, if accomplished, would be a most powerful witness to the whole town as his case is so notorious."

This shows that Bill D. (Alcoholics Anonymous Number Three) was obviously not the first drunk that they had tried to "fix." After Bill and Bob, "Dr. Roy H. McK." was the third. This happened even before they tried to fix yet another person, Eddy R., as reported in *Dr. Bob and the Good Oldtimers*. Eddy would have been A.A. #3 in June 1935, but he slipped. He eventually got sober in 1949 at the Youngstown, Ohio, Group.

The aforementioned letter is presently located at Bill Wilson's home at Stepping Stones, in its Foundation Archives, and a copy of it in the Cleveland Intergroup archives. It is believed to be the earliest correspondence known regarding Bill's association with Dr. Bob. It was written before Bill had moved in with the Smiths and after their first meeting at Henrietta Seiberling's home. Surprisingly, the letter—handwritten with pencil—reports an upcoming "audit" in connection with Bill's planned rubber machinery deal.

This contradicts the common story that the deal had already totally failed. And as the story goes, Bill was tempted by the bar noise in the Mayflower Hotel, afterwards made his miraculous phone call to Rev. Tunks, was put in touch with Norm Shepard, who then suggested calling Henrietta. Through her, Bill finally met Dr. Bob.

Another possible contradiction has been that during the 1930's, many people used the Mayflower Hotel as more of a place to get calls and messages rather than actually staying there. It has been reported that, quite often, people stayed (slept) at other hotels nearby but hung out at the Mayflower all day waiting for telegrams, phone calls and other messages. It has been suggested, but no documentation has been found yet, that Bill actually slept at the Portage Hotel and went to the Mayflower because of its more prestigious reputation.

But eventually, after two years of working with "rummies," Bill and Dr. Bob had helped to "fix" about forty seemingly hopeless alcoholics to achieve sobriety. Almost all these forty members of the yet unnamed society had attained at least two years of solid uninterrupted sobriety. And there were others who had difficulty maintaining a consistent sober status, yet they too continued to attend the Oxford Group meetings on somewhat of a regular basis.

It appeared to Bill and Dr. Bob that they finally had developed a workable solution to the age-old problem of alcoholism. They both felt it would develop into something tremendous if it could be kept in its original form and not diluted or changed by word of mouth as one drunk passed it on to another.

The two founders discussed the possibility of a book which would explain in detail the life-changing formula that people could follow. The book would contain stories—examples of individuals, hopeless alcoholics—who had attained and continued to maintain their sobriety. This book—when finished—would afford many thousands, if not millions, of alcoholics and their families, whom Bill, Dr. Bob, and the other early members could not personally contact, the opportunity that the founders had had for a changed life. The book would also insure, for generations to come, that this new way of life—as outlined in the book—would not become distorted or changed in any way.

Prior to the publication of the book, and while the first chapter was "being dictated," Henry G. P. ("Hank") wrote on what he called the "Sales Promotion Possibilities" and "The Market" for the book. Hank pointed out to Bill the following as to market potential:

1. Over one million alcoholics (Rockefeller Foundation)
2. At least a million non-alcoholics that have definite alcoholic relatives
3. Every employer of 100 or more people
4. Those that take an academic interest
5. Two hundred and ten thousand ministers
6. One hundred sixty-nine thousand physicians
7. The total would be well over three million prospects

Hank also had proposed a sort of outline for the book. The document containing the outline is located in the Stepping Stones

Foundation Archives. Even prior to Hank's marketing proposal and book outline, Bill had had similar ideas. Both had probably already discussed these ideas in general with one another. With the promotional opportunities which lay before him, Bill's mind had begun to work overtime. Not only would there be need for a book to carry the message, there would also be an even greater need for hospitals and even paid missionaries: hospitals to house the thousands of new converts, and paid missionaries to continue to carry the message and the book around the country, and eventually around the world. Bill's ideas were lofty indeed.

Even though the fledging fellowship had only a small band of forty sober drunks, Bill was thinking in the millions: not just in millions of new converts, but in millions of dollars as well. However, in order to make millions, they would need to obtain a good deal of money to promote this new idea.

There would have to be a campaign to raise funds. Alcoholism was a plague upon mankind, and the fellowship had found, he felt, the only cure that had worked. And it *had* worked, at least for them.

Bill had forgotten about the failures of the Washingtonians and of the Temperance Societies. He appeared even to have forgotten the new fellowship's own many failures. Yet Bill thought that, surely, the well-to-do would donate vast sums of money toward this worthy cause. Hadn't some of those same rich people generously supported the founder of the Oxford Group, Dr. Frank N. D. Buchman, and donated to other philanthropic causes? Bill Wilson and Doctor Bob felt that they could wipe out alcoholism with their simple plan. But Dr. Bob, though enthusiastic about this idea, did not wish to run off and do something rash.

He calmly suggested to Bill that they get the Akron fellowship together and get its opinions. They could all pray for guidance, and further discuss the idea. Bill was not too keen on Dr. Bob's idea for a meeting, because of the strong possibility that Bill would be voted down. Doc insisted. According to Clarence, Dr. Bob stated that he would not be a part of anything in which the others and God were not involved.

When Doc insisted, he usually got his way. For Bill knew that the majority of successful members were in Ohio, and that they were loyal to Doctor Bob. The few members in New York could not possibly carry out this plan without Akron's help. Bill acquiesced to Doc's wishes and called the members of the New York contingent to tell them of the plan.

The New York members apparently were fired up by Bill's flowery words and promises of fame and fortune. They told him they would vote on his proposal and get back to Bill within the next day or two.

The Ohio members on the other hand (who were in the majority, not only in sheer numbers, but in length of continuous sobriety) did not get so fired up. They held a meeting. They listened to Bill as he paced the room. Bill waved his hands, and at times pounded his fist on the table. The Akronites watched as Bill lit cigarette after cigarette, often letting the ashes drop on his suit. Bill was an excitable, "nervous man, whose clothing was always full of cigarette ashes. He spoke loud and was always moving around raising his voice for emphasis, and always wanted to be in the front of things" [*as he was described by Sue Smith-Windows, Dr. Bob's daughter, in a interview with her*].

The Akron meeting listened to all that Bill had to say and then listened to the few words that Doc had to say. Then they decided to have a quiet time and pray for guidance in this matter as they did in all important (and even in unimportant) matters.

The answer that came to them by guidance was almost unanimous, to the man. And they were against the idea of the hospitals and the paid missionaries. They were even against the idea of a massive fund-raising effort. They did, however, like the idea of the book. They voted to discuss it further, and prayed for more guidance. It seemed that they too, like Doc, could not be moved from their position. Yet the debate raged on.

Bill continued to promote his ideas to the Ohio members, with times of prayer in between. A final vote was taken upon the urging of Doc. When the votes were counted up, only the book idea and a proposal for a minimal amount of fund raising, "just to cover expenses," was passed. Clarence remembered being told by Doc that "It was real close, I think that it was passed by only one vote." Bill then returned to New York to start the book project, as he and Hank P. thought they were the only ones with enough expertise to do it. They were also going to try to raise some funds for this venture. Bill was met at the train station in New York by Hank, who was waiting for him, all willing and eager to promote this new money-making idea. Henry G. P. ("Hank") was the first drunk with whom Bill had worked who had stayed sober for any length of time. When Hank left A.A. at a later point, he had about four years of sobriety.

Bill had first met Hank at Towns Hospital, which was located at 293 Central Park West in New York City. This was the same hospital at which Bill had several times been a patient. It was there that Bill claimed to have had his "White Light" spiritual experience.

Hank was a red-headed dynamo salesman and promoter whose head, like Bill's, was always filled with grandiose ideas, or so Clarence felt. These ideas had gotten Hank into very high positions in life. However, because of his excessive drinking, Hank had been fired from a Vice President's position at Standard Oil of New Jersey. He then landed in Towns Hospital and was treated for chronic alcoholism.

But prior to going into Towns, Hank had started a new business venture (Honor Dealers with Bill W.) and opened a small office at 9-11 Hill Street in Newark, New Jersey. Soon after, they moved to another office in Newark, and it was in this small office space, on the sixth floor at 17 William Street, that A.A. had its first office. Ruth Hock, Hank's secretary, eventually became A.A.'s first secretary.

According to Clarence, Ruth was also one of the primary reasons Bill and Hank eventually had a falling out a few years later. Clarence told the author, "I don't remember exactly who was hitting on Ruth, but one of these birds had to go, it was a real mess."

Both Clarence and his wife Dorothy became very close with Ruth and, in later years, still remained friendly with her. Clarence thought that it was probably Hank who was the one who had made romantic advances towards Ruth and that Bill told him not to. But, as Clarence put it, nobody told Hank P. "No" and remained his friend. And certainly not his business partner.

In any event, when Bill returned from Akron in 1937, Hank and Bill compiled a listing of wealthy men who, they thought, would be willing to pour money into this noble cause. They had Ruth write numerous letters, and they personally called upon each and every one of the men on their list. They told each man of the "cure" that they had effected, giving themselves and other sober members as living proof of their success. After a great deal of effort, letter writing, cajoling, pleading, and "sure-fire" sales ploys, they had been unable to raise a single dollar. Nor were they able to arouse the slightest interest in the project in any other way.

Both men became despondent. It seemed that their grand scheme had fallen apart. Bill was prone to depression and, as early as the beginning of May 1935, he wrote Lois: "I am sorry I was blue yesterday." [This letter is located at the Stepping Stones Foundation Archives.]

There was absolutely no money to publish the book. Dreams of hospitals and paid missionaries seemed to vanish, gone up in smoke. However, Bill and Hank would not give up. They were driven men, determined to continue on. Continue against impossible odds to fulfill their dreams. Doc and the Ohio contingent continued with their prayers and continuously added to the numbers of sober alcoholics in their fellowship.

Then Bill came up with another idea. In the fall of 1937, he visited with his brother-in-law, Dr. Leonard V. Strong (Dr. Strong who was married to Bill's sister, Dorothy, was personal physician to the entire Wilson family, and was personal physician to Clarence's sister-in-law Virginia.) Bill told Dr. Strong about the bad luck that both he and Hank were having in raising the necessary funds to bring their project to fruition.

John D. Rockefeller's house in Cleveland

Bill also stated to Dr. Strong that he wished that he had entrée to John D. Rockefeller, Jr.

He was sure that if John D. were to take a personal, as well as financial, interest in this great humanitarian work, he would invest heavily in it. As Bill asked his brother-in-law, didn't Mr. Rockefeller fight vigorously for the Constitutional Amendment dealing with Prohibition and hadn't he given vast sums of money to that cause?

Dr. Strong listened intently to Bill. He tried to think if he could be of any assistance. After all, he was Bill's brother-in-law, and Bill was indeed staying sober due to this new way of life—a miracle indeed.

He remembered a young woman whom he had dated back in High School. This woman was the niece of Willard Richardson, who just happened to be head of all of John D. Rockefeller Jr.'s church charities. Strong remembered Richardson quite well, and also remembered that Mr. Richardson had solicited contributions from him on several occasions.

Dr. Strong told Bill he would contact Richardson and that he would, in fact, call him on the telephone at his office. During that phone conversation, Dr. Strong explained to Richardson the work that Bill and the others had been doing and about the great success that they had been having in working with alcoholics. Strong also pointed out, at Bill's insistence, the great need for funding and of the lack of success that they were having in securing it.

Willard Richardson became so excited about the idea that he suggested that Bill and Dr. Strong come over the very next day in order further to discuss the group's ideas and possibilities. Dr. Strong begged apology that he could not attend, but wrote a letter of introduction for Bill to Mr. Richardson which was dated October 26, 1937.

Bill attended the meeting with Richardson the next day, and after a lengthy conversation, both decided to set up another meeting. This meeting would be with some of Mr. Rockefeller's close associates. Bill felt that he was on his way to the top.

The proposal for this later meeting was outlined in a letter from Mr. Richardson to Dr. Strong, dated November 10, 1937. This proposal stated that they would meet in "Mr. Rockefeller's private board room." Present for Rockefeller's staff would be: 1) Richardson, 2) Albert L. Scott, Chairman of the Board of Trustees of the Riverside Church and President of Lockwood-Greene Engineers, Inc., 3) Frank Amos, an advertising man and close friend of Mr. Rockefeller *(Years later, in Frank Amos's obituary, he would be lauded as "one of the five men who founded Alcoholics Anonymous." The obituary pointed out that Amos had eventually served as a long-term trustee of what was to become the Alcoholic Foundation in 1938)*, and 4) A. LeRoy Chipman, an associate who looked after many of Rockefeller's affairs.

To add legitimacy, Dr. Strong was also invited, along with Dr. William D. Silkworth from Towns Hospital, a renowned expert of that day in the field of alcoholism. Dr. Silkworth would later write "The Doctor's Opinion" in the A.A.'s Big Book. Dr. Bob also decided to come, as well as John Henry Fitzhugh "Fitz" M., who was the son of a minister and a resident of Cumberstone, Maryland. Fitz's story "Our Southern Friend" appears in all four editions of the

Big Book. Also invited were other members of both the New York and Akron fellowship.

This meeting, which was held in December of 1937, proved to be one of the turning points for what was eventually to be known as Alcoholics Anonymous. The alcoholics who were present told their stories about how they were released from alcoholism. When they were through, Albert Scott, who was chairing the meeting, stood up and excitedly exclaimed, "Why, this is First Century Christianity! What can we do to help?"

The dollar signs in Bill's eyes lit up again. Here were Rockefeller's staff asking what "they" could do to help. Bill then began explaining a litany of things the fellowship would need. Money for paid workers and for chains of nationwide and, eventually, worldwide hospitals. The hospitals would be strictly for alcoholics. Then there was the book project and the other literature that paid missionaries would be using to help them in carrying the message. Of course, Bill explained, they would start off modestly; but eventually vast sums of money would be needed if this were to grow into a much-needed worldwide movement.

Being the promoter and one of the organizers of the project, Bill explained that the profits from the sales of hundreds and thousands of books would get this movement on its feet. However, for right now, they needed a vast sum of seed money to start.

As Dr. Silkworth and some of the alcoholics were caught up in the enthusiasm, many expressed pretty much the same opinion. Except, that is, for Doc and most of the Akron contingent present, who kept their reservations to themselves. They were reserving their right to question Bill's motives later.

After the alcoholics had their chance to speak, a most important question was asked of them—a question that would save A.A. for many years to come, a question that would save the alcoholics from themselves.

"Won't money spoil this thing?" they were asked. Bill and many of the other New York members sank down in their chairs. Dr. Bob felt God's hand in this reasoning. The question was repeated:

"Won't money create a professional class that would spoil their success of working man-to-man? Won't chains of hospitals, property and prestige, be a 'fatal diversion'?"

It seemed to Bill and the New York alcoholics that all of the complaints and votes expressed in Akron were coming up all over again—complaints that began both to haunt and send them into a state of discouragement and despair. But it was a saving grace that saner and sober non-alcoholic minds prevailed.

Frank Amos left for Akron that next week. Akron was chosen because it was the most successful in membership numbers and length of continuous sobriety. It was also the most probable site for the first of the alcoholic hospitals if any were created—this due in part to the fact that Dr. Bob, the proposed head doctor, lived in Akron.

Amos went over everything two or three times with a fine-tooth comb. He interviewed members of the medical community, families and members of the yet unnamed society, and the clergy who were involved with them. Amos attended meetings of the Oxford Group and scouted sites for the proposed hospital. He came away from the experience sold on the idea.

Amos returned to New York, as excited as Bill had hoped he would be. In preparing his report, Amos left out no details of what he had seen and found. This was indeed something worthwhile, he believed, something that Mr. Rockefeller would surely be interested in. It encompassed religion and medicine, and reclaimed the lives and families of those who were once thought hopeless. This society had found a solution and had brought it all together in one package.

In his recommendation to Mr. Rockefeller, he proposed that this new society be given the sum of $50,000, which in today's terms would have been equal to something between $4,000,000 and $6,000,000. (Weekly income for a simple job was $8 in those years.)

John D. Rockefeller Jr. read the report and intently listened to the glowing praises of this new work. After careful consideration, and taking into account the reasons for the demise of other such previous ventures, Rockefeller flatly turned down the vast money request that

Amos had proposed. Rockefeller stated in all honesty, "I am afraid that money will spoil this thing." He then outlined his reasons, which were almost identical to the concerns expressed by the Akron members. Again, thankfully, saner, more sober minds prevailed. At least for the moment.

It was at this point that Willard Richardson explained to Mr. Rockefeller, the desperate financial predicament that Dr. Bob and Bill were in. He said that in order for them to continue with this venture, they would need at least a little money, a stipend as it were.

Rockefeller pondered upon this for a moment and then agreed to place in the treasury of the Riverside Church the sum of $5,000. This amount was to be held in a special account so that Doc and Bill could draw upon it as they needed money. Rockefeller warned them, however, that if this new fellowship eventually were to become any sort of success, as he knew that it could be, it must become self-supporting.

Out of that $5,000 that was donated by Mr. Rockefeller, $3,000 immediately went to pay off the mortgage on Doc's home. This, it was reasoned, was so that Dr. Bob's mind would be set at ease since he had thought he wouldn't be able to provide a home to himself and his family. It was felt that release from financial insecurities as to his home would enable Dr. Bob to better care for the alcoholics that were placed in his charge.

The remaining balance of $2,000 was earmarked to be parceled out to both Bob and Bill in the amount of $30 per week. This amount would be used to provide the basic necessities of life for them and for their families so that they could continue working on the restoration of the lives of hopeless alcoholics. ($30 per week translated into late 1990's economics equals out to approximately $2,500 a week, four times what the average worker of that day earned).

Even though Rockefeller had agreed to give them only $5,000, this gave both Doc and Bill an above average income enabling them to devote more time and effort to the new cause. But the rest of the men who were at the meeting felt as if more could be done. They proposed that more immediate funding could be made available to this cause by establishing a tax free or charitable trust or foundation. They decided to make it a charitable foundation to make it more attractive to prospective donors and benefactors, since this would enable them to deduct, as a contribution, any donations or gifts from their personal and/or corporate income taxes. This idea was enthusiastically received by those in attendance at the meeting, especially by Bill and the New York contingent.

Through the help and assistance of Frank Amos, a young lawyer by the name of John Wood (at that time a junior partner in one of New York's better-known law firms) was retained to help bring the foundation idea to fruition.

Wood attended all of the business meetings and was instrumental in formulating this new foundation. After much discussion and argument, the fledgling venture was named "The Alcoholic Foundation."

To those gathered at the final vote, the name sounded just as important and prestigious as was the proposed work upon which they were starting. A trust agreement was drawn up, and a Board of Trustees was appointed—once again, only after hours of discussion and argument.

The Board, it was finally decided, was to be comprised of three non-alcoholics—Willard Richardson, Frank Amos and Dr. Leonard Strong, plus two alcoholic members—Dr. Bob and a New York member who, at a later date, returned to drinking, and had to be forced to resign. Therefore, this member shall remain nameless.

The momentous founding of the Alcoholic Foundation took place in May 1938. Yet, even though there was now a tax-free foundation, and though there were extensive efforts by the Board and a professional fund raiser who had donated his services and expertise free of charge, very little if any new funding was raised.

Sometime in the early spring (in March of 1938) the early members began writing the first draft of what was later to become known as the basic text of the new fellowship. This was the precursor of the book, *ALCOHOLICS ANONYMOUS.*

A twelve-page handwritten outline and certain suggestions for the book were found in the archives of the Stepping Stones Foundation in Bedford Hills, New York. Written at the bottom of the cover page, in Bill's writing, were the words, "Hank's Ideas." The author has verified that the outline was written by Hank P.

Hank's document contained an outline of the work, a listing of twenty-five occupations for the writers of personal stories, "Sales Promotion Possibilities, Suggestions for Chapter 1, Observations," and "Questions and Answers."

The "Questions and Answers" were as follows:

QUESTIONS AND ANSWERS

1. The question is often asked—where does the money come from this work?

2. How do I know this will work with me? Why is this method better than any other religious method? (It is not— this is only a step toward a religious experience which should be carried forward in Christian fellowship no matter what your church.)

3. Will I fail if I cannot keep my conduct up to these highest standards?

4. What happens when an alcoholic has a sexual relapse?

5. There is so much talk about a religious experience—what is it?

**Henry G. "Hank" Parkhurst, who wrote the chapter "To Employers"
in the Big Book and his personal story "The Unbeliever"**

On page eight of Hank's document, in the "Observations" section, there is something of an answer to the "religious" question. Hank wrote:

> *"One of the most talked about things among us is a religious experience. I believe that this is*

incomprehensible to most people. "Simple & meaningful words to us—but meaningless to most of the people that we are trying to get this over to.— In my mind religious experience—religion—etc.—should not be brought in. We are actually unreligious—but we are trying to be helpful— we have learned to be quiet—to be more truthful—to be more honest—to try to be more unselfish—to make the other fellow's troubles—our troubles—and by following four steps we most of us have a religious experience. The fellowship—the unselfishness—appeals to us.

"I wonder if we are off track. A very good merchandising procedure is to find out why people do not buy our products—it is good reasoning to find out WHY—I am fearfully afraid that we are emphasizing religious experience when actually that is something that follows as a result of 1-2-3-4. In my mind the question is not particularly the strength of the experience as much as the improvement over what we were."

Hank, when writing of the "four steps," was probably referring to the Oxford Group's Four Absolutes of Honesty, Unselfishness, Purity and Love. Prior to the A.A. Twelve Steps being written, the early A.A. members used these principles to keep sober, as well as other Oxford Group precepts.

Hank's ideas, as well as those from other members in New York and Akron, were guidelines for the writing efforts of AA's founders, who supplied their manuscripts. In any event Hank's outline appears to be the earliest known outline for the Big Book's contents. Hank wrote of the proposed book that it was "... for promotion of cure and understanding of alcoholism."

As a part of the fund raising for the book, Bill wrote his own story, including a report about Ebby's visit at his kitchen table, along with many other ideas which were taken directly from Oxford Group literature.

Bill was utilizing the office on 17 William Street in Newark, New Jersey, since Hank's business was almost defunct. Bill traveled daily to the office from his home at 182 Clinton Street, in Brooklyn Heights, Brooklyn, New York. He could write the rough drafts at home, bring them to Newark, and dictate to Ruth Hock what he had written the night before.

The drafts for chapters were circulated in rough and unedited form. These were sent to prospective donors. And then Frank Amos came up with another proposal. This once again gave Bill new hope.

**Ruth Hock (Crecelius), who was Hank P.'s
non-alcoholic secretary**

It so happened that one of Frank Amos's close friends was the Religious Editor at Harper's Publishing. The editor's name was Eugene Exman. Amos thought that Eugene might be interested in publishing the book.

Bill made an appointment and went to see Mr. Exman. Bill arrived at Exman's office with the unedited pages in hand (see Appendix "Bill's Original Story" for a one-page example). He spoke to Exman not only of the proposed book, but also of their struggles, failures, and successes. Bill went on to tell of their great plans and of Mr. Rockefeller's interest in the venture.

He then handed over the some 1200 lines typewritten by Ruth Hock. Exman was interested, much to Bill's relief. Exman asked Bill if the members could finish the book in a similar style and manner, though refined and edited from its rough form. He also inquired of Bill as to an approximate completion date.

Bill was excited. He answered, "It will probably take nine or ten months." Exman offered the movement a $1,500 advance on royalties which would be deducted from the account when the book was complete and was selling in the book stores.

Elated both with himself and with his apparent success, Bill went back to the Board of Trustees of the Alcoholic Foundation with the offer and told them of their coming good fortune. He emphasized the word "fortune."

It was their consensus that this was indeed the correct route to take. They considered how hard it would be for unknown authors to publish their own book about a cure for alcoholism, especially one written by people who were neither doctors nor psychologists. Harper's was a well-known publisher with an excellent reputation and had the means to market the book properly.

But a great deal of resistance developed in the New York A.A. fellowship. They insisted that the book be kept as a Foundation project, and not involve any outsiders or outside enterprise.

The Board was neither moved nor impressed with these arguments. So there were two factions, each unwilling to move from its position on this issue.

Bill was perturbed. He wanted to do what was right for the fellowship and for himself, but he was at a loss to know which course was right. He wanted to be on the side that was right.

So Bill went to his friend and business partner, Hank P., with his dilemma. Bill felt both he and Hank thought alike, and that he would get from Hank the answer he really wanted to hear. Furthermore, Bill had asked Hank to submit his personal story for inclusion in the book, a story which would later appear as "The Unbeliever," and was going to be included in all the sixteen printings of the First Edition. Bill felt Hank would return this favor.

Hank came up with the following reasoning: If Harper's, a well-known publisher, was willing to pay unknown authors an advance of $1,500 on the basis of a rough draft, he and Bill could, on their own, make millions. Hank was a salesperson of the first order and "sold" Bill on this idea.

Yet it was not so much a sales job as it was a reaffirmation of Bill's own thoughts. Since the Trustees had not as yet been able to raise one cent, and the prospects of their doing so seemed bleak, Hank suggested to Bill that they bypass the Foundation. He proposed to Bill that they put the book on a business basis and not a fellowship basis, and that they form a stock company to raise the much-needed capital, publish the book themselves, and make payment to the Foundation from revenues from the sale of books.

Bill went back to Harper's on his own, without informing the Board of Trustees. He spoke once again with Eugene Exman. He explained what he and Hank had discussed and asked for Exman's personal and business opinion. Bill was prepared for an argument and had formulated in his own mind, some sure-fire responses that he had rehearsed with Hank in order to bring Exman around to his point of view.

Much to Bill's surprise and consternation, Exman agreed fully with him. Exman explained that, contrary to his company's financial interest, he too felt the book should be published, **BUT** fully controlled by the Alcoholic Foundation.

Bill left the office feeling he had to convert the Foundation to his way of thinking. However, when he did meet with the Trustees in executive session, they did not feel as he had thought they would.

It was too late for that however. Despite their objections, Bill's mind was made up. The die was cast.

He had made his decision to bypass Harper's *and* the Foundation. Bill thought he could draw on the experience of the Oxford Group and on Hank's business expertise. Both Bill and Hank were fueled with high hopes and dreams of success. More importantly, to Hank at least, was the money. Hank had already started out on his well-planned and formulated sales campaign. He cornered every A.A. member that he could find. He spoke to everyone he knew. He utilized every sales ploy in the book and probably even some that to this day have yet to be written.

Hank was the ultimate high-pressure salesperson, so much so that Bill had to go around after him to smooth ruffled feathers, anger, and hurt feelings—this not to mention soothing the suspicions that were beginning to arise concerning the motives of Bill and Hank in all this promotion business.

The early members had firmly believed that recovery work was to be their life's avocation—for free. "No pay for soul-surgery" was an Oxford Group idea. To reclaim lives and "fix rummies" without thought of reward was their tradition. Yet Hank was stressing the millions of dollars to be earned—a dream also shared by Bill.

In only a few short weeks, the members of the New York contingent gave their consent, but it was only lukewarm, and given with reservations. Bill discounted the lukewarm response and reservations, preferring to claim their unanimous consent.

Dr. Bob eventually became sold on the idea and became convinced that he too should give his approval and consent—but he stipulated that this should not be made known to the Akron fellowship, until the proposal had the full approval and consent of the Board of Trustees of the Alcoholic Foundation. Finally after much pressure, the Board reluctantly let them go ahead with the proposed plan.

Bill and Hank began formulating a prospectus that would, hopefully, convince the alcoholics who were just beginning to see tangible results from their sobriety. Bill and Hank hoped to get them to part with money—money which would go toward a company that had yet to publish and yet to sell a single book.

Why the Book.

It has been estimated by the Rockefeller Foundation that there are over a million incurable, from medical or psychiatrical standpoints, alcoholics in the United States.

These men realize their vital need and are desparately seeking the answer. The book should be so written that it will prove the answer to these people.

The work has become so broad that full time assistance and direction is needed. This costs money (which has been offered by foundational funds) however the alcoholics believe it should come from within their own experience.

Copy of Hank's notes

Bill and Hank investigated cost factors, production, publicity, and distribution. Hank wrote in this document (a sort of outline and marketing plan combined) that the title page should read:

Alcoholics Anonymous
Published by
Alcoholics Anonymous, Inc.
A Non-Profit Organization for the promotion
of cure and understanding of alcoholism

(It should be noticed that this reference to a non-profit organization called "Alcoholics Anonymous, Inc." was a quite different set up from the Prospectus for the "One Hundred Men Corporation," where profits would go to the shareholders.)

Hank then went on in this document to suggest the following publicity:

> "Newspapers—When book is nearly ready to leave the presses a short mat article should be sent out to the 12,285 newspapers in the U.S. This article would briefly cover the work as it has gone to date. Case histories would be covered.—It possibly would be a brief case history of the work and announcement of the book. At least four news bulletins should be published at weekly intervals, ahead of the book."

Bill found a printer who had been highly recommended to him. He and Hank went to Cornwall, New York, in Orange County, to see Edward Blackwell, who was the president of Cornwall Press. The company was, according to Bill, "one of the largest printers in the United States."

While at Cornwall, Bill and Hank found the book would probably be about four hundred pages when finished, and would cost about thirty-five cents per copy to print. It was to have a retail selling price of three dollars and fifty cents, and a wholesale price of two dollars and fifty cents. Hank pointed out that the balance would be all profit.

The two left Cornwall secure in the belief that they would soon be reaping millions of dollars.

The Prospectus talked about 15,000 to 500,000 copies *(See the section on "Profits" in the copy of the Prospectus of the One Hundred Men Corporation reproduced after the end of Chapter 4.1 in this volume).*

But Hank's current outline included a chart which showed the estimated profits that would be realized from projected sales, respectively, of 100,000, 500,000 and even 1 million books.

The Trustees were strenuously objecting to the plan and stipulated that they would only tolerate the plan when and if royalties were paid to the Foundation. Bill readily agreed to this stipulation. He knew he would own at least one-third of the shares and, according to his agreement with the Foundation, would thus receive one-third of any profits. He surmised the profits from his 200 expected shares would be much greater than what could be received from any other payment.

The Trustees then reluctantly agreed to tolerate and accept the royalties, knowing that it would probably happen even without their consent. They felt that by agreeing, they would have some sort of hold on Bill and Hank and retain some checks and balances.

There remained only two more minor details to be worked out. The first concerned the fact that there was no publishing company incorporated. The second was that, without incorporation, they could not sell stock, and without stock there would be no capital to move onward.

Hank immediately solved these problems. None of the previously suggested names were eventually used. Someone came up with "Works Publishing". There are at least three explanations as to the origin of the name that they chose. The first is that one of the favorite Bible quotes in early A.A. was the passage in the Book of James which said that "Faith Without Works Is Dead." The second is that this first book was to be the first of many "good works" by the new publishing company. The third is that when the members of the group were questioned as to why this "cure" had worked when all others had failed, they simply replied, "It Works." In any event, the name "Works Publishing Company" was adopted.

According to "official" AA history books Hank went to a local stationery store and purchased a pad of blank stock certificates. He had Ruth Hock type across the top of each certificate "WORKS PUBLISHING COMPANY, par value $25.00." At the bottom of each certificate was typed "Henry G. P., President."

When Bill saw these certificates and read them, he was, to say the least, not too enthusiastic about Hank's being President of the company, especially when Bill himself wanted the honor. He was also quite annoyed at the obvious irregularity of Hank's doing all of this on his own, without consulting either Bill or the Trustees. But according to Clarence, Bill was probably more concerned with his own feelings rather than with any irregularities or with the consultation of the Trustees. Hank finally convinced Bill that there was no time to waste and argued "why be concerned with the small details?"

But there was one minor detail they had somehow managed to overlook, which turned out to be not so minor. That detail was that, despite all of their combined super sales efforts, they were unable to sell even one of the six hundred shares of Works Publishing, Inc. stock.

Not to be discouraged, Hank convinced Bill that they should go up to the offices of the *Reader's Digest* in Pleasantville, New York, to try and sell that magazine on the idea of printing a piece about the alcoholic society and about the forthcoming book. He and Bill believed that if *Reader's Digest* could be convinced, and indeed did print an article, the ensuing publicity would sell the book by "the car loads," and that this surge in sales would really convince "those tightwad drunks," as Hank described them.

Bill and Hank secured an appointment and went to Pleasantville to meet with Kenneth Payne, managing editor of the *Reader's Digest*. They outlined their intentions for the book, for publicity, and for the new society. They dropped the names of Mr. Rockefeller and of the others who were Trustees of the Alcoholic Foundation.

Payne was interested. He assured them the *Digest* would print such a piece when the book was ready for publication. He then told them he would, however, have to meet with and get the approval of other editors and of the staff before he could finalize any agreement with them.

Armed with this new possibility for favorable publicity from a national publication, Bill and Hank hurried back to New York City and began, once again, to sell their stock idea. Many of the once reluctant members began to sign up.

Many couldn't afford the full twenty-five dollars. So shares were sold on the installment plan: five dollars a month for five months. The Trustees pitched in as well. They were caught up in the new enthusiasm as were other friends of the movement.

Ruth then sent off copies of what she had typed to Doc in Akron. Bill also brought these copies to the weekly meetings of alcoholics who by that time were meeting in Bill's home. These same alcoholics had been asked to leave the Oxford Group meeting at Calvary Church in Manhattan.

Clarence remembered that they would "red pencil, blue pencil and any other kind of pencil" these drafts out in Ohio and then send the suggested corrections back to "Bill and the boys in New York." On the whole, the Ohio crowd approved of what was being written. Most of the drafts stressed the "spiritual side" of the teachings and principles of recovery, and Ohio had always held to the spiritual foundations of the program. This spiritual philosophy is still very much in evidence at many Cleveland meetings today.

A.A.'s new histories record that the New York "rummies," on the other hand, really tried to rip the book apart. They gave Bill a hard time with what he had written. The New Yorkers did not at all agree with the Ohio suggestions: they continued to try to downplay the spiritual and attempted to stress the "psychological and medical aspect of the illness."

Irving Harris's book about the Reverend Samuel Shoemaker, [20] the pastor of Calvary Church and the "leader" of the Oxford Group movement in New York City, says that the way in which the book treated the medical and psychological aspect was inspired by Dr. Silkworth. Harris says in this book that Silkworth told Bill:

> *"You're preaching at these fellows Bill, although no one ever preached at you. Turn your strategy around. Remember, Professor James insisted that "deflation at great depth" is the foundation of most spiritual experiences like your own. Give your new contacts the medical business—and hard. Describe the obsession that condemns men to drink and the physical sensibility or allergy of the body that makes this type go mad or die if they keep on drinking."*

Dr. Silkworth was referring here to William James's famous book, *The Varieties of Religious Experience*.[21]

Bill Wilson often stated that he had been an agnostic. And the New York group were stressing the medical and psychological aspects of recovery rather than the spiritual. But Bill did have his own private opinions in these matters. Thus he later wrote to an A.A. member in Richmond, Virginia, in a letter dated October 30, 1940, "I am always glad to say privately that some of the Oxford Group presentation and emphasis upon the Christian message saved my life." This same "Christian message" showed in the success that Ohio members were having. The more secular medical and psychological message resulted in greater failure and relapse into drinking within the New York membership.

After writing the first four chapters which were sent back and forth from Akron to New York, they realized it was time to write about how the actual "program of recovery from alcoholism" really worked. There was enough background and "window dressing" in the earlier chapters, they felt. They needed at that point to get to a description of an actual "program of recovery"—something that had eluded them thus far in their writings.

The book had been going slow, what with all the re-writes. Several of the subscribers, people who had purchased stock, were discouraged by the lack of progress and began to slack off in their payments. The New Yorkers wanted to see more tangible results. They wanted the book to be finished and their investment realized.

Bill was at near exhaustion due to the constant bickering and controversy. He said that "On many a day I felt like throwing the book out the window." But the book had to be finished if all of his dreams were to come true.

One of the legends as to how the Twelve Steps of recovery were written is as follows: Bill was lying on his bed at Clinton Street one evening. He was exhausted, discouraged, and at wit's end. He had a pencil in his hand and a legal pad on his lap. Nothing was coming to mind. He had reached a total impasse. He prayed for guidance, as had been the Oxford Group custom. Then, with pencil in hand, he began to write. He put down on paper what he felt were the basic principles which comprised the procedures that at the time were being utilized.

Bill felt that alcoholics would find loopholes within his summary of the original six "steps" that the alcoholic squadron of the Oxford Group had been using. He wanted to make sure that there was nothing that a "rummy" could slip through and use as an excuse.

When he finally put his pencil down, there were Twelve Steps. Bill felt he had found the perfect formula. He had relied upon God's guidance. He also felt secure in the knowledge that just as Jesus had Twelve Apostles who went forth to carry the Gospel (or Truth), this new—as yet unnamed—fellowship had Twelve Steps to help alcoholics recover and go forth to carry their "Truth."

This truth was RECOVERY—Recovery for the alcoholic who still suffered.

Bill no longer felt dejected. He felt renewed, even when that same evening, he was visited by two rummies who objected to the steps as Bill had written them. They loudly complained about the frequent use of the word "God" and of having to get on one's knees in the Seventh Step. Bill did not care. The Steps were to stand as they were.

But then Bill showed the Twelve Steps to the members of the New York contingent. Strong fights and heated discussions ensued. Some suggested "throwing the whole thing out." Some felt that there wasn't enough God mentioned. The latter, however, were in the minority in New York.

But even in New York, Fitz M. "insisted that the book should express Christian doctrines and use Biblical terms and expressions." Bill's opinion was now wavering back and forth.

Hank P., an agnostic like Bill, had realized God played an important part in his own recovery from alcohol, but wanted to use a "soft sell on this God stuff." But he did insist, "Not too much."

The person most vocally and most vehemently opposed to any sort of mention of God in any way was Jimmy B. Jimmy was a strident atheist. He wanted any and all references to God removed, not only from the Steps, but also from all of the earlier chapters of the Big Book. And he was insisting that God should not be mentioned in any of the later chapters as well. According to Clarence, "Jimmy remained steadfast, throughout his life, and 'preached' his particular brand of A.A. wherever he went." New York, Pennsylvania, Delaware, Maryland, Washington D.C., and later to California."

However, though, Jimmy was agnostic. His story, in the Big Book, mentions being alone in a room in New England with nothing but a Gideon's Bible. The NY men who usually provided the funds for anyone who wanted to return to the "nest" rejected him. (Bill's home on Clinton St. Brooklyn). He said, "My brilliant agnosticism vanished and I saw for the first time that those who really believed, or at least honestly tried to find a Power greater than themselves were much more composed and contented than I had ever been, and they seemed to have a degree of happiness which I had never known." He sold the samples of automobile polish because Hank had just fired him from Honor's Co. and made his way back to NY. As he entered Bill's, early in the morning, he inquired if they had had their "quiet time." The men saw his "altered attitude".

In forming A.A. in Philadelphia, he found he could not give away something he did not have. He says, "Then I found that as I give in to the spiritual or personality change I was getting a little more serenity. In telling newcomers how to change their lives and attitudes, all of a sudden I found I was doing a little changing myself."

He returned to Philadelphia for the 20th anniversary of A.A. and thanked a group, who had written him a thank you letter by sending a large ornately scribed Serenity Prayer. It is kept along with his first scrapbook at A.A.'s archives at SEPIA (South Eastern Pa Intergroup Assn.) Jimmy also kept a scrapbook when he moved to California. He was an early archivist of sorts in A.A. beginning in Feb. 1940.

However, although Jimmy never believed in God, he did later recognize that others did and that they too could be successful with their recovery by doing so. In a letter to Clarence and Dorothy Snyder, written before *The Saturday Evening Post* article came out in March of 1941, Jimmy said he had just moved to Landsdowne, Pennsylvania, near Philadelphia. He had "moved down on a new job two weeks ago," he said. And as soon as he had moved there, he started an A.A. group and began to carry his message of recovery. "Last week we had three at the meeting, and this week we have seven alkies. Several of them have been sober for a number of months on a spiritual basis and I do feel we have a swell nucleus started and they all want to go to work."

In 1947, Jimmy wrote a privately mimeographed history of Alcoholics Anonymous entitled *The Evolution of Alcoholics Anonymous*. Nell Wing said that it was the first historical piece that had been written about A.A.

Jimmy and his other atheist compatriots, along with the agnostic Hank, swayed the majority to their side. Bill had to give in. But not fully—Bill agreed to certain changes—he called them "concessions to those of no or little faith." These "concessions" consisted of including the phrase "as we understood Him" in the Third Step. Another was the eventual removal of the phrase "on our knees" from the Seventh Step. "On our knees" was in the pre-publication multilith or manuscript copy of the Big Book which was sent out to early members and prospective purchasers of the book. But when the first printing of the Big Book came out, "on our knees" had been removed.

There were many other changes made to "tone down" the wording of the book. (Compare the original section of Chapter Five, "HOW IT WORKS," with the prepublication multilith copy in

Appendix B, *"The Evolution of the Twelve Steps of Alcoholics Anonymous."*)

The Ohio membership was opposed to any changes in the drafts of the book. They had achieved great success using the original message. Their numbers were growing, and the members who were staying sober, were staying sober with little or no cases of relapse into active alcoholism.

Two years after the publication of the book, Clarence made a survey of all of the members in Cleveland. He concluded that, by keeping most of the "old program," including the Four Absolutes and the Bible, ninety-three percent of those surveyed had maintained uninterrupted sobriety. Clarence opined that New York's "moral psychology" approach to recovery "had nowhere near our recovery rate."

In later years he stated, "they [New York] keep making all of these changes, watering this thing down so much, that one day it will be so watered down that it will just flush down the drain."

He also said, when he was asked why he was so outspoken in his insistence on maintaining his program of recovery exactly as it was handed down to him by his sponsor Dr. Bob: "If you don't stand for something in this life, you're liable to fall for anything!"

Hank P. once told Clarence that it was he, not Bill, who wrote the chapter "To Employers." Hank told Clarence he "got no credit for it, not one damn mention from Bill."

Reportedly Bill wrote the chapter "To Wives." It is said Bill had once offered to have Doc's wife Anne Smith write the chapter, but Anne didn't want to do so. Clarence said she knew that Bill had not made the same offer to his own wife and Anne did not want to hurt Lois's feelings. Lois was in fact angered by the offer to Anne and was deeply hurt. Lois once said she had held a resentment over that for many years after the book had come out. She later wrote a small four-page pamphlet entitled "ONE WIFE'S STORY" which described her life with Bill. In it she stated,

> "Groups of the families of A.A.'s have sprung up all over the
> country with a three-fold purpose. First to give cooperation

and understanding to the A.A. at home. Second, to live by the Twelve Steps ourselves in order to grow spiritually along with our A.A. Third, to welcome and give comfort to the families of new A.A.'s."

This pamphlet was produced before the name Al-Anon was in existence. Lois inscribed to the author on his copy of the pamphlet, "This was one of the very early pamphlets." When Al-Anon finally did arrive, Lois, one of the Co-Founders of Al-Anon, learned to "detach with love" regarding to her long-standing resentment toward Bill over the chapter "To Wives."

While the "Program" portion of the book was being written, the New York and Akron members were submitting their personal stories of recovery. In New York, Bill and Hank edited the stories submitted by the New York contingent. Many of them objected to the way their stories were being totally changed by this editing. In the Archives of the Stepping Stones Foundation in Bedford Hills, New York, there are several of these handwritten and edited stories which were submitted for the book.

In Akron, Jim S., who was an Akron newspaper reporter and early member, interviewed and helped write and edit all of the stories that came from the Akron area, and eventually all the New York stories as well. Much of this writing took place around the kitchen table in Dr. Bob's home.

Jim S. was one of the men who had visited with Clarence in Akron City Hospital and had told Clarence the story of his own recovery from alcoholism. Clarence had been asked by Doc to submit his story, and as he went over it with Jim, explained to Jim that he was having problems with his wife. Clarence and Jim tried to slant Clarence's story to appease Dorothy and, by doing so, bring the two closer together. Neither Jim and Doc liked this attempt at appeasing Dorothy and they admonished Clarence for his impure motives. Despite this, Clarence's "slanted" story was published "as is."

The Big Book was almost ready for publication. But there was one little problem: the book did not as yet have a name. Nor did this new fellowship of nameless drunks. Everyone was asked to submit names for the book, and more than one hundred titles were actually considered. The following were some:

1) "The James Gang," taken from the Epistle of James in the Bible, on which some of the recovery program was based.
2) "The Empty Glass," "The Dry Life," or "The Dry Way."
3) "The Way Out," a title which was abandoned after an extensive search conducted in the Library of Congress showed that there were already twelve other "The Way Out" books in publication. The members decided that it would be too unlucky to be number thirteen.

Bill had even proposed calling the book and naming the fellowship "The B.W. Movement," naming it after himself. This particular title did not meet with much approval from the Akron group, who were fiercely loyal to Dr. Bob. About that story it says in *AA Comes of Age* on page 165:

"I began to forget that this was everybody's book and that I had been mostly the umpire of the discussions that had created it. In one dark moment I even considered calling the book The B. W. Movement. I whispered these ideas to a few friends and promptly got slapped down. Then I saw the temptation for what it was, a shameless piece of egotism."

Another popular title that was proposed was "One Hundred Men." This was popular due to the fact it showed the obvious success of the movement and also that one hundred was a nice round figure. Actually there were—at that point—only some forty sober members between Akron and New York, with the vast majority being in Ohio. However forty men didn't seem as persuasive as one hundred.

As to the number 100, the meetings then were open not only to the alcoholics, but also to their families as well. The wives (and the one or two husbands of the women members) were added to the number forty, and it amounted to around a hundred people who were attending meetings.

There was one hitch to this title however. The hitch came from one of the women members: Florence R., who was the only woman member in New York, objected strenuously. Her story was submitted and printed in the pre-publication multilith edition, and she did not want to be "one of the boys." In the multilith edition, her story was typed out with a typographical error in the title: "A Femine Victory." The error was corrected in the actual printed first edition, so the title of the story was given correctly as "A Feminine Victory" in all sixteen printings of the first edition.

Florence unfortunately did not maintain her sobriety on a constant basis, and it was reported that she committed suicide in Washington D.C. during an alcoholic depression. We have since learned that she may have died from complications of pneumococcal meningitis according to WAIA (Washington Area Intergroup Assn). The death certificate says she died April 19, 1943 at Gallinger Municipal Hospital. Her story was taken out when the second edition was printed in 1955.

But in deference to Florence, they agreed that the title should not be "One Hundred Men." They did, however, continue to describe the book on its title page as "The Story of How More Than One Hundred Men Have Recovered From Alcoholism." This angered Florence very much. By the time the second printing of the first edition came out in March 1941, the title page had been changed to "Thousands of Men and Women."

The origin of the actual Big Book name, *Alcoholics Anonymous*, will probably forever remain unknown. Some have said it came from someone's describing the movement as a bunch of "anonymous alcoholics" who met for their recovery. Others said, "We were nameless drunks at a meeting." The most accepted version is that a writer from the *New Yorker* Magazine by the name of Joe W. apparently coined the phrase. (Joe remained sober only periodically, and according to Clarence, never really "got the program.")

The name *Alcoholics Anonymous* was definitely in use however by the late summer of 1938. At that point, the name was mainly used in connection with the title of the book, and only to a smaller extent as the name of the fledgling fellowship. Meetings, both in New York and in Akron, were not as yet being called Alcoholics Anonymous meetings. They were still, in actuality, Oxford Group meetings. The Akron group meetings were still officially Oxford Group meetings, and the New Yorkers—who Clarence believed had been asked to leave the Oxford Group meetings somewhat earlier—still had no other name for their gatherings. As Clarence once explained, the New York contingent had been asked to leave the Oxford Group because the "drunks and pickpockets" were no longer welcomed. This, he stated, was due to the large number of members who showed up drunk at meetings, and from those members who picked the pockets of the well-to-do Oxford Group members who were also in attendance.

By the end of January 1939, the Big Book manuscript was ready for publication. Not all of the stories were completed or submitted as yet, however twenty-one of them were finished. Four hundred copies were multilithed—run off from a master copy typed on an ordinary mechanical typewriter of the kind used in offices at that time—and were spiral bound. They were packed to be shipped from the office on William Street in Newark, New Jersey.

There was one other error, which may or may not have been typographical. It even appeared on the title page. The book was entitled "ALCOHOLIC'S ANONYMOUS" with an apostrophe in the word "Alcoholic's." It is not found on all copies.

Some of the copies were sent out to members, doctors, clergy and other friends of the movement for their comments, criticism and evaluation. The balance of the copies were sold to people who had ordered the book before its final printing. There was no notice of copyright nor notice of the multilith being a review or loan copy. Since the multilithed manuscript was published, sold and distributed to the public without these notices, according to the Copyright Act of 1909, it and all subsequent printings were forever in the public domain.

These original manuscripts are very rare today, and less than fifty are probably still in existence. Many are in deteriorated condition.

Reproduced copies are available to interested parties at the Archives at the General Service Office of Alcoholics Anonymous in New York City.

The multilithed pre-publication copy contained the original "explanatory" chapters, including the chapter entitled "The Doctor's Opinion," which was written by Dr. Silkworth of Towns Hospital in New York City. Dr. Silkworth did not have his name printed in the book until the second edition, which came out in 1955.

This multilithed manuscript contained twenty-one personal stories. Eight were those of New York members—seven men and one woman. Thirteen stories were those of Akron members or people who were attending the meetings in Akron. Twelve of those stories were written by men, and one — "MY WIFE AND I" — was submitted by a couple, Maybell and Tom L.

One of the stories was written by a man who lived in Grosse Pointe, Michigan. At the time the book was being written, he was living with Dr. Bob and Anne Smith. He had been sent down to Akron by the Michigan Oxford Group for help because there were "no drunks" in the Michigan group at that time. This man was Archibald "Arch" T. He later returned to Michigan and started A.A. in Detroit. Archie's story was printed in the first edition as "THE FEARFUL ONE," a title which was changed to "THE MAN WHO MASTERED FEAR" in the second, third and fourth editions.

Another story from a man who was attending the Akron meetings, was the "HOME BREWMEISTER." This man was Clarence H. Snyder, whose story appeared in all the first three editions of the A.A.'s Big Book.

Of these twenty-one stories in the manuscript edition, all save one made the first printing of the first edition. That one was "ACE FULL-SEVEN-ELEVEN." Its writer was a member of the Akron group, who did not like the changes that were being made in the book. He also, as Clarence remembered, did not trust Bill Wilson— he felt Bill "was making money on the deal"—and also did not like the promotion angle that was being presented. The man asked that his story be removed from the final copy sent to the typesetters, so it never appeared in the first edition. His was the only story that talked about the addiction of Pathological (compulsive) Gambling, as well as that of alcoholism. His story ended with the line "His will must be my bet – there's no other way!" Clarence remembered that this man never returned either to gambling or to drinking.

The New York A.A. Archives does not release the names of any of the writers of the stories in the A.A.'s Big Book, so all of the names mentioned in this present book were made available to the author by Clarence Snyder, with the exception of the name of the man who wrote this story, since Clarence could not remember his name.

But the Original Working Manuscript of Alcoholics Anonymous, on page 172 in the Hazelden reproduction (Personal Stories page 62 in the typewritten manuscript) has the story "ACE FULL—SEVEN—ELEVEN" x-ed out, with a handwritten note in pencil saying:

Del T____'s story —
Thought the book was racket
and so with drew this.
w.a.w.*

We believe that these initials are w.g.w.

So his name was apparently Del T. His was the only story that talked about the addiction of pathological (compulsive) gambling, as well as that of alcoholism. His story ended with the line "His will must be my bet— there's no other way!" Clarence recollected that this man probably never returned either to gambling or to drinking.

When the Big Book was ready for its final publication date, ten new stories were added. Four came from New York members, four from Akron, and one from Cleveland. The Cleveland story was "The Rolling Stone" by Lloyd T. He got sober in February 1937 and initially stayed with the Oxford Group in Akron when the Cleveland group broke off. However, he too eventually came into A.A. and stayed sober.

There was one story that was supposed to have been written by a man from California. This story, "THE LONE ENDEAVOR," was written by a man named Pat C. According to the story printed in the book, he had gotten a copy of the multilith and got sober through it alone, without any personal contact. He then wrote to the Newark office, and they answered him, asking for permission to print his letter in the book. Permission was granted by return mail.

In Jim B.'s historical account, *Evolution of Alcoholics Anonymous*, he related this story and added, "Our New York groups were so impressed by his recovery that we passed the hat and sent for him to come East as an example. This he did, but when the boys met him at the bus station the delusion faded, for he arrived stone drunk and as far as I knew, never came out of it." Other sources have it that he came out and stayed out after this event.

There was one Al-Anon type story that was included in the ten new ones. Its title was "AN ALCOHOLIC'S WIFE," by Marie B. She was the wife of Walter B., whose story "THE BACKSLIDER" also appears in the book. We call this an Al-Anon story, probably the first on record, because Mary B. herself was not an alcoholic. In her story she wrote, "Since giving my husband's problem to God, I have found a peace and happiness. I knew that when I try to take care of the problems of my husband I am a stumbling block as my husband has to take his problems to God the same as I do."

Meetings in the early days were somewhat different from those held today. There were really no "closed" meetings, that is, meetings which could only be attended by those who had a problem with alcohol or thought they had. Meetings in the early days were open not only to alcoholics but also to their families.

Henrietta D. (wife of Bill D., whose story "Alcoholics Anonymous Number Three" appears in the second, third, and fourth editions of the Big Book) wrote a letter describing her early experiences at the meetings in Ohio. In it, she also described her first meeting with Anne Smith on Friday, June 28, 1935. The letter reads:

> On Friday night, when I went to the house on Ardmore
> Avenue, I met the most thoughtful, understanding person I

have ever known. After talking with her for a while, I addressed her as Mrs. Smith, and she said, "Anne to you my dear." She wanted to remove all barriers. She wanted God to have full credit for this wonderful thing that had happened to her. Bill W. was there at this time. After they talked with me for a while, Anne asked if I would like to "go all the way with God," I told her I would. She, Anne, said we should kneel, which we all did, and told me to surrender myself to God and ask Him if he had a plan for me to reveal it to me... She taught me to surrender my husband to God and not to try to tell him how to stay sober, as I tried that and failed. Anne taught me to love everyone, she said, "Ask yourself, what is wrong with me today, if I don't love you?" She said, "The love of God is triangular, it must flow from God through me, through you and back to God."

The author has wondered if this triangular description could be one of the reasons that the triangle and circle later became the symbols and registered trademarks of A.A. A.A.'s had the triangle within the circle, and Al-Anon (still) has the circle within the triangle.

In her letter, Henrietta D. continued to describe what was probably the first Al-Anon meeting in the world. She wrote:

> In the early part of 1936, Anne organized a "Woman's Group" for wives of alcoholics, whereby in her loving way, she tried to teach us patience, love and unselfishness. Anne made it very plain to me from the beginning, that she wanted no credit for herself.

Anne explained to Henrietta that there was only one purpose for the wives and the alcoholics both. It was to "know and follow God's plan." After meeting with Anne, Henrietta described a phenomenon often experienced by others who had met with Dr. Bob. She wrote: "I was completely sold on A.A."

In reviewing Henrietta D.'s account, the author is reminded of Anne Smith's remarks in her *Spiritual Workbook*:

1. A general experience of God is the first essential, the beginning. We can't give away what we haven't got. We must have a genuine contact with God in our present experience. Not an experience of the past, but an experience in the present—actually genuine.

2. When we have that, witnessing to it is natural, just as we want to share a beautiful sunset. We must be in such close touch with God that the whole sharing is guided. The person with a genuine experience of God with no technique will make fewer mistakes than one with lots of technique, and no sense of God. Under guidance, you are almost a spectator of what is happening. Your sharing is not strained, it is not tense.

Anne was living "witness" to what living these precepts could produce in a person. Early A.A. accounts often record that everyone who came into contact with her could feel the presence of God and the peace and serenity that Anne possessed.

Two stories which appeared in both the multilith and the first edition where those of two brothers—Richard "Dick" S. (whose story is "The Car Smasher") and Paul S. (whose story is "Truth Freed Me!"). Ironically, it was Paul and not Dick who eventually died as a result of an automobile accident on September 19, 1953. However, both brothers remained completely sober until their respective deaths.

Dick S., whose story "The Car Smasher" was in the first edition

This ends the review of the writing of the book. All that then remained was to get the finalized and approved version of the book to Cornwall, New York. Hank, Ruth Hock, Dorothy Snyder (Clarence's wife), and Bill went together to a hotel in Cornwall. There they checked and corrected the galleys and got the book printed.

But there remained another detail. How were they going to pay the Cornwall Press the money necessary to print their book?

PROSPECTUS
THE ONE HUNDRED MEN CORPORATION

FOREWORD

Before considering the attached proposal, certain information should be known by the reader.

Informed doctors and psychiatrists consider true alcoholism just as much a diease as cancer. The bodies of those subject to alcoholism have become abnormal in reaction and mind even more so. This has been called an allergy. Many alcoholics are men of exceptional character and willpower, as proven by the type of men that make up Alcoholics Anonymous. Among the recoveries are men from every profession, and practically every type of business. People not familiar with the subject think alcoholism is a habit based upon physical craving. This is absolutely not true, for when not drinking, no physical craving exists. This is proven by the following fact: Physicians state that a maximum of six months abstinence removes any physical craving and yet it commonly occurs that men start to drink again after having been confined in an institution for as much as a year. It has been repeatedly stated by the world's leading doctors that they have no answer save for the very mildest of cases.

It is an indisputable fact that over the past four years over one-hundred true alcoholics have recovered, who from the standpoint of medicine and psychiatry, were considered hopeless. These men have dubbed themselves Alcoholics Anonymous.

Another indisputable fact is that during 1937, thirty-five percent of the life insurance turn downs were due to alcoholism. A realization is coming to public, professional and business men that there exists today an alcoholic problem which takes its place in seriousness with cancer and syphilis. Magazine and news articles on the subject bring incredible response.

The name Alcoholics Anonymous has been adopted because of the nature of the work, because of the desire to keep away from notoriety, and because the work is strictly non-sectarian.

BRIEF RESUME OF THE WORK OF
ALCOHOLICS ANONYMOUS

About four years ago William G. Wilson had been pronounced an incurable alcoholic. Doctors and psychiatrists have agreed that the only way out for the true alcoholic is through a so-called spiritual experience and it matters little what form this experience takes.

In November of 1934, a school friend came to Mr. Wilson's house with certain information that has undoubtedly saved his life and the lives of many others. Mr. Wilson's friends outlined a procedure for a simple spiritual approach, and through its use Mr. Wilson was released from alcoholism.

At that time certain ideas came to him which form the basis of the events which have since transpired. Mr. Wilson realized first of all, that to be acceptable to the ordinary men of the world, the spiritual feature must be simple and understandable. He saw that the particular spiritual approach presented to him had these characteristics, and could even be further simplified and made effective. Because the approach had the elements of universal appeal, he wondered why so comparatively little success had been secured from the spiritual approach with other alcoholics. He conceived the idea that it was because the matter was so often presented to an alcoholic by a non-alcoholic; that there was not sufficient basis for initial mutual confidence. He realized that one alcoholic could gain the confidence of another to an extent that no other person in the world could.

The idea took hold of Mr. Wilson's imagination, for he envisioned one alcoholic helping another; that one helping still another and so on. After his release from Towns Hospital, Mr.

ALCOHOLICS ANONYMOUS

Wilson began to return there to talk to some of the patients. Several caught the idea and bear witness today to the effectiveness of those first approaches.

It occured to Mr. Wilson that accurate and reliable medical information should be in the possession of every alcoholic when he approached another alcoholic. With such equipment the new prospect could be readily persuaded that he was hopeless; that he is, in actual fact at the jumping off place.

Being convinced there was no other way out, the new man would look with more favor and willingness upon a spiritual method in spite of any prejudice he might have had.

In the spring of 1935 Mr. Wilson went to Akron, Ohio, on business. While there he communicated his ideas to three other alcoholics. Leaving the three men, he returned to New York in the fall of 1935, continuing his activities there. These early seeds are now bearing amazing fruit. The original Akron three have expanded themselves into more than seventy. Scattered about New York and in the seaboard states there are about forty. Men have even come out of insane asylums and resumed their community and family lives. Business and professional people have regained their standing.

In all, about two-hundred cases of hopeless alcoholism have been dealt with. As will be seen, about fifty percent of these have recovered. This, of course, is unprecedented—never has such a thing happened before.

This work has claimed the attention of prominent doctors and institutions who say without hesitation that in a few years time, as it gains impetous, thousands of hitherto incurable cases may recover. Such people as the chief physician of Charles B. Towns Hospital and psychiatrists of the Johns Hopkins Hospital at Baltimore express such opinions.

THE PRESENT PROGRAM

It has been felt vitally necessary to spread the work widely and get it on a sound basis rapidly.

The first step has been the establishment of a trust known as The Alcoholic Foundation. This trust is administered by a board of three well-known business men who are non-alcoholics, and by two members of Alcoholics Anonymous. The articles of the trust specifically set forth that non-alcoholic members shall always be in a majority of one over the alcoholic members. The Alcoholic Foundation will, in order to obviate any possible criticism, administer the financial affairs of the group.

When it is considered that there are an estimated million alcoholics in this country the obligation for wide spread of the work may be perceived. Education and instruction should be made available to every one touched by a drink situation. An understanding of the nature of the disease and its cure must be mastered by wives, relatives and employers of alcoholics. A definite program of attitude and action should be offered every-one concerned. It is felt that these aims may be gained by the publishing of an anonymous volume based upon the past four years experience.

The publishing of this book, to be known as "One Hundred Men," is the subject of the attached material. The Alcoholic Foundation will receive an author's royalty as a donation for the furtherance of the work.

Considering the necessity for a volume of this kind; its being based upon actual experience; the publicity that has been assured; and the tremendous amount of good inherent in its results; anyone must agree with a former editor of the New York Times, who after reading the first two chapters predicted a sensational sale. (Ten chapters have now been written).

ALCOHOLICS ANONYMOUS

THE PROPOSAL

It is proposed to form—
"THE ONE HUNDRED MEN CORPORATION."

PURPOSE

To publish the book—"One Hundred Men."

ASSETS

Money has been subscribed to maintain the author for five months. A completely equipped office.

THE ISSUE

Sufficient $25.00 par value shares to promote publicity, sales, and publish the book. Shares either payable in full at time of subscription, or five dollars for each share subscribed at time of subscription and five dollars per share each thirty days for four months after subscription.

THE CORPORATION

Stock—Non-Assessable.　　Delaware Corporation.

FACTS

The following facts are pertinent in considering the possible success of the volume—"One Hundred Men."

1. Publicity
2. Established Publishers' Opinion
3. The Possible Market.

PUBLICITY—1. Of publicity value is the fact that the foundational soundness of the work is verified by letters from The Johns Hopkins Hospital, and the chief physician of Charles B. Towns Hospital, one of the foremost alcoholic institutions in the United States. Furthermore the work has been investigated and justified most thoroughly by private parties from an outside source.

2. The syndicated magazine **This Week**, (included with Sunday New York Herald Tribune and many other Sunday newspapers) has expressed an interest in running a page two article regarding the work and the forthcoming book. The editor prophesied from fifteen to twenty thousand inquiries from the weekly circulation of five million two hundred and fifty thousand. This syndicated magazine section for Sunday newspapers is second only to the American Weekly used by Hearst papers.

3. The Readers Digest, in a personal interview with the Managing Editor, stated that the work and the forthcoming volume were of such interest as to justify their placing a staff writer on it and running an exclusive article just prior to publication of the volume.

4. Mr. Wainright Evans, established author, wrote Mr. Bigelow, Editor of Good Housekeeping magazine, a letter regarding the work. Two of the members of Alcoholics Anonymous in company with Mr. Evans called upon Mr. Bigelow who requested Mr. Evans to submit an outline of the completed article which he believed would be used by the magazine just prior to the issuance of the book.

5. A fact pertinent to one's calculations as to the possible public interest should be the results of the publication last spring of an article entitled "The Unhappy Drinker" in the Saturday Evening Post. The Post commented that more inquiries came to them from this than from any other article they had ever printed.

6. Approximately a year ago a very obscure article was published by Doctor Silkworth in a small New York Medical journal. He barely alluded to this work, simply saying that such a thing was happening. He was amazed by the hundreds of inquiries received from lay people all over the United States.

7. Established publishers have said both directly and by implication that this volume seems assured of the most unusual publicity preceding publication of any book they have known.

ESTABLISHED PUBLISHERS OPINION—Established pub-

lishers must practically see a sure fire book in order to make an advance to an author. Furthermore they are exceptionally careful that this advance is conservative in order that it may be returned from royalties on sales. Harper & Bros. after reading the first two chapters, investigating the publicity, and talking to two members of Alcoholics Anonymous, offered fifteen hundred dollars as an advance against royalties. This is impressive in view of the fact that five thousand volumes would need to be sold to repay the advance.

In the course of publishing investigation, these same two members of Alcoholics Anonymous called upon Mr. Walsh, owner of the John Day Publishing Company, publishers of such volumes as The Good Earth, The Importance of Living, etc. This call was made upon the basis of a personal friendship with Mr. Walsh and as a consequence the advice given by him was upon a friendly basis rather than securing the publishing of the book. Not only did Mr. Walsh give invaluable printing, credit, and sales information, but predicted an unusual sale for the volume. He said, and gave reasons for his opinion which will be outlined later, that he could not see where this venture would gain through using an established publisher.

THE POSSIBLE MARKET—It has been estimated that there are over a million alcoholics in the United States and that every family seems touched by the problem. If this is so, and we have been assured that there has never been any published work that not only gave the answer, but told a man what to do to recover, then this book should have an incredible sale.

One Hundred Men will not only have an appeal to the alcoholic layman, and those affected, but should appeal to the five hundred thousand Clergymen in this country, the three hundred and fifty thousand Physicians, and the twenty odd thousand established Psychiatrists. We know that the problem is one of pressing concern to large corporations, and we know also that special reprints should be interesting to insurance companies.

Taken these few fundamental market facts into consideration, along with the publicity that seems assured, who can estimate the possible sale?

CORPORATE SET-UP

The corporation is set up on a budget that runs to April 1st. By that time the book will be out and further sales plans will need to be made upon experiences to date.

However for full protection of the shareholders the shareholders procedure will be set up in the articles of the corporation.

On each of the first 1000 books, eighty cents will be apportioned among the shareholders who have made a cash subscription.

On each of the second 1000 books, seventy cents will be apportioned among the shareholders.

On each book over 2000 books and until the subscriptions have been returned, sixty cents will be apportioned to the shareholders.

The difference between the above payments and the gross profit will accrue in the corporate treasury. It is planned to call a stockholders' meeting in March, 1939, to vote as to whether the corporation shall distribute cash on hand to the stockholders, or continue maintaining headquarters for the direct sales of the book.

BUDGET TO APRIL 1st, 1939.

Author	$1,000.000
Directional and Sales Promotional Work	1,800.00
Office Rent	480.00
Stenographer	650.00
Office Expense (estimated)	240.00
Incidental Expenses	500.00
Printing Plates	700.00
1000 Volumes	350.00
Art Work	250.00
	$5,970.00

Of the above, there has been extended as a loan to insure the writing of the volume $1,500.00

COSTS

Printing (highest figure assumed by Mr. Walsh)

per volume...	$. 34
Royalty (to Alcoholic Foundation)	.35
Packaging, drayage, etc. per volume...............	.05
	.74

SALES FIGURES

Retail price.......................................	$3.00
Jobbers discount (maximum 46%).................	1.38
	1.62
Printing, royalty, and packaging	.74
Gross profit per volume sold through book stores ...	.88

Mr. Walsh estimated that as a result of the publicity, one volume at least would be sold for every two volumes through book stores. For direct sales the following costs would prevail.

Printing	$ .34
Royalty (to Alcoholic Foundation)	.35
Package, drayage, addressing......................	.12
Postage (highest)	.12
	.93
Gross profit one direct sale.......................	$2.07

Taking the estimate of one direct sale for two book store sales, we have the following set up:

Gross profit two book store sales @ 88 cents	$1.76
Gross profit per volume one direct sale...........	$2.07
	$3.83

Dividing by three we have an average gross profit of $1.276 per volume.

PROFITS

As said before any accurate estimating of profits cannot even be approached.

For anyone who wishes to draw their own estimate, the following figures and facts are given:

It would take sales of the first 5000 volumes (basis Harpers advance offer) by April first to assure subscribers money. Inasmuch as the budget has been designed to defray all expenses of operation to April 1st, profits up to that date are gross profits, without deductions.

On the other hand if office were maintained through April, May and June and five thousand volumes only were sold, the returns to the shareholders would be slightly over fifty percent. As mentioned before, decision as to continuance of the office through April, May and June, will be made at the stockholders' meeting in March, 1939.

If, on the other hand, any success such as has been predicted accrues, the following profit projection would seem possible.

By June first the subscription would have been returned. Then, if the following sales are reached the profit per share would be:

15,000 volumes first year—per share return after money back . . . . . $ 10.00
25,000 . . . . 30.00
50,000 . . . . 75.00
100,000 . . . . 150.00

Although it seems ridiculous, one estimate has been made of half a million volumes within two years time. Should this come, over nine hundred dollars per share would be returned.

OPERATION OF THE
ONE HUNDRED MEN CORPORATION

During the time of the writing of the book, and while sales promotional and directional duties are going on, the necessity of an office is apparent.

Among other sales promotional possibilities that must be followed up is the offer of Floyd Parsons to write an article based upon the book for the Saturday Evening Post. Mr. Parsons is very well acquainted with the editor and believes an article would be acceptable.

Most of the church organizations have their National Offices in New York City. These must all be followed up. The National Library Board has its headquarters in New York City. This must be canvassed, as must the American Medical Society. It may be possible to have articles in those publications.

Some of the larger purchasers beside the jobbers must be approached. It is customary for sales to people such as Macy's to be made direct by the publisher.

On April first, when the book has been published, the decision will be reached by the stockholders as to the continuance of the office. If sales are going at a very rapid rate, there would be no question as to the necessity of the office.

There is naturally a question as to what would be done after April first if an office is not necessary. One of the usual printing services extended by book printers to publishers is that of shipping. The printer will attend to all details such as billing, collecting the money, and shipping for a publisher at cost. In other words, it is possible to turn over to a regular book printer all physical detail except writing, selling, and publicity.

A fact not generally realized is that book publishers do no printing. The printing, the art work, and all work attendant to

ALCOHOLICS ANONYMOUS

issuing the book is done by specialized book printers. One of the duties of the management of the corporation will be attending to the printing details. Mr. Walsh of the John Day Printing Company recommended any one of three printers competent to handle all details.

Another question is that of distribution and credit to book stores. There are only three book jobbers in the United States; any one of whom covers the entire country. Their credit is of the highest and they in turn take off the publishers hands all questions in regard to credit risks to the retail store. We have been told that we will have no trouble in securing any one of these three jobbers.

Taken all in all, there are plenty of details to be taken care of and sales promotional work to be done between the present time and April first.

Works Publishing Company, par value $25.00.

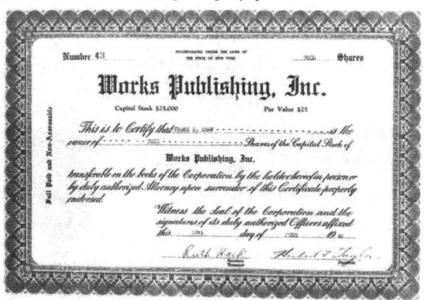

This is a 1940 version of the certificates.

SUBSCRIPTION

Date..............................

On the basis of being a charter subscriber, I hereby subscribe for...................................

Twenty Five Dollar par value non-assessable shares of The One Hundred Men Corporation to be formed.

My check for ....

is attached which is in full payment — partial payment.
(CROSS OUT ONE)

In case this check is partial payment, I agree to pay an equal amount in thirty, sixty, ninety, and one hundred and twenty days from this date.

Signed _____

Street Address_____

City _____

State_____

CHECKS MAY BE MADE PAYABLE TO:
THE ALCOHOLIC FOUNDATION

                or to — HENRY G. PARKHURST, Inc.

PLEASE MAIL TO:

HENRY G. PARKHURST, Inc.		WILLIAM J. RUDDELL
17 William Street	or	108 Harvey Street
Newark, New Jersey		Hackettstown, New Jersey

**Hank, Ruth, and Bill were utilizing the office on
17 William Street in Newark, New Jersey**

Chapter 4.2

THE BOOK

"Publication"

PRELUDE

Take, Oh take the gift I bring!
Not the blushing rose of spring,
Not a gem from India's cave,
Not the coral of the wave —

Not a wreath to deck thy brow,
Not a ring to bind thy vow, —
Brighter is the gift I bring, —
Friendship's pearly offering.

Take the BOOK! Oh, may it be
Treasured long and near by thee!
Keep, oh keep the gift I bring, —
Love and friendship's offering! [22]

— The Temperance Token

Ed Blackwell of the Cornwall Press told both Bill and Hank that he could not go ahead with the book printing until and unless they came up with some money—at least enough to cover the cost of the paper. Both men pleaded with Blackwell. Both had come this far. Could he not do them a favor for this worthwhile cause, they asked? They tried many sales ploys, and even dropped the name of Mr. Rockefeller.

But Blackwell was not about to print the book on credit. He held fast to his requirement for payment up front. Bill and Hank drove back down to New York, disappointed once again. Disappointed but undaunted.

Sales of shares of Works Publishing, Inc. were progressing very slowly. According to a printed financial statement that was issued in June 1940, there were at that time six hundred and sixty shares sold. Four hundred and five of them were owned by the Alcoholic Foundation. Forty-four individuals had subscribed to, and purchased one hundred and seventy-four shares. Five individuals received eighty-one shares given to them for "services rendered."

At twenty-five dollars per share, the total share offering should have produced $16,500. But as of June 30, 1940, only $4,450 had been received.

By the time the book was being printed, less than six hundred and sixty shares had been sold. The multilith printing had cost one hundred and sixty-five dollars to print. And this was for four hundred copies.

By June 1940, the Cornwall Press had been paid two thousand four hundred fourteen dollars and seventy-one cents. (This included the printing plates which had been valued at $825.) All of this outlay of money, but not a single book had been ordered.

Bill Wilson had loaned the movement one hundred dollars. Charles B. Towns of Towns Hospital loaned the Foundation two thousand, five hundred and thirty-nine dollars. A Mr. William Cochran of the Cochran Art School of Washington, D.C., had been persuaded to loan the Foundation $1,000 at the insistence of Agnes M., who was the administrator of Cochran's school and was the sister of Fitz M. whom Bill had helped sober up in New York. Agnes had been so grateful for her brother's rebirth that she did all that she could do to help.

Bill and the Foundation finally did manage to raise the necessary funds to cover the initial printing costs. Bill, Hank, Dorothy Snyder (Clarence's wife, who at that time was visiting with her sister in Yonkers, NY) and Ruth Hock went to Cornwall, New York, to oversee the printing of the book. This was the first of many trips made to the little hamlet of Cornwall before the final galleys for the book were approved as ready.

The paper had been ordered. The book was to be printed in the thickest, cheapest paper possible. Bill, Hank, Dorothy and Ruth wanted to have the book appear much larger than its approximate four hundred pages. They wanted potential purchasers to believe they were getting something substantial for their money.

The Big Book's girth was expanded even further by having the printer print each page with unusually large margins surrounding the text. This promised a very large and heavy volume. Thus the book came to be known as the "Big Book."

The book's binding was red in color. Blackwell had an overage of red and explained to Bill and Hank that he would give them a special deal on this material. Ever cost conscious, Bill and Hank accepted. In fact, they even felt the color red would make the book more attractive and marketable. Red stood for royalty, so they thought.

The first printing was the only one on which a red binding was used. All the other bindings, except for that used with the fourth printing, were in various shades of blue. The fourth printing, due to another overstock of binding material and thus lower cost, was bound in green as well as in blue. There was a typographical error in the first printing, despite all efforts to an error-free volume: on page 234, the second and third line from the bottom was printed twice. This error was removed from subsequent editions.

A New York City based artist and member of the fellowship, Ray C., was asked to design the dust jacket. He submitted a few different ideas for consideration. These included one which was blue and in an Art Deco motif, and another which was red, yellow and black with a minimum of white. The latter had the words Alcoholics Anonymous printed across the top in large white script.

Hank and Bill chose the red, yellow and black mock-up and the jacket became known as the "circus jacket" due to its loud and circus-style colors. Bill and Hank felt this dust jacket stood out and was eye catching. The unused blue jacket is still located at the Archives at the Stepping Stones Foundation.

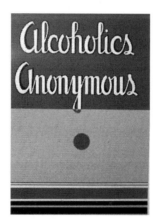 

Ray C.'s story, "AN ARTIST'S CONCEPT," appeared only in the first sixteen printings of the first edition. His story was preceded with a quote: "There is a principle which is a bar against all information, which is proof against all arguments and which can not fail to keep a man in everlasting ignorance—that principle is contempt prior to investigation." It says there it was from Herbert Spencer, though nobody has yet to find this quote in any of Mr. Spencer's works.

Research now shows that Spencer, though credited with the quote, never actually penned it, and that the original author of that quote seems to have been William Paley (1743-1805).

And though Ray's story was removed from the second edition, the so-called Spencer quote was retained, and it can now be found at the end of Appendix II on Spiritual Experience in the Big Book at page 570.

The alcoholics were ready to go. They had a book that told of their experiences. They had a program of recovery that was outlined within the pages of the book. And they were conducting meetings of the alcoholic squadron of the Oxford Group. But even though there was an Alcoholic Foundation and references had been made in correspondence to "we of Alcoholics Anonymous," the alcoholics' meetings were not yet actually called "Alcoholics Anonymous meetings" or "A.A. meetings," although the gatherings were being held in both Brooklyn, New York and Akron, Ohio.

Bill and Hank had sent out four hundred copies of the multilith (which promised a book to follow when it was finally published). They sent letters and post cards to doctors, clergy and others. They sat back and waited for their Post Office to deliver sacks of mail containing thousands of orders for their books. And with the thousands of orders, they also expected thousands of dollars which would accompany them.

They waited and waited. Each day they called the Post Office, asking where the responses were. They were often told that none had arrived. Four thousand seven hundred and thirty books had been printed. Yet as of June 30, 1940, only two thousand, four hundred and five had been sold. They recorded "163 books outstanding against accounts receivable," and they recorded that two hundred seventy-nine books had been distributed free of charge.

In other words, from the publication of the first printing in April 1939 through June 30, 1940, a period of fourteen months, Bill and Hank still had one thousand eight hundred and eighty-three copies unsold.

Bill and Hank were once again dejected. Cartons upon cartons of books remained in stock in Cornwall, New York. Ed Blackwell would only release books that had already been paid for. Thus, unless the Foundation sold some from their stocks, they couldn't sell the remaining volumes in Cornwall. "You've got to have money to make money," they must have thought.

By this time, the New York contingent was having major doubts they would even get back their hard-earned investment. They also began to doubt Bill.

In Akron, Doc was also feeling heat from Ohio members who had invested. Though these people were still attending the Oxford Group meetings at T. Henry and Clarace Williams' home, they had hoped on something more when the book came out. They weren't sure what that something was, but it would come, they believed.

Unbeknown to all something was about to happen—something that would change the course of the history of the yet unnamed fellowship. That something would come the very next month.

On April 11, 1940, Bill and Hank wrote a letter to the Trustees of The Alcoholic Foundation. It started off: "We, William G. Wilson and Henry G. P_____, hereby desire to waive any and all interest that we have in the Works Publishing Company, the book 'Alcoholics Anonymous,' or any other source of income that may accrue to Works Publishing Company, in favor of The Alcoholic Foundation." They relinquished their 200 shares each of Works Publishing Company to The Alcoholic Foundation. They went on to say: "It is further a requirement that royalties of 10% on the book 'Alcoholics Anonymous,' past and in the future, shall be paid to Robert H. Smith and his wife Anne Smith, during their lifetime; such payments to be in addition to any other grants that might be given to them by The Alcoholic Foundation." Both William G. Wilson and Henry G. P_____ signed this letter addressed to The Trustees.

Chapter 4.3

THE BOOK
"The Break From the Oxford Group"

"He who would accomplish little must sacrifice little; he who would achieve much must sacrifice much; he who would attain highly must sacrifice greatly." [23]

"The dreamers are the saviours of the world." [24]

By April of 1939, the Cleveland contingent had grown to eleven and then fourteen "rummies," and also included some of their spouses. All traveled back and forth to the T. Henry and Clarace Williams' home at Akron every Wednesday night.

Unlike New York, which had only one Roman Catholic member, the majority of the Cleveland contingent was Roman Catholic. And it was said the Catholic Church did not want its members participating in open confession. Clarence remembered that these Catholic members had been warned against confessing their sins "one to another" without a confession to a priest. These alcoholics told Clarence that they were about to be excommunicated from their Roman Catholic Church if they continued to attend Oxford Group meetings.

In her book *Sister Ignatia: Angel of Alcoholics Anonymous*, on p. 31, Mary C. Darrah wrote the following as to how these men were discouraged from attending the Oxford Group meetings:

> "They returned home and told their parish priest that they had finally found the answer to their drinking problems at a meeting in Akron. But when the priest learned of the Alcoholic Squadron's alignment with the Oxford Group, he forbade the men to return because of the group's suspected Protestant overtones."

Each Wednesday, on the way back from the Akron meetings the "boys" would stop off for ice cream or coffee. They would engage in a critique of that night's meeting and what had transpired there. They expressed to Clarence, with growing concern, that they might not be able to continue with going to the meetings due to their church's objections. And they also feared that without the fellowship afforded to them at the weekly meetings, they might resume their drinking—probably sooner than later.

This problem caused on-going discussion between Clarence and Doc. Clarence was insisting something had to be done. Doc, however, did not wish to be disrespectful to the very Oxford Group people who had saved his life and stated that nothing at all could, or would, be done.

At around this same time, Clarence had arranged for Albert R. "Abby" G. to be placed in Akron City Hospital for his alcoholism. Because Clarence had to go to work the next day and couldn't take the day off, he asked Bill Wilson if Bill could drive Abby down from Cleveland to meet Doc at the hospital. As Clarence remembered it, Bill and Dorothy (Clarence's wife) "packed Abby into a car and hauled him off to meet Doc in Akron."

Consistent with the newly established custom in those early days, when a "rummy" was in the hospital, the members of the group not only visited with the patient, they also visited with his spouse and family members. They took the family member to the Oxford Group meeting in Akron while the alcoholic was still in the hospital.

One particular night during Abby's hospitalization, as Clarence remembered it, Clarence was visiting with Grace G., Abby's wife. Clarence told Grace he was about to lose all of the Catholic members because they could no longer attend the Oxford Group meetings. Clarence told her their parish priest forbade it.

Clarence said to Grace: "Now that we've got this book here, the Twelve Steps and the Four Absolutes, there was no need to go to the Oxford Group any longer." But the problem was, Clarence told Grace, that Doc refused to leave the Oxford Group and Clarence was in a dilemma about disobeying his sponsor.

Clarence added that many of the early members didn't have jobs or were just beginning to pay off old drinking-induced debts. They couldn't afford to rent any hall or room in Cleveland in which to hold their own and separate meetings. Grace looked at him with a shocked expression on her face. She told Clarence that the Cleveland Group could meet at Abby and Grace's house, free of charge, for as long as they wanted to.

Abby was a prominent patent attorney in Cleveland. He represented people who held patents, and he held the rights to numerous patents himself. The G.'s had a very large house; and, ever since their children moved out, the house had seemed empty to them. They would both enjoy having the people around and it would be good to hear the sounds of laughter within its walls once again, Grace told Clarence. She also said that many meetings in their home would be a good way to help insure that her alcoholic husband would remain sober.

Grace G. was beginning to set the stage for a new meeting in Cleveland even while Abby was still "fogged up" and in the hospital. Clarence, through what he felt was an act of Divine intervention, had just found a home for his "boys."

Abby's story ("He Thought He Could Drink Like a Gentleman") appears in the second and third editions of the Big Book, and Abby recalled, in that story, some of his memories concerning Clarence. His first impression, when Clarence first started trying to twelve step him, was that Clarence was a little "touched." He felt that Clarence must have some kind of mental problem because of the way he was always chasing him around the place to "fix" him. Clarence, on his side, often related the story of how Abby was to come into what was to be A.A.

Clarence's sister-in-law, Thalia, a local beautician, was the wife of the man who had thrown Clarence out on the docks in New York. Abby's wife Grace was one of Thalia's best clients. One day, Grace appeared to "fall apart" in the beauty shop. In the midst of the hysterics, Grace told Thalia about Abby's drinking and about how it was driving them further apart. Grace told Thalia that Abby's being constantly drunk was going to drive her crazy. Grace continued, telling Thalia that Abby's drinking was also hurting his law practice.

Grace said that at fifty years old, Abby was acting like a helpless child when he was drunk. At this point, Grace began to sob uncontrollably. She couldn't go on with her story. Thalia then took Grace into the back room and related to her the story of what had happened to Clarence and told her Clarence could "fix" her husband. Grace stopped crying. She thought that this could possibly be the answer to all of her prayers. She invited Thalia over to her home. She asked if Thalia could also bring Clarence with her so that he could speak with her husband about this "cure."

Abby disliked Clarence right from the start. As soon as Clarence and Thalia walked through the door of the G. home, Abby developed a definite attitude. Abby was a college graduate and a well-known and formerly respected lawyer. Clarence was a high school dropout and a car salesperson. Clarence said of Abby, "He looked down his nose at me due to my lack of education."

Abby felt that, even though he was still drinking and was about to lose everything, including his marriage and his business, he was still smarter and had "more on the ball" than Clarence.

After being insulted and snubbed, much to the embarrassment of Grace, Thalia and Clarence left. They departed after spending about an hour at Abby's home trying to speak with Abby. Clarence and Thalia made their apologies and told Grace that if she ever needed them for anything she should call. Grace should call they said, even if Abby never decided to get sober. They told Grace they would pray continuously for the both of them. They further explained that, with prayer, Abby didn't stand a chance of staying with his old drinking ways.

When Clarence left the house he was not discouraged about Abby's eventual recovery or about the new meeting place. He had his family, the other members of the Cleveland contingent, and Grace on his side. He knew none of them would stop praying until Abby got better.

Clarence began to chase Abby all over town. He would often show up at the saloons which Abby frequented and "haul" him home. "We kept selling this guy. We went after him constantly,"

Clarence said. After pursuing this course of action for a period, Clarence almost felt like giving up. But he didn't.

During this period of time Bill Wilson was visiting Cleveland to promote the Big Book. Clarence convinced Bill to go talk with Abby. Clarence said Bill really "didn't want to go, but he did anyway." Clarence knew from experience that Bill could throw around a lot of four or five syllable words. He had "a different line of B.S. than I did," said Clarence.

While Bill and Clarence were at Abby's home, and during one particular conversation, Abby challenged Bill "to tell me something about A.A." Clarence recalled that Abby had actually challenged Bill to talk about "this cure, this group of anonymous rummies."

In his story Abby said, "I do recall one other thing: I wanted to know what this was that worked so many wonders, and hanging over the mantel was a picture of Gethsemane; and Bill pointed to it, and said, 'There it is.'"

Abby then agreed to go to the hospital the next morning. Clarence had to go to work the next day, so Bill and Dorothy agreed to take him there. They then called Doc on the phone to make arrangements regarding the admission.

The next evening, while at Akron City Hospital, and after visiting with Abby, Clarence held yet another conversation with Doc about the Roman Catholic boys in the Cleveland contingent. Clarence related:

"I says, "Doc you know these fellows can't come." I says, "They can't belong to an Oxford Group." I says, "We don't need all this folderol of the Oxford Group. We can eliminate a lot of this stuff. We have a book now with these Twelve Steps, and we have the Four Absolutes, and anyone can live with that."

Doc says, "Well you can't do that,' he says, 'you can't break this thing up."

I says, "We're not breaking anything up. All I'm interested in is something with more universality so that anybody can belong whether they have a religion or believe in anything or not. They can come."

He says, "Well you can't do that."

I says, "We're gonna do something."

And he says, "Like what?"

And I says, "Well we'll see like what!"

At this point in time Clarence was almost fifteen months sober and was telling Doc, his sponsor, what to do.

On the way back to Cleveland that night, Clarence and the Cleveland contingent stopped off for another of their critiques. Clarence informed them that Grace G. had offered them the use of her home as a meeting place. He then reviewed why they had to make a break with the Oxford Group so the Roman Catholic members could continue to attend and still stay on good terms with their church.

Clarence went on to say that since they had the book, the Twelve Steps, and even a name—the name from the book—they could do this. There was further discussion, some of it heated.

Even though a few of those present disagreed, the majority was for Clarence's idea. Lloyd T., Charlie J. and Bill J. were the most outspoken against Clarence's idea; and they refused to budge from their position. Even when the break did finally come, these three still considered themselves Oxford Group members. Yet all, except for Bill J., eventually left the Oxford Group and came into A.A.

On Wednesday, May 10, 1939, the Clevelanders went to the Oxford Group meeting at T. Henry and Clarace Williams' home. At the end of the meeting, Clarence announced that this would be "the last time the Cleveland contingent would be down to the Oxford Group as a whole."

He announced the Cleveland Group was going to meet the following night, May 11th. He said, "We're gonna start our own group in Cleveland." He told the Akron fellowship, "This is not gonna be an Oxford Group. It's gonna be known as Alcoholics Anonymous. We're taking the name from the book; and only alcoholics and their families are welcome. Nobody else."

He then told all present where the new group—the Alcoholics Anonymous meeting—was going to meet. Clarence announced

"We're gonna meet at 2345 Stillman Road, Cleveland Heights, at Al and Grace G.'s home."

Doc stood up and said, "You can't do this."

Clarence replied, "There's nothing to talk about."

The meeting almost turned into a riot as the Cleveland Group got up as a whole and walked out. But not as much of a riot as the one which occurred the next day in Cleveland.

Chapter 5

How It Worked

"Proceed with imagination and real faith—expect things to happen. If you EXPECT things to happen, they DO happen. This is based on FAITH IN GOD, not on our own strength. A negative attitude toward ourselves or others cuts off God's power; it is evidence of lack of faith in His power. If you go into a situation admitting defeat, of course you lose."

— Anne Smith's Oxford Group Diary

Chapter 5.1

"The First A.A. Meeting in the World"

"A.A. spoke to us, not with the accusing voice of those who had never known the tragedy of alcoholism, who had never suffered distraction; it spoke to us out of the experience of those who had suffered just as we had suffered and who had found how to break the chains. It told us simply that we had been trying to meet our problems without surrendering those things that keep us tied to the wheel. We had been trying to pull ourselves together with a will too shattered to be able to succeed." [25]

On May 11, 1939, one month after the Big Book had been published, a meeting was held. It was a meeting of Alcoholics Anonymous, held by and for alcoholics and their families only. Historian Mary C. Darrah, wrote:

In the years 1935-1939, the Oxford meetings provided a group experience for the early alcoholics. A.A. did not meet as a separate group officially *named* Alcoholics Anonymous until May 1939 at the home of Abby G. in Cleveland.

Nell Wing[26] stated in an interview with the author: "Clarence was rightly the first to use the initials, A.A." She was, however, referring to Clarence's use of the initials "A.A." and not to his use of the name Alcoholics Anonymous.

Clarence Snyder

A fellowship of anonymous drunks had in fact existed prior to May 11, 1939. But it was the Cleveland meeting which first used the name *Alcoholics Anonymous* that it took from the book. Cleveland's May, 1939 meeting is the first documented meeting which used the name Alcoholics Anonymous, separate and apart from the Oxford Group.

According to the records of the Cleveland Central Committee's Recording Statistician, Norman E.—records which were compiled in the middle of June 1942—the following took place:

> On 5/10/39, nine members left the Akron meeting of the Oxford Group to form the G. group. The location of the group was 2345 Stillman Road, Cleveland Heights, Cleveland, Ohio. The sponsors of the group were: Clarence Snyder, Al G., Geo. J. McD., John D., Dr. Harry N., Lee L., Vaughn P., Chas. J., and Lloyd T. The first secretary of the group was Clarence Snyder.

The preceding information was taken from a survey form sent out to all Cleveland groups on June 18, 1942. The G. group information was filled out and signed by Albert R. G., and dated June 24, 1942. These original forms are part of a collection of original Cleveland memorabilia and records in the possession of Clarence H. Snyder, which he delivered to the author prior to his death.

The first A.A. meeting in the world was not uneventful. According to Clarence, the entire group from Akron showed up the next night and tried to "discourage" the Cleveland meeting from happening. "Discourage" was a very mild term, according to Clarence, and he used it sarcastically. He said:

"The whole group descended upon us and tried to break up our meeting. One guy was gonna whip me. I want you to know that this was all done in pure Christian love.. A.A. started in riots. It rose in riots."

Clarence was often quoted as saying, "If you don't stand for something, you're liable to fall for anything." And on May 11, 1939,

Clarence stood his ground, as did the other members of that first A.A. group. Thus A.A., as such, began in Cleveland, Ohio.

In a letter to Hank P., dated June 4, 1939, Clarence wrote: "Bill J. and I and Clarace Williams, and etc., etc. had a knockdown dragged out affair a couple of weeks ago and they have chosen to leave us alone and confine their activities elsewhere. We lost the activities of three or four rummies but I guess it had to be that way. Life is too short and there is too much to be done to spend any time or energy carrying on any comedy or petting business with any Oxford Group or any other group."

In the same letter, Clarence described how the Cleveland meetings were being conducted: "Not too much stress on spiritual business at meetings."

Clarence always felt that overt spirituality belonged between a "baby" and his sponsor. Prayer and Bible reading was a prerequisite, Clarence felt, but only at home. His 1939 letter went on:

"Have discussion after meetings of any business or questions arising. Plenty of fellowship all the time. Leaders of meetings have been chosen so far by seniority in the bunch."

The meetings were very simple. They opened with a prayer or the reading of a verse from the Bible. This was followed by the leader's speaking for one half hour to forty-five minutes. Then the meeting was over.

At least the "official" part of the meeting was over. The remainder of the evening was spent with members and their families in fellowship with each other. "Plenty of hot coffee and doughnuts to go around," said Clarence. In Cleveland, there are still some meetings that are held in this manner—a short "lead," questions, and then fellowship.

The Cleveland meetings continued to grow as the members went forth to "fix rummies as an avocation." In an undated meeting roster for the G. group, which Clarence gave the author, and which is probably from the summer of 1939, there is a listing of twenty-six typewritten names, addresses and phone numbers. It contains an additional thirty-five handwritten names in Clarence's handwriting at the bottom. The roster has first and last names in the typewritten part, but most of the handwritten names use only first initials and last names.

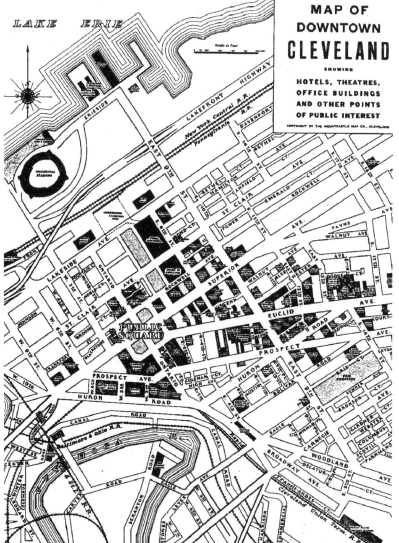

Among the names listed are: Clarence Snyder, Dr. Robert Smith, Richard S., Albert G., Warren C., William H., Jack D., Charles J., George McD., Clarence W., Glenn W., Dr. Harry N., and Vaughn P.

The author dates this roster to the summer of 1939 because Dr. Bob's name appeared on it, and Clarence said Dr. Bob attended the Cleveland meetings over the summer of 1939. Also, Warren C.'s name appears on the roster, and Clarence said he had twelve-stepped Warren in July 1939. (By the Fall of 1939, the Abby G. group had split and formed three separate groups.)

There was even some local radio publicity that Clarence appeared on, in late May or early June, which brought inquiries into the New York office for information on "The Alcoholics Anonymous."

In a letter to Clarence from Bill Wilson's secretary Ruth Hock, dated June 22, 1939, Ruth attached a listing of inquiries about Alcoholics Anonymous. Some of these had come from as far away as London, Ontario, up in Canada. Ruth wrote at the head of the list:

> Route
> Soulsaving Snyder
> Lyndhurst to Canada.

Included in Ruth's letter was a request that, "Something should be done about knockdown drag out affairs at Lyndhurst, Ohio— S.O.S." It is not clear whether Ruth's reference to "knockdown drag out affairs" alluded to the Cleveland break with the Oxford Group, or to the fact that Clarence and Dorothy were having severe marital problems at home. (The first Cleveland meeting was in the Cleveland suburb called Cleveland Heights, while Clarence lived in the Cleveland suburb called Lyndhurst.)

Ruth Hock was extremely close to both Clarence and his wife Dorothy, and remained so even after they eventually got divorced. Ruth continued to correspond with, and visit both of them at their respective homes. She maintained this close friendship until each had passed on.

There were many interesting stories connected with the summer of 1939 in Cleveland. It was in that first summer that A.A. began to grow. Along with the growth there came success, joy, sorrow and the inevitable growing pains.

Chapter 5.2

HOW IT WORKED

"Summer of '39"

"When we reach 100, we are all going out and celebrate and get good and drunk together. If we ever should get all of these birds drunk at the same time and in the same place, the Russian invasion of Finland would look like bedtime at an old woman's home."[27]

". . . and thus Cleveland became the testing ground for what Alcoholics Anonymous was to be."[28]

Late one evening, Edna McD., who was a nurse at the local Cleveland Tuberculosis Society, called Clarence. She told him about her husband, George, who was a drunk. George McD. was what Clarence called a "high bottom drunk," someone who as yet "hadn't gotten down to the skids." Edna had heard about the wonderful work that "the Alcoholics Anonymous" was doing in Cleveland. In her phone call, she became very emotional and started to cry, and the words began to get stuck in her throat. She unfolded a tale of woe to Clarence, a tale with which he was not unfamiliar.

Edna told Clarence that George had gone out to a Hockey game drunk. She said, "George blew off his big mouth; and some fellow told him to shut it …. beat the socks offa this poor guy, this George. They gave him an awful beating."

Edna said that while she was "pouring" George into bed, after he had somehow managed to get home, she had told him about this group of drunks that was having a great deal of success with men such as himself. She told George she was going to call one of these men that very night. George had told her to go ahead and then proceeded to fall asleep in mid-sentence.

This was the call Clarence had received. He told Edna that unless George wanted help, he couldn't give it to him. Clarence then offered his support to Edna if she ever wanted to talk, and gave her a few phone numbers of the other wives who would be there for her as well.

The next morning George's head was pounding. He was beaten and bruised. Upon Edna's insistence he decided to quit drinking. Edna gave him Clarence's phone number and then handed him the phone. George dialed the number and, when Clarence answered, he asked for help. Clarence "qualified" him over the phone, and then made arrangements for him to go into Akron City Hospital.

In the early days, all new prospects were hospitalized for at least five to seven days, depending upon the severity of their physical dependence and condition. Clarence called Doc to finalize the arrangements and then called George back to tell him to get ready to go into the hospital. Clarence told George that he was picking him up that evening. Clarence gave George a list of what to bring and what not to bring.

When Clarence arrived early that evening, he asked Edna a question that she never expected to hear. He asked her if she had any alcohol in her home. She was taken aback. "I thought this cure was to stop my George from drinking? What do you want with liquor?" she asked.

Clarence explained to her that on the way to Akron, George would be "hollering" for alcohol every five minutes. Since "this was the last that he was ever going to have, you might as well give it to him and keep him happy on the way down," said Clarence.

Clarence, George and Edna started on the almost forty-mile trip, and every time Clarence gave George a drink, Edna made a smart remark. She berated George, Clarence said. She didn't stop talking and nagging all the way down to Akron. There were times, Clarence said, that he didn't blame good old George for drinking. He thought to himself that if he had a wife like that, he didn't know if he himself would want to stop.

They finally got to the hospital and had George admitted. It was then in the solitude and quiet of the waiting room that Clarence realized that he would have to make the forty-mile trip back with Edna. Alone.

This was not a prospect to which Clarence looked forward. For "some unknown reason," said Clarence, he went to Doc's house. Doc wasn't as yet home. However, his wife, Anne was. Anne was sitting in the living room with Arch T. from Detroit.

Archie T., founder of A.A. in Detroit

"A little skinny guy, scared of everything," said Clarence of Arch. Arch had spent weeks and weeks at Doc's. He was being baby-sat. He wasn't drinking, but his mental and spiritual condition wasn't improving either. He was in a strange city, with even stranger people. He had already been at the Smith's home for about five months, and he was afraid to leave his room.

Arch and Anne were sitting and talking, so Clarence and Edna sat for a while and spoke with them. Clarence was trying to stall the inevitable; but when Edna kept insisting it was time to leave and to start back to Cleveland, Clarence came up with what he thought was a brilliant idea. He told Arch that all of the rummies in Cleveland were driving him crazy. Clarence said, "I am so busy, will you come up with me to Cleveland and please help me?" In the back of his mind, Clarence felt he should take someone along for the ride as self-protection.

"Archie looked at me as if he were hit with a club," said Clarence. "Nobody ever asked Archie to do anything because he felt that he was absolutely worthless and useless to society," Clarence related to the author.

Anne, however, thought that it was a great idea. Anything that would help Arch to get out of his room was brilliant. She told Arch, "You heard Clarence. You're going with him. Run upstairs, and get your sweater. You're going with him."

Arch was dumbfounded. He nervously looked back at Anne, then to Clarence, and back once again at Anne.

"Git," she said, and he ran up the stairs.

He got his sweater and came back down. He looked imploringly at Anne who stood her ground. Despite Arch's sad face, she didn't budge.

Arch reluctantly got into the back seat with Edna and settled in for the long ride. Clarence breathed a sigh of relief and sank back into the driver's seat. He relaxed as they drove back to Cleveland. Edna was off his back.

The next day, Arch seemed somewhat different. Maybe it was the fear that Clarence would force him to suffer another long ride with Edna, or maybe it was something else more profound.

Arch got so busy with A.A. in Cleveland that he appeared to change right before Clarence's eyes. Arch went to hospitals and dry-out places, helping drunks all over the place. He got so busy and so far in over his head that he forgot all about his fears and phobias. Surprisingly, he became a big asset to Clarence and became "one of the boys." He eventually went back to Akron a new man. Within a few months he returned to Grosse Pointe and started the first A.A. meeting in Detroit.

It was either in the late summer or early fall of 1939 that Clarence received a phone call from a man named Jerry, an insurance man that he once known. This man was not an alcoholic, but he had seen the change in Clarence. He had seen what this new way of life had done for him.

This man told Clarence of a friend who was locked up in "this gooney roost way out in the woods." The man's wife had him probated there. He was a journalist, and he had been kicked off of almost every newspaper in northern Ohio. The insurance man told Clarence that he "is a good newspaper man; he ought to be salvaged."

Clarence went out to this sanitarium to visit with this other fellow. He brought the A.A.'s Big Book for him to read, and after speaking with him for a while, Clarence realized the man wasn't all that "nuts." Clarence decided that if he were able to get the man out and maybe get him a job on a newspaper, A.A. could get some well-needed publicity.

"Jerry [the insurance man] and I went out to see the journalist's wife," Clarence said. "We talked her into getting him released." With a car salesperson and an insurance man working their combined sales pitch on her, the wife didn't stand a chance. She signed the release papers, and Clarence went to get the newspaperman out of the sanitarium.

Clarence contacted some people in the newspaper business, and with some connections, got this man a job at the Cleveland *Plain Dealer*. This man was so grateful that, on October 21, 1939, the first of a series of seven articles about Alcoholics Anonymous was printed. The first article was entitled, "Alcoholics Anonymous Makes Its Stand Here."

He was such a good reporter that he was able to have this series printed very shortly after he got the job. The newspaperman was Elrick B. Davis, and he enabled one of the first pieces of major publicity that A.A. ever had.

The articles were written with such sensitivity and insight that many people felt Mr. Davis must be a member of A.A. But Clarence would neither confirm nor deny Davis's membership status. *(There are other stories that have been told about how Clarence met Mr. Davis, but this was the one that Clarence related to the author.)*

The newspaper series produced hundreds of inquiries from all over—not just from Ohio. They poured in from all over the country. "'Cause somebody would cut those things out and send 'em up to Uncle Slug up here in Nebraska someplace, and you know, people would write in," said Clarence. Even the New York office got numerous inquiries.

Every Monday morning, Clarence would meet with members of the Cleveland group. Just like a sales manager, he would distribute a handful of the inquiries to each of them. "I'd tell 'em to go out and report to me Wednesday what you did with 'em," he said.

The "rummies" would run wild with these inquiries, Clarence said. The meeting at Abby's home began to fill up with alcoholics, and they were beginning to run out of room at Abby's house. Another problem developed—a problem that had very little to do with the obvious overflow of alcoholics meeting in the house at Stillman Road.

Some of the more "intellectual" members were offended by Clarence's getting the publicity in the Cleveland *Plain Dealer*. He was accused of getting paid for the articles. They also accused him of being paid a percentage for everyone who came in. Clarence never learned where this percentage gossip came from.

No one was making any money on the meetings or from the publicity. Clarence told the author they never had enough money even to reimburse Abby and Grace for the coffee and doughnuts—this even on an occasional good night when they passed the hat and collected some change.

These same Cleveland members also expressed a fear they would eventually have their photographs printed in the pages of the newspaper. They wanted to remain a nameless and faceless society of ex-alcoholics, and on that point, Clarence couldn't have agreed with them more. He tried to explain to them that all he wanted to do was spread their message of hope to other still sick and suffering alcoholics, the same kind of people that they once were.

Arguments ensued. Fist fights almost occurred. The very Irish Catholic members who had been the subject of Clarence's arguments with his sponsor, and with whose continued recovery he was so concerned, accused Clarence of selling them out to the news media. Several times Clarence tried to reason with them. He told them, "All of this was crap, all hot air." They wouldn't listen; they were having none of Clarence's explanations.

What happened next was another first for A.A. The objectors all got together and decided to take a vote. In true democratic fashion, they voted with closed ballots. The result of that vote shocked Clarence beyond belief. They voted him out of A.A.

"So I'm the first guy ever voted out of A.A.," said Clarence. Fortunately, there was another group of members who didn't agree with the outcome of the vote. However, they were outnumbered, and no matter how hard they tried, they couldn't do or say anything that would change the other faction's minds.

Clarence pulled no punches. He spoke his mind as openly and honestly as he could. Dr. Ernest Kurtz, author of *Not-God: A History of Alcoholics Anonymous*, wrote of Clarence that he had an "abrasive" personality. Clarence had much to do with the early beginnings and growth of Alcoholics Anonymous in its formative years. But Bill Wilson's secretary, Nell Wing, observed to the author, "If he could have not been the kind of antagonistic person that he was, he could have possibly been a tri-founder."

But Clarence was a perfectionist. He pushed himself in the banking business to be the best. He had made himself "the best drunk" he could, and he pushed for the best A.A. possible, as he put it. He always tried to live up to the Four Absolutes of Honesty, Unselfishness, Purity and Love. And he believed that he had gotten a message to carry to the still sick and suffering alcoholic, both inside and outside of the rooms of Alcoholics Anonymous. And carry it he did.

Chapter 5.3

HOW IT WORKED

"Cleveland Continues To Grow"

Tradition One: "Our common welfare should come first; personal recovery depends upon A.A. unity." [29]

Tradition One (long form): "*Our A.A. experience has taught us that* .... Each member of Alcoholics Anonymous is but a small part of a great whole. A.A. must continue to live or most of us will surely die. Hence our common welfare comes first. But individual welfare follows close afterward." [30]

"For as the body is one, and hath many members, and all the members of that one body, being many, are one body .... God hath tempered the body together .... That there should be no schism in the body; but that the members should have the same care one for another." [31]

Clarence was fond of saying "All you need to start a meeting is a resentment and a coffee pot." He felt that if there were any *real* unity, all that there would be in the world is one very large and boring meeting. He said, "A.A. didn't start, or grow, in unity. A.A. started and grew in riots."

Clarence also said, "When we had our first 'unity' in Cleveland, we didn't split into two groups. We did one better. We split into three." Group Number Two in Cleveland was called the Borton Group. This group met at the home of T. E. Borton, a non-alcoholic friend of the A.A. fellowship. The meeting was located at 2427 Roxboro Road in Cleveland. Its first meeting was held on Thursday, November 16, 1939.

The number of members that left the G. Group was forty. The sponsors of the Borton Group were Clarence, Jack D. and Clarence W.

Almost immediately thereafter, in another show of what Clarence sarcastically called A.A. "unity," they split again on November 20th. Out of the Borton group was born the Orchard Grove Group. The Orchard Group met on Monday nights at 15909 Detroit Avenue.

The Orchard Group later changed its name to the Lakewood Group. There were eleven original members of the new Orchard (Lakewood) Group, and its sponsors were William E. B., Warren F. C., William R. L., and Edward H. The group's secretary was Elvira B., William B.'s wife.

According to the records of Norman E., recording statistician of the Cleveland Central Committee, the phenomenal growth of these two break-away groups was recorded as follows:

> Membership of the Borton Group in the first six months— seventy-five members. Membership in the first year one hundred and thirty-eight.

> Membership of the Orchard Grove Group in the first six months—twenty-five. Membership in the first year was forty-five.

> The membership of the meetings was doubling every six months.

A.A. in Cleveland was on the move. Soon after the original split, Clarence received a phone call from a Louis Seltzer, who was editor of the *Cleveland Press*, a Scripps-Howard newspaper. Seltzer knew of the A.A. movement and gave it his support for many years.

Seltzer told Clarence that he knew of a man in whom Clarence might be interested. This man, Clarence was told, was a good newsman. He was, said Seltzer, "worth salvaging; and if you can find him and fix him, I will pay for all expenses."

Ever interested in furthering the A.A. cause, Clarence asked Seltzer where this man might be found. Seltzer told Clarence that the man would probably be located on skid row, in the Eagle Avenue section.

Clarence immediately sent out a couple of the members of the group to look for the man. Armed with a description, they went from building to building. Eventually they found him in an abandoned warehouse. He was lying on a cold damp concrete floor.

It was already winter in Cleveland, and this man was more dead than alive. He had one collapsed lung, and there was a surgical tube sticking out of his chest from the other. He appeared unconscious and was on the verge of freezing to death. He could hardly breathe. So while one of the men stayed with him, the other went to call Clarence.

Clarence called Seltzer and told him of their finding his man and told him that they would be taking him to a hospital for help. Clarence got into his car and went to pick up this new prospect. The prospect was then taken out to the Post-Shaker Sanitarium on East Boulevard and Fairhill Road in Cleveland.

Clarence told me that Sara Post, who was the owner and superintendent of the facility, had turned her family estate into a sanitarium for mental patients. According to Clarence, the building was three or four stories tall and had the capacity to hold about one hundred people.

The state of Ohio had at that time recently opened a new facility for the treatment of the mentally ill on the outskirts of town, and the Post Sanitarium was, as a result, losing many of its patients. Sara Post was looking for people to fill the empty beds.

The state had been paying Ms. Post three dollars a day for the housing and care of these mental patients. This came out to a total of twenty-one dollars a week for each of them.

Clarence had suggested to Ms. Post during one of his many scouting missions for new hospital beds closer than those in Akron, that she could get alcoholics in there as patients for about forty dollars a week.

Ms. Post at first didn't want anything to do with the alcoholics and had rebuffed Clarence's offer. Clarence remembered that she had told him forty dollars a week wasn't enough. Clarence had retorted, "We don't bring stars out here. We bring people who are really in a fix." He explained to her that alcoholics were no worse than mental patients, saying "Most of 'em won't eat for the first few days; and if you taper 'em off of booze, they'll stay calmer than those loonies."

According to Clarence, Sara Post did not like alcoholics. She told Clarence that one of her nieces had married an alcoholic and that it had almost ruined the niece's life. The man's drinking had almost killed her, Sara said.

Clarence reiterated his offer of forty dollars a week, reminding Sara that the amount was almost twice what the state of Ohio was currently paying. He also reminded her the state was sending her less and less people all of the time, ever since opening their new facility. He pointed out that the state was only sending her people they felt they didn't want to handle. She was, he said, receiving their worst and most uncontrollable patients.

Finally, Sara Post agreed to accept alcoholics at her facility. She did however insist that she didn't want to "taper them off" of alcohol. Clarence took the man that they had found in the abandoned warehouse to Post-Shaker and tried to have him admitted there. But Sara took one look at him and emphatically stated that she didn't want him there at all.

Clarence then explained to her that Louis Seltzer, of Scripps-Howard Publications, was going to pay for all the man's expenses. Clarence pleaded that they should and could do all that was necessary to save him. Clarence even offered Sara more money and told her that he would bring in all necessary medical help at no extra cost to her or her facility. Sara Post held her ground. Clarence increased the money offer once again. But Sara Post, Clarence stated, said it was not the money, nor the physical condition of this man that concerned her. She said she had personal reasons for not wanting him there.

Then Clarence learned that this particular man was the same man who had married Sara's niece and nearly ruined her life. Clarence reminded her that, despite her personal objections, she was getting paid for all of the expenses that this man incurred.

He said this was a business proposition, and that her personal feelings towards this particular man, whatever they were, had no place in the treatment of alcoholics in general.

Clarence then gave her what was to be the clincher. He told her that if she didn't accept this man as a patient, and at the originally agreed upon price, he would pull out all of the alcoholics that were currently there and never send her another one. She immediately put aside all of her personal feelings and reservations, and the man was admitted that same day.

This man spent six to eight weeks in the hospital. At times no one was sure whether he was going to live or die. He did, however, eventually begin to recover physically, and then from his alcoholism.

The patient accepted the A.A. program as it was presented to him by the members who came to visit with him. He "took his Steps," as they were given to him by Clarence, and as his physical condition improved, he began to speak with the newer prospects as they arrived.

When he was well enough to leave the hospital, Seltzer said the journalist could go anywhere in the country that had a Scripps-Howard newspaper. He was promised that all of his expenses would be paid, and he was guaranteed a position on the newspaper.

The journalist was so grateful to Clarence and to the A.A. members in Cleveland for saving his life that he wanted to stay right there in Cleveland. Clarence acknowledged that the journalist was indeed a good A.A., and was welcome to stay. In fact, Clarence said he would love for him to stay. But he reminded this man that the weather in Cleveland was not conducive to his continued recovery on the physical level, considering his weakened lungs. They discussed the options with Seltzer; and the three finally decided upon Houston, Texas.

After a long and drawn out good-bye, with the A.A.'s Big Book in hand, the journalist boarded the train for Texas. While on the train, he had the time to write a series of articles. They were similar to those that had appeared in the Cleveland *Plain Dealer*.

When the journalist arrived in Texas and started his job on the *Houston Press*, he convinced that newspaper to print this series. The man was Larry J. He also found a minister on skid row in Houston, and the two of them started what was to be the first A.A. meeting there.

The *Houston Press* series became the basis for the first pamphlet ever published by Alcoholics Anonymous through Works Publishing, Inc. This pamphlet, which was simply entitled "A.A.," was written by an unnamed Cleveland member and included all of the articles in the *Houston Press*.

Bill Wilson was constantly amazed at the growth and apparent success that Cleveland was having in sobering up alcoholics. He visited there every time that he went to Ohio. Bill later wrote in *A.A. Comes of Age*:

> *Yes, Cleveland's results were of the best. Their results were in fact so good, and A.A.'s membership elsewhere was so small, that many a Clevelander really thought A.A.'s membership had started there in the first place. The Cleveland pioneers had proved three essential things: the value of personal sponsorship; the worth of the A.A.'s Big Book in indoctrinating newcomers, and finally the tremendous fact that A.A., when the word really got around, could now soundly grow to great size.*

Clarence was a dynamo. He wanted the best for himself and "his boys" in A.A. He refined the art of A.A. sponsorship to the point that Nell Wing, Bill Wilson's secretary, commented to the author that Clarence was probably the "one man responsible for sponsorship as we know it today."

Clarence wanted the meetings and the organization to run like a top-notch business (but without the business end of it). So he developed an idea for officers at the meetings, an idea that would not depend upon individual personalities which would eventually get in the way of progress. A rotation of officers was instituted so that everyone could have a chance to participate and give some input. This was done by election and by seniority in the group. Clarence promoted that idea so that no one person, including himself, could possibly take over. At times however, Clarence did try to take charge and control, especially when things weren't going his way. Often, however, the members called him on this behavior and often, though reluctantly, he changed.

Clarence established a standard format for the running of the meetings so that there would consistency from one meeting to the next. This, he felt, would insure that alcoholics, both the "old timers" and the new members, would feel at home wherever they went. As to this contribution, Nell Wing stated, "It was Clarence who was probably responsible for meetings as we now know them."

Clarence often seemed to be a visionary. But Clarence was his own worst enemy. His personality got in the way of his being recognized for these accomplishments. Many felt Clarence was arrogant and antagonistic. But he was steadfast in his ideology and principles—principles he carried with him until his death.

Clarence was never one to be publicity shy, nor was he one to shun any offer of help—no matter what the source, no matter what the consequence. He was open to anybody if he felt it was for the betterment of A.A., and for the betterment of the quality of life that the A.A. way afforded alcoholics and their families.

Chapter 5.4

HOW IT WORKED

"Other Publicity"

Tradition 11: "Our public relations policy is based on attraction rather than promotion."

—*Twelve Steps and Twelve Traditions*

"Who ever was attracted to a bunch of drunks? We had to sell this thing, permanent recovery. We sold it in bars, in the alleys, in the jails and in the newspapers."

—Clarence Snyder in the A.A. *Grapevine* (Apr 1946)

During the period Clarence was still drinking, his wife Dorothy had gone to Reverend Dr. Dilworth Lupton. Lupton was, at that time, pastor of the First Unitarian Church, located on Euclid Avenue and East 82nd Street in Cleveland.

Dorothy had often implored Reverend Lupton to intervene with, and speak to, Clarence. And this Lupton did, on several occasions. But Clarence, at that time, was unable and unwilling to quit drinking. Eventually, the Reverend gave up and told Dorothy to turn her husband's drinking problem over to God. She told Lupton that that was exactly what she was doing when she had asked Lupton for help. But Lupton explained to Dorothy that he could do nothing further than what he had done, and that the only thing left was prayer. Lots of prayer.

When Clarence had left the hospital and begun attending meetings of the Oxford Group in Akron, Dorothy once again went to the Reverend Lupton. This time it was to interest him in coming to observe the miraculous "new cure" in action.

Lupton had explained to Dorothy that, as far as he was concerned, as long as this "cure" was a part of the Oxford Group movement, it didn't stand a chance and that he couldn't become a party to it. "Nothing good could come out of the Oxford Group," Clarence remembered Lupton saying to Dorothy.

After Clarence and the Cleveland contingent had broken off all ties with the Oxford Group, Dorothy once again approached Reverend Lupton. This time she brought with her the A.A.'s Big Book and the names of a few Roman Catholic members. One name was that of Joe D., whose story "The European Drinker" was in the Big Book. The fact of Joe D.'s association with this new Cleveland group was to be the proof to Reverend Lupton that the alcoholic fellowship had indeed broken with the Oxford Group.

Lupton thanked Dorothy for her continued interest in his meeting with her husband and for her desire for him to see this new "cure" in action. Lupton promised Dorothy that he would look into and investigate this new movement and get back with her at a later date.

Lupton read the Big Book, and seeing its potential, called her asking her to meet with him at her convenience. Her convenience, as it turned out, was right there and then. The two of them—Lupton and Dorothy—continued to meet, discussing the possibilities, and began formulating a plan of action. Lupton offered to assist Dorothy in any way he could with this new movement.

Dorothy Snyder was an instrumental part of the beginnings of A.A. in Cleveland. She was close with Anne Smith, Dr. Bob's wife, in Akron; and she was intensely proud of her "new" husband. Sue Smith-Windows of Akron, Doc's daughter, recalled to the author that her "mom [Anne Smith] really liked both of 'em." She was referring to the closeness that her mother had with both Clarence and Dorothy.

Clarence made an appointment to meet with Reverend Lupton. When he arrived, Reverend Lupton did not at first recognize him at all. There had, of course, been a profound change in Clarence. After speaking for several minutes, Clarence was able to convince Lupton that, indeed, he was the very same man who had visited with him a couple of years earlier.

Clarence told Lupton the story of A.A. and of the trials and tribulations that preceded its formation. He told him of his drinking years, of how he met Dr. Bob and Bill Wilson, and of the split from the Oxford Group. Lupton listened intently and was almost sold on the idea. But he wanted to know more.

Lupton was invited to visit and did in fact attend several meetings of the Cleveland group. He even invited nine of the alcoholic members to his home to be "interviewed" by himself and a "prominent physician and a psychiatrist." Apparently, all the members passed this interview with flying colors. These men and the stories of their changed lives, were proof enough to Reverend Lupton of God's work amongst them.

On November 26, 1939, the Reverend Dr. Dilworth Lupton preached to his congregation a sermon concerning this new "cure." The sermon was entitled "Mr. X. and Alcoholics Anonymous." [32]

Dorothy, in her zeal to promote this new movement, had informed a reporter friend from the Cleveland *Plain Dealer* about Lupton's upcoming sermon, and she asked the reporter to attend and possibly write a review. The reporter accepted Dorothy's invitation and did attend the sermon.

On November 27, 1939, the Cleveland *Plain Dealer* printed the sermon and it was met with a positive reaction by the readership. It also brought about some inquiries about the new movement and cries for help by both alcoholics and their families.

The sermon was later printed in pamphlet form by Lupton's church. It was pamphlet Number Forty-six, and was priced at ten cents. It was titled "Mr. X and Alcoholics Anonymous," the same title that was given to the sermon.

Mr. X was Clarence Snyder and in a letter from the Reverend Dilworth Lupton to Clarence dated June 24, 1942, Lupton wrote, "I am very happy that I was able to have something to do with the beginnings of the Alcoholics Anonymous in Cleveland." This was in response to Clarence's thanking Lupton for the important role he had played in the beginnings of the movement. The Lupton sermon in the Cleveland *Plain Dealer* brought in over one hundred inquiries. These inquiries continued through April 16, 1939. This was the day that Rollie H., star catcher for the Cleveland Indians baseball team, held a news conference.

Rollie H. announced to the world that his past erratic behavior was due to excess booze and that he was, in fact, an alcoholic. Rollie also announced that he had been dry for one year "with the help of, and through, Alcoholics Anonymous." This statement was printed in the April 17, 1939 edition of the Cleveland *Plain Dealer* and in newspapers throughout the nation. This startling announcement, and the resulting publicity, brought in over one thousand inquiries from around the country. This deluge was followed by approximately eight hundred inquiries when an article was published in *Liberty* magazine on September 30, 1939.

The *Liberty* article was entitled, "Alcoholics and God," and was written by Morris Markey. The Markey article was the first piece of national publicity A.A. had ever received. Many of the inquiries from the Markey article, as Clarence remembered, were from "the over-religious in the southern states." The Rollie H. articles had brought in inquiries from around the United States. They were from people coming from all walks of life.

According to Sue Smith-Windows of Akron, Rollie was "a better catcher drunk than most were sober." She related to the author a story about the way Rollie happened to get into the Oxford Group. She said that the team manager offered a large sum of money to the Oxford Group to "fix" his star catcher. The Oxford Group refused the offer of money, but did agree to help. They explained to the baseball manager that Rollie had to be hospitalized in order to get that help. He did go into the hospital. However, he was definitely not a volunteer.

Sue related how other team members conspired to have Rollie hit by a ball that was to be thrown specifically for the purpose of injuring him. Not seriously, but enough for him to be taken out of the game.

When the pitch came, Rollie was hit. Despite his protestations, he was advised by the team doctor to go to the hospital and get "checked out." When he arrived there, he was placed under the immediate care of Dr. Bob. Within a very short period of time, Rollie began his indoctrination into the Oxford Group and eventually into A.A.

There were several other pieces of publicity that originated from the Cleveland area in those days. Some in the form of pamphlets that the members were having printed on their own and would hand out to anyone who would read them. Sometimes they convinced the local papers to print reviews of the meetings or the pamphlets.

Carl S., who was sponsored by Larry J. from Houston, Texas, had moved to and started meetings in the Miami, Florida, area and Carl requested some of this early publicity in a letter he wrote to Clarence on December 18, 1940. The letter said:

> *Would be glad to see samples of the printing the boys are having done, if any is available. We are all ready to pounce on the prospects these articles will develop.*
>
> *We had our first meeting last night, for the Flowing Orange Juice Annual Bowl Session, or whatever you want to call it, there were five of us there. Ruth Hock sent me some names, and we have one guy from the New York Lodge, Charley C., an actor now at liberty. Joe T., a Miami Beach resident, and a good sound self-instructed A.A., is going to be a great force in working up an active gang here.*
>
> *We called on a man whose wife had sent in to Ruth, and found he had been released from jail, but he was now at work on a construction job. He is to be our first convert, and tho he has a colorful history of exploits here, and is well celebrated as a "hard man to handle when he gets his skin full" as the police say, he is a fine fellow if sober!*
>
> *It seems Sunday night, he and his dog went out for a stroll, to replenish his supply after the police had taken it from him owing to a disturbance during the afternoon he figured in, at the beach. Due to his keen appreciation of religious worship, he and his dog decided to "take over" a Negro church*

gathering and prayer, and when they arrived, he was in the middle of an extemporaneous sermon on the Evils of Law Enforcement, and also on the middle of the deposed preacher's stomach. He and the dog were removed to his regular cell at the local ice-house for some quiet meditation and recovery.

This gives you a slight insight on the local situation as we find it, in launching our first efforts here in Sunny Southland of tropical wonders.

The beginnings of A.A. were filled with pathos and with dissention. There were trials and tribulations as the message of hope was carried to the still sick and suffering alcoholic.

On the other hand, as the previous quoted letter exemplifies, A.A. was made as much fun as possible. Clarence had a great laugh over this story. So did all of the others at the meetings to which he brought it.

Publicity brought new members as well as new tales. Some were funny and some, more often than not, were sad. But publicity was not the only way to which A.A. was enabled to grow by leaps and bounds in Cleveland. It also grew due to the personal contact of one drunk with another: one in recovery to one who was still suffering. This was Cleveland's—and Clarence's—personal mission.

Chapter 5.5

"Personal Contact - Attraction Rather Than Promotion"

"Certainly we were not in any way psychic or advanced in spiritual growth, but just very ordinary human beings, who had had more suffering and worry than the majority and who had known tragedy after tragedy." [33]

Cleveland, Ohio was a hub of A.A. activity in late 1939. Clarence went about his sales job both in his career as a salesperson and as an A.A. member. Personal contact with prospective members, as well as with those who were attending meetings, was what made the membership grow in numbers and in strength of sobriety.

Clarence believed that in order for a prospective member to get well, his entire family had to get well also. Members of the group visited the homes of those who had sent in inquiries arising out of newspaper and radio publicity. A.A.'s spoke with the wives and husbands of the alcoholics either prior to, or during their hospitalizations. Family members were invited to attend meetings, were given a copy of the book, *Alcoholics Anonymous*, and were told to read the daily devotional in *The Upper Room* every day.

Members of the A.A. group shared with the prospective A.A.'s and their families their own personal stories as to how they got well and how A.A. had restored their family life and belief in God. This personal sharing gave hope to newcomers and families that they too, had a chance at a better life.

Clarence went around to the local doctors, social workers, lawyers, judges and service organizations such as the Lions, Kiwanis and Rotary. He spoke to all about A.A. and the work the movement was doing in Cleveland. He appeared on local radio stations and spoke about how A.A. was restoring the outcasts of society to the status of productive citizens.

A.A. members roamed the streets and alley ways speaking with drunks; leaving copies of the A.A.'s Big Book with those who showed even the slightest interest in stopping drinking. The A.A.s went into bars and abandoned buildings, seeking out prospective members.

Numerous letters from wives and husbands of alcoholics flooded the Cleveland A.A. post office box after the appearance of each Letter to the Editor, article, and radio program concerning A.A. Each letter was answered with a phone call and a personal visit to the homes and offices of the writers.

One letter came from a woman in Zanesville, Ohio, and concerned her husband whom she called a "hopeless case." Clarence went to speak with this woman and then with her husband. After Clarence had told each his story and how he had been restored from the ravages of alcoholism, the husband consented to being hospitalized. He was placed in one of the local hospitals and was visited daily by A.A. members who told him their own stories. The man was convinced that he too wanted what they had. He was taken to a meeting upon leaving the hospital and then, in Clarence's terms, was "taken through his Steps."

The man's wife became involved in his recovery and attended meetings with him. She too began to recover, both in attitude and in spiritual reliance on God. In later years, she wrote to Clarence, thanking him for all the efforts he had made in getting her husband better. Clarence responded that it was not he who had restored her husband and their marriage. He responded to her letter of thanks, by giving all of the credit to God and to their commitment to each other and the A.A. movement.

This man never had another drink for the rest of his life and continued to correspond with Clarence, informing him of his A.A. "birthdays" and of how he too was carrying the message to others.

Another of Clarence's "babies" was Irwin "Irv" M. He lived on Eddington Road in Cleveland Heights, and was a salesperson who had lost several accounts due to his drinking. Clarence had "pulled" Irv out of a bar at the request of Irv's wife and had "convinced" him that he "needed to be fixed." Irv had a difficult time sobering up, but was sold on the idea of A.A. and of helping others.

Irwin sold venetian blinds and travelled around the country doing so. Wherever he went, he started A.A. meetings. And Irwin was a high-pressure salesperson in and out of A.A.

He was Jewish, weighed 250 pounds, and kept slipping back into active alcoholism. Still, he was a driving force in the early days of A.A. In the book *Dr. Bob and the Good Oldtimers*, Bill Wilson is quoted as saying, "The prospect of Irwin as a missionary scared us rather badly." In a letter to Clarence, dated May 22, 1940, from the Hotel Virginia, in Columbus, Ohio, Irwin wrote, "This is the first trip in one year that I was sober. Thank God." This was the first of many letters that Irwin wrote Clarence in which he told of his "slips," of regaining his sobriety, and of carrying the message by starting meetings.

Irwin, due to his widespread sales territory, also received constant lists of inquiries which Ruth Hock had received at the New York A.A. office. Irwin followed up on them with the same gusto he used in his sales pitches. In a letter to Clarence, dated September 18, 1940, he wrote:

> *You know that list that Miss Hock sent me from New York. Well I stuck my neck out, because it sure kept me busy, but am beginning to like it now. I contacted two men in Indianapolis and they are starting a group there. I contacted four but 2 stuck, the others were a doctor who wouldn't admit he was alky and another Bozo who could handle it. However I am trying to do my share. I am thankful to providence that I started a few men on the road to health and they are also thankful. That's what makes me feel good.*

Irwin, in his travels, also started groups in Atlanta, Georgia and throughout the South. In a letter dated March 28, 1942, from Knoxville, Tennessee, Irwin's wife wrote to Clarence that "Irwin started another club in Charleston, W. Va." According to a book on A.A.'s history in West Virginia, *Fifty Years of Freedom in the Mountain State*, "Irwin was recognized as the 'sponsor' of that first Charleston Group."

Personal sponsorship was another hallmark which came out of Cleveland. Each member and prospective member was indoctrinated with the idea of having and then becoming a sponsor. The idea of sponsorship, as A.A. knows it today, originated in Cleveland.

A.A. members were taken through the steps by their sponsor after being hospitalized for a short period. On their release, they were then taken to meetings and told they were to carry their message of hope to others as an "avocation" without personal monetary gain. In 1943, Clarence wrote a pamphlet on sponsorship which was published by the Cleveland Central Office in 1944. This pamphlet was entitled *A.A. Sponsorship—Its Opportunities and Its Responsibilities* (see appendix D). The pamphlet outlined what a sponsor is and what he or she does. In its conclusion, Clarence wrote, "If you're going to be a Sponsor ... be a good one!"

Clarence often remarked: "Who wanted to be attracted to a bunch of drunks?" He pushed A.A. down people's throats if he felt that they needed it. He knew that A.A. had saved his life and the lives of countless others, so he was always promotion minded. And in February 1940, what Clarence characterized as one of the biggest promotions to that date took place in New York City.

Chapter 5.6

HOW IT WORKED

The Rockefeller Dinner
February 8, 1940

January 30, 1940

To Clarence Snyder,

... I am glad to hear of the good work you are doing.

Sincerely Yours [signed]

Dr. Emmet Fox, Pastor
Church of the Healing Christ
Hotel Astor, New York, N.Y.

Bill Wilson had once again gone back to Willard Richardson to ask for more financial help. The Big Book had been published. Meetings were growing. Yet no significant money from book sales had been forthcoming.

Henrietta Seiberling had admonished Frank Amos that "money would spoil this thing." But Amos's report was so glowing and promising for the movement that he again approached Mr. Rockefeller for money, and Rockefeller decided once again to help out.

John D. Rockefeller, Jr. promised Bill he would invite all of his friends to a dinner in order that they too, could hear about this wonderful movement which was now officially known as Alcoholics Anonymous.

Alcoholics Anonymous had its legal trust, the Alcoholic Foundation, and the founder had a book. Mr. Rockefeller therefore told Bill that all of his (Rockefeller's) friends would receive copies of the book at the dinner in the hope they would be able to help the movement out in some manner.

Bill once again envisioned millions pouring into the Foundation. The hope of hospitals, paid missionaries, offices and sales probably flashed before Bill's eyes.

Doc Smith was called so he could make plans to attend this event, and he was asked to bring along "some of the boys." Clarence was told by his sponsor, Doc, that he (Clarence) was to attend.

The well-oiled machinery of the Rockefeller empire was put to work. One hundred eighty-seven engraved invitations were sent out. They read as follows:

Mr. John D. Rockefeller, Jr.
requests the pleasure of your company
at dinner
on Thursday, the eighth of February
at seven o'clock
The Union Club
Park Avenue and 69th Street

Mr. William G. Wilson, author of
"Alcoholics Anonymous"
and Dr. Harry Emerson Fosdick
will speak on an Effective control of alcoholism

R.s.v.p.
30 Rockefeller Plaza   *Business Suit*

Of the one hundred eighty-seven invitations that were sent out, one hundred and twenty-seven people sent their regrets. Sixty people, including among them members of A.A., responded in the affirmative.

Of the sixty who attended, several were or became great friends of the A.A. movement. These included: Frank Amos, Gordon Auchincloss, Dr. R. E. Blaisdell, Horace Crystal, A. Leroy Chipman,

Leonard V. Harrison, Dr. Foster Kennedy, Dr. W. D. Silkworth, Dr. Leonard V. Strong, Jr., and Wendell L. Wilkie.

Among the A.A. members who attended were Bill Wilson, Dr. R. H. Smith, Fitz M. from Washington, D.C., and Bert T. and Bill R. from New York. Clarence Snyder represented Cleveland.

Clarence had boarded a Pullman train in Akron at six P.M. on the evening of February seventh along with Doc for the long trip to Jersey City, New Jersey. Clarence was in car 102 and occupied Lower Berth #4. He paid $3.95 for ticket number 685. He was excited once again to be visiting New York City, and with the prospect of meeting John D. Rockefeller, Jr. This was Clarence's first time back in New York since he had gotten sober.

The menu for the dinner, which was printed on a Union Club card, was dated February 8, 1940, and contained the following:

MENU

STUFFED TOMATO WITH CRAB MEAT

BLACK BEAN SOUP

ROAST BREAST OF DUCKLING
APPLE SAUCE
LIMA BEANS
BROILED SWEET POTATOES

MIXED GREEN SALAD
MICHEL DRESSING

BOMBE UNION CLUB
CAKES

DEMI TASSE

After the dinner, Nelson Rockefeller made apologies for his father, John D., who could not attend due to illness. Nelson Rockefeller then turned the meeting portion of the gathering over to Mr. Albert L. Scott (Mr. Scott had been in attendance at the original meeting with Mr. Rockefeller in December 1937).

After making a few brief introductory remarks to those assembled, Mr. Scott introduced Bill Wilson. (Quotes from the dinner were taken from the "Digest of Proceedings at Dinner given by Mr. John D. Rockefeller Jr. in the interest of Alcoholics Anonymous at Union Club, New York City, February 8, 1940," which was made available by the Rockefeller Archives in Tarrytown, N.Y.)

Scott said: "I first want to introduce my friend Bill Wilson, who is at my right. Of this group, Bill Wilson here has been the leader. He is almost, if not entirely, the originator of the undertaking."

Clarence vividly remembered being taken aback by these remarks. He felt his sponsor, Dr. Bob, was once again being demoted to the post of "forgotten co-founder." Clarence wanted to get up and clarify this glaring oversight to Mr. Scott, and he indignantly started to rise. Clarence remembered that Doc Smith placed his hand on Clarence's arm and quietly asked Clarence to remain seated. Doc then explained to Clarence that his (Doc's) purpose there was not to receive any applause, but rather to lend support to the movement. He went on to tell Clarence that he was content with taking a back seat, and didn't mind that Bill was once again in the spotlight. Clarence remembered Doc's saying: "Bill eats this stuff up." Doc told Clarence to "let him have his day."

Clarence was very protective of Doc. He felt that Doc was "getting a raw deal in all of this." Clarence continued to protest throughout his life that Doc always got "the short end of the stick," especially after Doc had passed on and "Bill was left to his own devices." These "devices," Clarence always felt, had been kept in check while Doc was alive by Doc's gentle persuasion which would "calm him [Bill] down."

In any event, Bill Wilson began his talk by saying: "If there is one thing that most people would like, it is to recover the good things they have lost. With us who have been alcoholics one of those good things is the regard of our fellow men." Bill then proceeded to thank all of those present for coming to the dinner as "a mark of renewed confidence."

Bill then related the story of Roland H.'s visits with Dr. Carl Gustav Jung in Switzerland and how Doctor Jung had told Roland that he *must* experience a "so called vital spiritual experience." Bill then went on to say that Dr. Jung had told Roland: "I don't know whether the lightning will hit you or not. You might try. Otherwise you may as well shut yourself up, because if you don't, you will die."

Bill then told those assembled of his own experiences with alcoholism and how it had affected all areas of his life.

Bill also related how Roland had carried the message of the Oxford Group to an old drinking friend, Ebby T., and he told how Ebby had then eventually carried the message—"I've got religion"—to him. Bill spoke briefly of what went on during Ebby's crucial visit with him, and of the events leading to his spiritual experience in Towns Hospital.

Bill told of his meeting Dr. Bob, and of their adventures over the summer and fall of 1935. And he then spoke about returning to New York City and trying to work with other alcoholics just as he had done in Akron, or as Bill put it, "as an avocation—and that is what it is with all of us—I did some work here in my spare time." Bill W. also related some of the background concerning the writing of the Big Book and its history to date.

And he then talked a little about what A.A. was doing around the country and of its successes. He began with Cleveland and with Clarence:

> "One of these fellows was a chap who is here tonight, by the name of Clarence Snyder. Clarence began to work around among people in Cleveland ... so little by little a nucleus was formed in Cleveland of people who were getting well."

Bill then briefly discussed the success that they had been having in Chicago and New Jersey:

> *"Of all the people who have been seriously interested in this thing since the beginning, one-half have had no relapse at all. About 25% are having some trouble, but in our judgment will recover. The other 25% we do not know about."*

(In comparison with today's recovery rates, these 50%–75% figures on recovery are quite impressive.)

At the end of his talk, Bill turned the meeting back over to Mr. Scott, who in turn introduced Dr. Foster Kennedy, who made a few brief remarks. The Reverend Dr. Harry Emerson Fosdick was then introduced to speak. Dr. Fosdick ended his talk with the following words:

> *"Last of all, I admire the quietness, the anonymity with which this movement is carried on. Very small overhead financially, no big organization, nobody making anything out of it, no high salaried staff, people for the love of it sharing with others the experience that has meant life to them—that is good work. No one is a prophet, but I suspect that there is a long road ahead of this movement."*

Remembering these remarks, Clarence recalled to the author:

> *"It's a far cry from what A.A. is today. What with the millions of dollars in rent and salaries, millions of dollars going to one individual in royalties—where are the people doing it for the love of it, doing it as an avocation?"*

After all of the speakers were done, the A.A. members mingled and spoke one-on-one with those present. What Clarence observed and heard there disturbed him greatly. He told the author he felt that the New York A.A.'s were "trying to put the bite on the rich people who were there." He remembered feeling ashamed of their performance.

Later, after all of the guests had left, hands were shaken and thanks were given to Mr. Rockefeller and to his staff for a beautiful meeting and a wonderful meal. All of the A.A.'s then went down the street, as Clarence put it, "to one of them Greek restaurants to have a critique."

Clarence remarked to the author that Bill Wilson was "walking four feet off of the ground—he knows that he's gonna get millions from these people." Bill told Clarence at that time, "You'll get out on the road and start groups. That will be your thing to do. We're all going to get busy with all these millions."

Clarence then looked at Bill and replied, "Bill, we aren't gonna get anything out of these people." He told Bill he was ashamed concerning the "bunch of bums who you brought in to panhandle these rich guys." But Clarence felt that Bill didn't really hear what he (Clarence) was saying, and that Bill was too involved in his "schemes."

Soon after they had returned to Akron, Doc and Clarence were informed that Rockefeller had only given a mere $1,000 to the movement. With the sale of the Big Books to Mr. Rockefeller and to those who "got the hint" in the accompanying letters, A.A. received an additional $2,000. Three thousand dollars in total, all from a group of men, many of whom were worth many millions.

Clarence stayed in New York for another week, attended meetings, and spoke. In a February 19, 1940 letter from Bert T., a Trustee of the Alcoholic Foundation, Clarence was told,

> *Everybody liked your talk at the Sunday meeting, and Bill said he wished you had been able to give it at the regular Tuesday meeting. However, most of your talk has been passed around by word of mouth and I am glad of that.*

Even though the dinner was a financial disappointment to the alcoholics, especially Bill, it inspired them to continue full force in carrying the message to the still sick and suffering alcoholic. And Bill felt the ensuing free publicity from the dinner would probably make up in other donations and membership what they had "lost" on the dinner itself. The message was important: *the message must go on.*

ALCOHOLICS ANONYMOUS HAS BUT
ONE PURPOSE: TO HELP THE SICK ALCOHOLIC
RECOVER IF HE WISHES.

*This was the quote that was in the beginning of
most early A.A. literature.*

Chapter 5.7

HOW IT WORKED

Trials and Tribulations of 1940

"You know when I came back to Cleveland I thought A.A. here stunk and kept getting drunk to prove it. After I was completely batted around by John B. it finally dawned on me that I never accepted the third step." [34]

1940 was a year of growth and challenge. The original three groups, the G. Group, the Borton Group and the Orchard Grove Group (later called the Lakewood Group), split up into four more groups during 1940.

On May 1, 1940 the West 50th Street Group broke away from the Orchard Grove Group taking four members with them. The West 50th Street Group had their first meeting on May 8th. By the end of its first year, that group had eighty-seven members. They met at 3241 West 50th Street on Wednesday evenings. Its name was later changed to the Brooklyn Group.

On August 27th, the Berea Group formed and met at the home of Bob J. It had nine members and at the end of its first year, had grown to thirty members. On September 3rd, the group moved from the home of Bob J. to St. Thomas Episcopal Church Parish Hall in Berea.

On September 20th the Westlake Group branched off from the Orchard Grove Group and began meeting at the Hotel Westlake. When the Westlake Group left Orchard Grove, it took thirty members with it. The group later became the Lake Shore Group.

On October 15th, the Sunday P.M. Group branched off from the Borton Group and took thirty members with it. The Sunday Group first met at the Hotel Hollenden and later moved to the Central YMCA.

The growth of A.A. in Cleveland was phenomenal. Clarence tried to be the leader but was meeting with a lot of resistance from the members who felt that their brand of A.A. was better than his, and therefore started meetings of their own.

In a letter to Ruth Hock, dated January 5th, 1940, Clarence described how Doc led one of the meetings:

> *Doc led our meeting last night and never have I heard him in such fine fettle. I have noticed a vast improvement in Doc since he pulled his gang out of the Williams'. He now speaks with authority, and without any pussyfooting, and I believe he looks 10 years younger.*

In the Hock letter, Clarence continued:

> *The Akron bunch and us are all still busy. We have over 120 alkies in the Cleveland bunches now, and since the holidays, things are picking up again. We had very few casualties, and most of them minor this past month.*

Clarence was working overtime in his efforts to "attract" new members. He continued to speak at various organizations and even contacted one of the local radio stations concerning the possibility of a weekly radio program on A.A.

However, the WGAR Broadcasting Company wrote its regrets to Clarence on April 27th, stating:

> *We have gone over the possibilities of a series of radio programs in connection with Alcoholics Anonymous and we find that we are incapable of working out a plan by which these programs could be written and produced properly to maintain audience interest from week to week and at the same time protect the best interests of your organization.*

The broadcasters returned to Clarence the Big Book he had sent them and said: "[We] wish your organization a continuation of the fine success which it has had to date."

Clarence did manage to write some radio talks and get them on the air. But he also met with resistance from certain A.A. members regarding this publicity. He gave their complaints no heed, and continued on with his work.

Letters were coming in from all over Cleveland. Clarence followed up on these as best he could and handed some of the inquiries to the others. It was a difficult period in Cleveland, what with all of the people coming into A.A. and the problems that they were having at meetings.

There were those who still believed that hospitalization was a necessary part of the recovery process. Others, like Warren C., who had not been hospitalized, felt that alcoholics could get well by attending meetings without the benefit of being in a hospital. Controversy raged on about this matter well into the middle forties.

The publicity brought about its own problems. Members felt that they should remain anonymous, but the articles, letters, and radio programs were bringing in people who were simply curious about this strange group of ex-problem drinkers. Other members felt that the new blood was necessary for the continued growth and recovery of the membership. These felt that their purpose was to carry the message of recovery to the still sick and suffering. And how better to do this than by continually bombarding the public with facts about the existence of A.A. and what it had done for its members?

Clarence was "called on the carpet" numerous times for using his full name wherever he went. Some of his programs and flyers said, "Clarence Snyder of the Alcoholics Anonymous will speak on this new cure for Alcoholism." These even listed Clarence's place of work so people could contact him.

Arguments over publicity increased when in the later part of the year, Clarence was contacted by the New York A.A. office concerning a proposed article in *The Saturday Evening Post*.

The *Saturday Evening Post* was sending an investigative reporter to Cleveland to "expose" A.A. for what the magazine thought it was: another get-rich scheme that was using the alcoholics for the benefit of a few men.

Clarence ran through a gauntlet of angry inquiries from members about the proposed article. On the one hand, how were they to maintain their anonymity? On the other, if the article were favorable, how were they to keep up with the assured influx of new people it would bring?

Clarence assured members that the article would not endanger their meetings or anonymity. He also told them that they could handle any influx of new members if it were done properly. But there were even more trials and tribulations during early 1941 when the article did finally reach the public.

During this time, Clarence was having his own personal problems. His marriage to Dorothy was rapidly going down the tubes. He told the author, "We were more on the outs than not."

Though she liked the changes in Clarence, Dorothy still could not stand what she believed Clarence had become: the long and lonely evenings, the phone calls in the middle of the night, the dinners that went cold and uneaten on the kitchen table, and the arrogance she saw emerging. It appeared to Dorothy that Clarence's whole life had become A.A. work. He neglected her and their young son in favor of the sick and suffering alcoholic.

There was no balance in their lives. Despite the fact that Clarence preached family unity to the other members, he had none in his own life. Dorothy was beginning to get fed up with Clarence and his way of dealing with their personal problems. She began discussing divorce with him, and he was having none of that.

A.A. had become Clarence's new addiction; and as with his drinking, it was beginning to destroy his family once again. Dorothy spoke with other A.A. members, and with Doc and Anne Smith. She shared this problem at meetings with other wives. If Clarence wasn't going to change and they could not work out their problems, she would have to leave him.

Clarence was so absorbed in his A.A. work that he could not see that he was once again about to lose his wife and son. He tried to back off in his A.A. work and found he was becoming miserable. Without his family, he would lose; and without his A.A. involvement, he felt he would also lose.

Dorothy was a moving force within the A.A. movement, yet she found the time to be a mother and tried to be a wife. But Clarence was unable to separate his home life from his A.A. life. Their problems continued and escalated.

And so, on August 20, 1940, Clarence and Dorothy were divorced. In a letter to Ruth Hock in New York, Clarence wrote:

> *O well, it is about in line with about everything else I hear about myself, including being engaged to seven different girls, secretly married to four, drunk and disorderly, married to an heiress and engaged to two others, and a wife beater. So what the hell. On the contrary, I am doing fine, officially single, sober (3 years), don't ever expect to slip, don't beat anyone's wife, no heiresses have proposed to me, but just going along. Have been fired out of the finance business and am now selling Fords .... Have had a lot of interesting experiences in the past 3 years and have since listened to some screwy ideas. Which convinces me that all the nuts aren't alkies .... All in all it's a great world.*

About the same time, Dorothy wrote Ruth Hock, saying:

> *Dear Sugar-Puss, tell Bill that Prince Blue-Flame is getting a divorce from his "100% I Am" wife—said that a man needed a woman—I gather that spiritual mysticism wasn't enough.*

About this time, Clarence's address changed from 1552 Biltmore Avenue in Lyndhurst, Ohio, to his employer's address: "c/o E. D. Latimer & Co., 5363 Broadway Avenue, Cleveland."

Officially single, Clarence was free to continue on with his A.A. work. Clarence also agreed to pay support for his son. In his separation agreement, Clarence agreed to pay "of his earnings the sum of $40.00 per month, the said payments to be made monthly until the said Richard Snyder shall have attained the age of twenty-one years and/or shall have become self-supporting at which time the said payments for the said child shall cease."

Clarence also agreed to a life insurance policy "in the Phoenix Mutual Life Insurance Company for the sum of Five Thousand Dollars ($5,000.00) consisting of three separate policies."

Due to his fluctuating income, Clarence had difficulty maintaining the monthly child-support payments and the insurance premiums. Dorothy had to pay the policy premiums and kept "hounding" Clarence for payments and upkeep on the insurance well into the early 1950's, as Clarence put it.

In a letter to Clarence dated January 23rd, 1949, Dorothy wrote:

> *I believe, in all fairness, you will agree that I have had the heavy part of this bargain ... even to taking over the insurances (which were loaned to the hilt) when you agreed to take care of them. I have consistently made less than you but at no time have I made any demands on you, even when you told me you were making $800-$1,000 per month, nor have you ever offered to do more.*

Chapter 6

Growth and Movement

"We are thinking deeply, too, of all those sick ones still to come to A.A.—thousands, surely, and perchance millions. As they try to make their return to faith and to life, we want them to find everything in A.A. that we have found, and yet more, if that be possible. On our part, therefore, no care, no vigilance, no effort to preserve A.A.'s constant effectiveness and spiritual strength will ever be too great to hold us in full readiness for the day of their homecoming." [35]

Chapter 6.1

The Saturday Evening Post Article

"From Cleveland, by various means, the movement has spread to Chicago, Detroit, St. Louis, Los Angeles, Indianapolis, Atlanta, San Francisco, Evansville and other cities." [36]

In late 1940, *The Saturday Evening Post* commissioned one of its staff writers to do an exposé on Alcoholics Anonymous. His name was Jack Alexander. This man was famous for his articles exposing fraud and wrongdoing in the *Post*.

Alexander's initial objective was to "get all of the dirt" on A.A. and print it in the *Post*. But his investigation convinced him of a different story, and he set about writing an article in a national publication, which would put A.A. "on the map."

In a letter written from Ruth Hock to Clarence, which was undated and written in pencil on yellow legal paper, the following was stated:

One of their staff writers is definitely on the job and is now doing the rounds of some of our New York meetings. He will be out here to attend at least one Cleveland and one Akron meeting and is going to look you up for a talk. He is a very thorough person and we all feel that the result will be one exceptionally good article which should mean a lot in many ways. His name is Jack Alexander and I think he will be out here in about two weeks.

Ruth went on to discuss the fact that the *Post* would not do the article without photographs. She knew that this was a touchy issue with the Cleveland members and wrote:

We would like you to put out some gentle feelers on the picture situation but wouldn't like to see you have people on your neck by trying to force the situation—so, sort of try out the lay of the land and let us know. If the crowd will get together, the Post staff photographer will take the picture. So we are for a bigger and better A.A. very soon.

When Jack Alexander did arrive in Cleveland, he spoke with Clarence about photographs; and Clarence convinced him that a local photographer would probably do a better job with the expected photographs. Clarence reasoned that the Cleveland members would probably feel more comfortable with a local photographer.

Clarence selected the Art Miller Studios. In a letter to Bill Wilson, dated January 19, 1941, he wrote, "This photographer, Al Miller, is reputed to be one of the best in his line. In fact, there are only three places in Cleveland that have equipment to match his."

There was however, one little glitch that developed. About five hundred of the Cleveland members gathered for a group picture. Clarence wrote Bill, "I saw the negative of that picture and just to make you feel bad, it would have been a dandy."

But the photographer lost the negative and the picture was never printed. When asked why there was only one photo taken, Clarence wrote:

Of course, we all like to play safe (since we're sober) and the question has been asked me 521 times, "Why didn't he take several pictures while he was about it?" My answer, because

I asked the very same question, and he stated that "It isn't necessary and he never does and nothing can happen."

Because of Miller's loss of the negative, there was a delay in getting photos for the article, something neither Bill nor *The Saturday Evening Post* cared for. Clarence wrote Bill that the *Post* "wasn't satisfied with the hospital pictures, but for the life of me, I or no one else can understand why. So we took 5 more hospital pictures, all of which look good, and sent them on." One of these hospital photos appeared in the *Post* article. Another, showing Clarence on the right, can be found here:

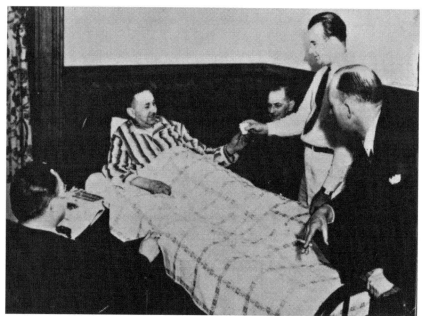

Clarence is on the right, smoking a cigarette

Clarence asked Bill about the possibility of getting a preview of the article, stating:

I was preparing the groups for any eventuality and would like to have some angles for my own benefit. We have had publicity before and I fully realize all the angles involved, the magazine, the editor, the reader and the subject. I understand all of that and I am in a diplomatic way trying to smooth the path for a lot of objectionable criticism from some of the more touchy or critical brethren, who mean well but have some queer ideas about such things. We have had over 700 contacts here and have prepared a couple more sanitarium set-ups to take care of any possible overflow of inquiries .... We are prepared for a rush, if one occurs, in any degree. With all the members we have, it will not be difficult to absorb any amount now.

The New York office was also gearing up for the article. In a "Memorandum to the Board of Trustees of the Alcoholic Foundation" dated February 19th, 1941, Bill Wilson wrote the following:

An article is to appear on March 1st in The Saturday Evening Post. This piece will be the feature number of that issue. The name Alcoholics Anonymous will appear on the outside cover of the magazine. Our message will be brought straight to the whole nation—nearly every one of at least a million alcoholics will hear of us. Three years ago The Saturday Post published an article called "The Unhappy Drinker," an interesting piece by a psychologist and an alcoholic. The Saturday Post offices were flooded with letters and telegrams—some 8,000 in all. The Post had to hire an additional staff of girls to give these people even a nominal reply, let alone a follow up—as we must. Last week Mr. Sommers, one of the editors of the Post, told me that a far greater response was expected from the coming article on A.A.

Therefore we must base our budget upon at least 10,000 inquiries. This means that this office will have fully three times as much work to do as it had the year past. By no stretch of the imagination could our present office force handle the situation.

The March 1st issue of *The Saturday Evening Post* was a best seller. Apparently every A.A. member bought a copy of the article, and it reached the millions of other *Post* readers. A.A. had become "national," and most of the members were proud of the way that A.A. had been portrayed. Some, however, did not approve of the article, and they expressed their opinions at the groups. Several Cleveland members stated they didn't think that their treasured and precious anonymity would now be protected and preserved. Some actually dropped out of A.A., but many of these did later return.

The office in New York was pleased with the results, stating in a proposal to all A.A. groups:

> *As anticipated, The Saturday Evening Post article of last March produced a flood of inquiries which, combined with our normal mail, brought the total number of letters received since then to 5,139. Each has received a personal reply. 15,000 pamphlets and 1,749 books have been shipped since March 1st. Besides, an extensive correspondence has been maintained with the groups. A.A. membership has more than doubled, standing now above 4,000 members. Office activity continues at a high rate and is thus far in line with our original estimate of 10,000 inquiries for the fiscal year.*

The Cleveland membership also grew. In 1941, Cleveland added fourteen new groups. Six of these were established between April and May after the *Post* article appeared.

A.A.—nation-wide, and especially in Cleveland—was on the move.

Chapter 6.2

Cleveland A.A. Grows in Leaps and Bounds

LUNCHEON—MAY 26TH, 1941—MONDAY
Speaker—Mr. Clarence Snyder, Ford Salesman,
E. D. Latimer and Co., 5362 Broadway
Subject—"Alcoholics Anonymous"

This movement, rapidly gaining in momentum, offers the first uniformly successful hope for a large group of people. There is much all of us would like to learn of this. The program has received favorable comment in other clubs as being most instructive. [37]

The year 1941 was a banner year for the growth of A.A. in Cleveland. The first group formed that year, on Friday, January 3rd, was organized and called the Lee Road Group. It met at 1637 Lee Road. A second Lee Road Group was formed as part of the original group and it met for the first time on Monday, January 6th, at the same address. This meant there were now nine meetings in the Cleveland area.

A tenth meeting—the Crawford Road Men's Group—had its first organizational meeting on February 12th with twelve members present. Its second organizational meeting (which was probably its first regular meeting) was held on February 19th, with seventeen members present. The Crawford Road meeting was held originally at 1779 Crawford Road. Clarence described its origins as follows:

> *There was a time in A.A. that people were coming in so fast, we had a hard time absorbing them on a one-on-one basis ....*
> *I was trying to figure out how to teach A.A. in classes to people. The problem was, where to find a place to teach these classes. This was because we had no money, which added to the problem.*

One of the 1941 inquiries which came in to the *Cleveland Plain Dealer*, was from a Walter B. Of him, Clarence wrote, "He lived down on Crawford Road." Clarence took this inquiry and went to visit with Walter. When he arrived, Clarence found the address to be a funeral home. Clarence was told that Walter was living out in the back in the carriage house.

When Walter answered the door he was wearing a beret. Of meeting him, Clarence said, "He was very affable, very polite and very drunk." Walter invited Clarence inside, and Clarence said, "Lo and behold, this place was a theater." Walter loved the theater so much that he set up his home as one. Clarence described the "theater" as being made up of a "couple of hundred theater seats, a stage, and props." On the other end of the building, Walter made his living quarters. Besides Walter, there was no one else living there except for "this Great Dane, his best buddy," as Clarence described the Dane.

Walter's hobby was putting on amateur theatrical events for the neighborhood. Most people didn't come to these because Walter was always drunk and making a fool of himself.

Clarence took a look at this theater and told Walter, "You are a gift from heaven." Walter was dumbfounded. He didn't understand what Clarence was talking about. But Clarence felt he had just found the right place for holding the A.A. classes. It was perfect, Clarence thought.

The A.A.s took over Walter's home. As Clarence said of the new classes:

> *"All these men, who were just wandering around with no place to go anyway, were told to go to this place. They came to be taught this program. By the end of the first year, the Crawford Road Men's Group had one hundred and thirty-five members. This was from a core group of only ten."*

Clarence told the author about one of Walter's neighbors, an elderly woman who once inquired about what was going on. She wanted to know about all of these strange men coming and going, the laughing and carrying on. She asked if they were drunk. Clarence told her that none of them drank even though they were once hopeless alcoholics. "You mean they don't drink?" she asked.

Clarence replied, "Nope, and they never will drink again." He explained to her a little about the A.A. program and told her his own story.

The Lady proceeded to tell Clarence that she had a boy who was "on the bum," and asked, "Can you fix him?" Clarence asked her where the boy was. She told him her boy was somewhere on skid row in New York City, and that he hadn't contacted her in a long time. Clarence told her about Bill Wilson, and gave her Bill's number.

This woman also had a daughter who was living in New York, and the daughter was given Bill's number in case she ever saw her brother. The brother had been an advertising manager for Calvert Distillery and got fired for drinking too much. "I guess he must have believed his own ads," Clarence observed. Shortly afterward, the brother contacted his sister for help, and the two got together. The sister gave him Bill's number, and the man joined A.A. Clarence recalled that this man never drank again and went on to become the first editor of the *A.A. Grapevine*.

On August 20th, 1941, the meeting at Walter's "theater" had to move. The announcement for the new meeting read as follows:

We have moved to our new meeting place at 8920 Euclid Ave. 2nd floor of the Euclid-Bolton Garage Building. A new and larger meeting place, seating approximately 150 people, located on the south side of Euclid Ave. between East 89th St. and East 90th Street.

There is ample parking facilities in the neighborhood for those who drive.

A Special and Interesting Meeting is planned for MEN ONLY Wednesday P.M. Aug. 20, 1941. Our first meeting in our new quarters.

Phone RA.   *5759 W.E.B., Secretary*

On April 21st, 1941, the Miles Avenue Group was formed in Cleveland. It branched off from the Borton Group and had its first meeting on that Monday at 10203 Miles Avenue. William H. and Frank W. were the group's sponsors. There were twenty original members; and by the end of the first year, the Miles Group had eighty-five in attendance.

Cleveland's group number twelve was the Collinwood Group. It first met on Thursday, April 24th at the Arnold Hall on East 152nd and St. Clair. There were fourteen members present. It had branched off from the Lee Road Friday Group, and its sponsors were Dan M., Franklin S., Tom V. and Harvey B. S. On June 25th the group moved to 14709 St. Clair Avenue and met on Wednesdays. At the end of the first year, the Collinwood Group had eighty-five active members.

Group number thirteen was the Shaker Group. It was formed on Monday, May 4th, 1941, and met at the Shaker Junior High School. It had branched off from the Borton Group with ten original members and increased to twenty-three active members by the end of the first year. The first Secretary was Thomas C. B.

Cleveland's next group was formed on May 16th, 1941. It was the Avon Lake Group and it met for the first time on Wednesday at the home of Dr. P. The group then later moved to the Avon Lake Town Hall and met on Fridays. This group had branched off from the Lake Shore-Cleveland Group with eight original members. It later moved to the American Legion Home in Lorain, Ohio. Its sponsors were Dr. P., John B., John M. and Tom S. (Tom was one of Clarence's "babies").

The next group was not only a first for Cleveland, it was a first for A.A. as a whole. Group number fifteen was the Women's Group. Marion R., the group's secretary, wrote, "I believe it is most interesting to know we are the first women's group in the U.S."

The first meeting of that women's group was on Tuesday, May 20th, 1941, and it met at the Colonial Hotel. There were sixteen original members. The sponsors of the group were Marion R., Lila D., H. M. and Mary S. On May 27, the women began holding their meetings at the "homes of girls" and later moved their meetings to Wednesday nights at 12214 Detroit Avenue.

Clarence had always fought for women to be able to come into A.A. But Dr. Bob had been against this idea, stating that he felt women members would be too distracting and would cause problems, not only for the male members, but for their wives as well. Also, Clarence felt, Bill Wilson was not too "keen on the idea" of women in A.A. But Clarence believed the meetings should be open to any person who had a problem with alcohol, and that women were certainly not immune.

Six more meetings were formed between May 23rd and November 26th, 1941: The first of these was the Lorain Avenue Group, which met on Monday, May 23rd at 11934 Lorain Avenue. It had twenty original members and had branched off from the Brooklyn Group.

Next, the West Side Men's Group was formed and had its first meeting on September 4th. It first met at 11107 Fortune Avenue with eight original members. They later moved their meeting to Tuesday nights at Pilgrim Church on West 14th Street and Starkweather. The sponsors of the West Side Group were Howard E., Norman J., Elmer H., Regis L., Jim C., Bob T., Bob F. and Jim S. At the end of its first nine months the West Side Group had one hundred and thirty-three members. The group was a special interest group of sorts, as was explained by its secretary, Dr. H. C. R., who wrote, "This group is solely for recreation purposes …. Requirement of membership is good standing in a parent group."

The Collinwood A.M. Group had its first meeting on Wednesday, October 1st and met at 14709 St. Clair. There were fifteen original members, and by the end of its first year the group had fifty-eight active members. The sponsors of the group were Al R., Don M., Frank S. and Bill C. It had branched from the original Collinwood Group.

The next group to form was the Lorain Group which met on Wednesday, October 22nd at the Antlers Hotel. There were fifteen original members, and at the end of the first six months, there were thirty. The sponsors of that group were Tom S., Don W. and Frank B. Both Tom and Don were Clarence's "babies."

The West 25th Street Group first met on Thursday, October 30th at West 25th Street and Erin. It had thirteen original members; and at the end of its first year, there were fifty active members. The sponsors of the group were H. H. F., Tom C., Clayton B. and Tom L. This group had branched off from the Brooklyn Group.

The Lee Road Wednesday Men and Women's Group held its first meeting on November 26th at Lee and Mayfield. There were fifty original members, and at the end of the first six months, there were seventy-five. The sponsors of the group were Albert R. G. (from the original G. Group), Stan B., B. McD., F. D. The Lee Road Group had branched off from the Thursday and Friday Lee and Mayfield Groups.

There was one other Cleveland Group, which for some reason Clarence couldn't recall. It did not make the list compiled by Norm E., Recording Statistician of the Central Committee, and was not listed among the original twenty-nine groups from May 11, 1939 through July 24, 1942. This was the Heights Group Friday, which first met on January 3, 1941 at 1637 Lee Road. It had twenty original members and had branched off from the Heights Group Thursday. Original members included George McD. and D. B. H.

There were two out-of-town groups formed in 1941, which sprang directly from the Cleveland Groups. The first was the Douglass Group, which met on Tuesday, November 11, 1941, at the Grace Episcopal Church in Mansfield, Ohio. It had seven original members, four of whom had come from the Borton Group. At the end of six months, there were fourteen active members. The sponsors of the group were Marion D., Ralston Fox S. and C. T. "Duke" P. (from Toledo).

The other out-of-town group was the Geneva Group, which first met in Geneva, Ohio on September 8th. On January 30, 1942, it moved to Ashtabula, Ohio, and changed its name to the Ashtabula Group. This meeting met bi-monthly since its members were still going to Cleveland to meet at the Borton Group every other week. The sponsors of the group were Jack D., William F., Harry S., Al S. and Pete S.

Clarence and "the boys and girls" were thus very busy during 1941. They were running around, answering inquiries, and starting meetings. They were also beginning to form what was probably the first local Central Office of A.A. The only other A.A. office was that of the Alcoholic Foundation in New York City.

Chapter 6.3

Cleveland Central Office Formed

The legitimate object of Government is to do for a community of people whatever they need to have done, but cannot do all in their separate and individual capacities.

Abraham Lincoln

Being mindful of the need and usefulness of a central committee, our two meetings have been marked by an outstanding atmosphere of fine fellowship and co-operation between the groups. We have had excellent attendance and much interest is being shown by all committee members in the furtherance of our fellowship.

> **Bulletin to All Groups—regarding the second meeting of the Cuyahoga Central Committee, August 15, 1941 ...**
> **Clarence H. Snyder, Chairman**

In the late Spring or early Summer of 1939, the A.A. Association had been formed in Cleveland so that prospective members could have their hospital and sanitarium bills paid in a timely manner. This Cleveland committee was the forerunner of the Cleveland or Cuyahoga County A/A Committee, or "Central Committee," as it was later called. The A.A. Association kept track of alcoholics in the various centers for detoxification and kept records of their accounts there. If the bills were not paid, the Association either called up on members to pay them, or in cases where this was not possible, the Association would accept payment responsibility for those members from funds set aside for such a purpose.

That there was still no official Central Committee in operation as of February 21, 1941, seems evidenced by a letter to the editor in the *Cleveland Press* by Clarence. In that letter, Clarence told what

Alcoholics Anonymous was all about and used the address of the Alcoholic Foundation. He listed it as "30 Vesey street, Room 700, New York City." Clarence then also gave his own address at 8803 Euclid Avenue, Cleveland.

In his February, 1941, letter to the *Cleveland Press* Clarence wrote that A.A members accomplished their sobriety by following a specific pattern. He said the member must:

Have a sincere desire to quit drinking forever.

Recognize the allergy and compulsion for lifetime.

Recognize his ailment as a disease.

Accept God and live by four simple principles: honesty, unselfishness, purity and love.

Clarence continued his letter to the *Press*, by suggesting that one read "our book 'Alcoholics Anonymous,' a book written by alcoholics, for alcoholics, at the Cleveland Public Library." Clarence added:

The several thousand people (over 700 in Cleveland alone) who have thus far found life and hope through this means, is ample testimony that the day of miracles has not passed.

On March 2, 1941, only one day after the Jack Alexander article appeared in *The Saturday Evening Post*, a meeting was held in the office of the Cleveland Switchboard Co. The purpose was to form the Cuyahoga County A/A Committee.

The announcement card for the meeting read as follows:

MOTION by B___, second by C___—that a CLEARING HOUSE COMMITTEE be formed, and that it be composed of two (2) members from each and every A/A Group in Cuyahoga County. This Committee to have NO AUTHORITY to commit, involve or bind any one or all of the Groups in Cuyahoga County in any manner whatsoever without referring proposed ideas, plans or propositions to each individual Group for its acceptance or rejection. MOTION was carried.

COMMITTEE MEMBERS: Kindly conform to this important rule.

C. H. Snyder, Chairman.

The meeting was held, and the motion was carried. But there was a movement to oust Clarence from the position of Chairperson. Clarence wrote Bill Wilson on March 4, 1941, asking Bill for help with this "revolution." It seems the Cleveland members were still complaining about what had transpired with the articles in the *Cleveland Plain Dealer*. Clarence wrote:

> *They wanted to know how much the Plain Dealer pd. me. Why I didn't put it in the kitty. Where did I get the authority etc. etc. etc. Not one kind thing said in my behalf. This from persons I had picked out of the gutter and worked on and gave unceasingly and unselfishly of fellowship and whatever I could. Experience then, the resentment and hatred has been there. They have gone out of their way on numerous occasions to embarrass me.*

These disgruntled members voted Clarence out of office, just as they had voted him out of A.A. during the original split of the Cleveland Group. They elected Bill H. as chairperson and wanted nothing to do with Clarence.

Clarence's ego was wounded. He wrote Bill Wilson, stating that Bill should "pay no attention to this so-called Cuyahoga County committee as yet. Continue to send me the names as always, and they will be followed and taken care of in a conscientious manner as always."

About the same time, there were a number of Cleveland members who objected to the Alcoholic Foundation's call for contributions and refused to support the New York office. As to this issue, Clarence added in his letter to Bill:

> *About the foundation money plan, don't concern yourself about that here. I wish I had known about it before Bert T____ blew in. After this revolution subsides, I can get you all the dough for the foundation that will be needed from our part of the country. And believe me when I tell you I can get it where no one else can.*

Dissention continued in Cleveland for several months. A Cleveland Committee did not develop until August of 1941. A bulletin to all groups, sent out that August, said:

> *At the second meeting of the Cuyahoga Central Committee meeting, held Friday evening, August 15th, the following committees were appointed by the chairman.*

The "chairman" at that time was once again Clarence Snyder. Three committees were formed: one was Entertainment, with Al "Abby" G. as chairman, one was Finance, with Wm. "Bill" H. as chairman and one was Hospital, with H. L. M. as chairman. Each of the three committees had six members from different groups around the Cleveland area. The terms of office for committee members was to be three months "or until the chairman's term of office expires, or until replaced by the chairman."

Rotation of officers was one of Clarence's ideas. This was to insure an equal and representative voice from within the fellowship. Also introduced at this meeting were the "new A.A. Pamphlets." The author believes these were probably similar in content to the earlier *Houston Press* articles by Larry J., the man whom Clarence sponsored, who had moved to Texas to start A.A. there.

On August 19, 1941, a meeting of the Finance Committee of the Central Group Committee was held. Its minutes suggested to

"... the representatives of the groups that they in turn propose to their respective group that they deposit with the Finance Committee the Sum of one dollar each week beginning January 1st 1942."

It went on to state that:

> *Such funds are to be used for the purpose of defraying normal expenses of the Central Committee Group such as P.O. box rental, postage and such other incidental expenses as may be required .... [And to] make contributions to the Foundation in New York and such other charities as may be recommended to the finance committee by the various groups and approved by the finance committee.*

A bulletin to all groups from the "third meeting of the Cuyahoga County Central Committee, held Tuesday evening, August 26th," announced plans for a Halloween Party and a New Year's Eve Party which was to include "all the combined groups." The bulletin also announced the availability of two A.A. pamphlets:

1) the *Houston Press* articles written by Larry J., and
2) the articles in the *Cleveland Plain Dealer*.

The bulletin also asked if anyone was interested in a bowling league. Thus the Fellowship was not only concerned with the meetings and 12 Step work, but was also involved in social activities.

About this time, Clarence proposed a dinner to "Honor Dr. Bob Smith" and it was planned for October 5th. Clarence felt his sponsor, Dr. Bob, should be honored for his untiring efforts in "fixing rummies."

At first the Dr. Bob dinner was set for the Lake Shore Hotel at 12506 Edgewater Drive in Cleveland. The Hotel had room for 450 people. Announcements were sent out to all of the Ohio groups, as well as to those in surrounding states. The event was to involve not only the dinner, but "an afternoon full of special events." All of this was to cost $1.35 per person.

The response was overwhelming. The reservations were reaching the 450 person cut-off. They had to decide what to do. Would they turn people away? They decided to move the location. Clarence contacted all of the local hotels and found one, the Hotel Statler, which would accommodate more than 600 people.

When built, the Statler had cost over $2,500,000 and was one of the largest hotels in Cleveland. The hotel negotiated a deal similar to the one with the Lake Shore Hotel. The price for the room and the meal was still low.

At a

cost to the committee of $1.00 per person, the menu was to consist of:

Half Grapefruit
Pan Fried Veal Cutlet
Potatoes Croquette – Peas au Beurre
Vanilla Ice Cream with Raspberry Ice
Cakes – Coffee

Invitations were sent out to Bill Wilson and others, and local groups contributed to help pay the train fare to bring the speakers out to Cleveland. Invitations were then sent out once again asking people to attend and informing them of the change of location. In a letter to Clarence dated September 30, 1941, Jim B. of Detroit wrote, "I shall deliver your affectionate message to Archie (Arch T.) but, sorry to say, he told me Sunday, he was not planning on making the trip." Jim's letter thanked Clarence for the invitation and for the information as to the change of location and informed Clarence of other Detroit members who would attend.

October 5, 1941 finally arrived. According to the press release from the Central Committee, "approximately 850 attended" the dinner, and "about sixteen out-of-town groups were represented at this assembly."

A newspaper article about the dinner was headed, "900 Reformed Alcoholics Hold Anonymous Dinner." The turn-out had been so great that the article ended with the following:

"The Statler's ballroom seldom has entertained a larger crowd than that which attended the dinner. Extra tables were set on the balcony and in the corridor."

As M.C. for the event, Clarence wrote a schedule of events on the back of the card which announced the meeting. It was written in pencil, and read as follows:

Invocation
Dinner Announcements

Introductory Talk and Welcome to guests
Introduction – Out of town guests
Central Committee
Mr. & Mrs. Borton – Women's Group
Grace G. – Edna McD.
Dorothy S. – Mrs. Doc Smith
Henrietta Seiberling – Wally G.
Bill D. – Bill Wilson
Doc Smith – Closing Remarks
Prayer

Dr. Bob Smith was overwhelmed by the response. He spoke briefly and tried to downplay his role in the founding of A.A. Everyone was pleased with the outcome. In the *Bulletin to All Groups*, dated October 17, 1941, Clarence wrote,

"Everyone was gratified to learn that we didn't go in the red on our appreciation dinner. In fact we came out 90 to the good."

On October 21st, the Central and Group Hospital Committee met with 14 groups represented and two absent. They adopted the "rules and regulations ... for general use by the Hospitals and the Sanitariums accepting A.A. patients" (see Appendix G).

The Committee continued to meet, formulate policy, set social events and inform the groups of current events concerning A.A.

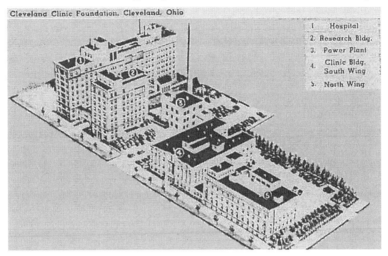

members. Clarence had an idea for a newsletter which would inform members of A.A. news and contain a meeting directory. The other purpose for the newsletter, which was to be called the *Cleveland Central Bulletin*, was to inform the membership of the whereabouts of members who were serving in the Armed Forces.

Eventually, the Central Committee decided they needed an office, and on February 8th, 1945, the A.A. Cleveland District Office opened. And though it has changed addresses many times since 1945, that District Office has continued to respond to the still sick and suffering alcoholic.

In a pamphlet put out by the Cleveland District Office in 1962 the following statistics were given:

> *Since the Office door opened on February 8th, 1945, more than 12,910 calls for help have been received. Of these, 7,878 were reported receptive and already started on their way back to a New Life. During the same period, hundreds of speakers have been supplied to groups and various organizations ... also thousands of packages of literature have been sent out to everyone seeking information regarding Alcoholics Anonymous.*

Personal contact, sponsorship, literature, a newsletter, rotation of officers, and a tremendous recovery rate were to become the trademarks of Cleveland A.A. And Clarence had fought for all of this because he wanted the still sick and suffering alcoholic to have the same chance that he had gotten. His sponsor, Dr. Bob, had given him a ministry: to help the alcoholic get well, if he wished to get well. Clarence wanted the best and did his utmost to see that Cleveland got it.

We here set forth the "Aims, Purposes and Functions of the Cleveland Central Committee." The source, an original document, was early and undated:

Aims, Purposes and Functions of the Central Committee

I. To promote unselfishness, unity and understanding among all groups: e.g.—

As individuals, we should never forget our purpose in being associated with our fellowship. Our membership is composed of persons from all walks of life, many different types of background, various stages of mental, physical and spiritual development; various temperaments, social set-ups, religious beliefs and creeds. All of us have reached the same extremity. All of us are trying to maintain sobriety, and live like human beings are meant to live. We are all interested in helping others like us to share what we have found.

The fact that we are such a cosmopolitan and democratic fellowship accounts for the fact that we have numerous perspectives among the members of our fellowship. No individual or group in our fellowship is perfect, nor perhaps will ever be, and by the same token, no individual or group is one hundred percent wrong. We feel that every one and every group has a place in our plan, and can contribute constructive ideas and suggestions for the benefit of our movement as a whole. We believe that any difference of opinion arising between individuals and groups can be brought to a satisfactory compromise, through the patient application of the principles of Love, Unselfishness, Tolerance and Understanding. By meeting together, we can get acquainted, and come to realize that no matter what our perspectives may be, we all have about the same problems, and in really understanding the other fellow, we find that he is not such a blackguard after all.

It is needless to expound at length on the merits of Unity. In our case, however, a greater unity and understanding can be responsible for the salvaging of futures, homes and lives. A duty rests upon us to discharge an obligation that no person or group of persons but us can handle satisfactorily. By one hundred per cent co-operation, can't we do a much better job of discharging that duty?

II. To establish a uniform hospital technique: e.g.—

Many constructive measures have already been worked out by the Hospital Committee; case histories, group hospital committees, new hospital connections, standard regulations for entering patients; visiting, handling "slips" etc. Much money has been saved the hospitals who co-operate. Our position with the hospitals has been strengthened. Constant attention must be paid to our hospitalization set-up, for the good of the fellowship as a whole.

III. Establishment and maintenance of a suitable promotional program: e.g.—

We want and need new members. They want and need us. Promotion of our plan is very important. It is a discharge of a duty. In the past, most of our promotional work has rested on too few of the members. Some members have done much toward helping, by sending out pamphlets at their own expense. Some groups have also done this.

Many of our members have found us through the medium of newspaper and magazine articles; talks before clubs and organizations; from physicians; members of the clergy; social and civic organizations; the courts, and others. The proper type of publicity is very beneficial to our ends, but the very nature of our work makes it necessary that we be certain, insofar as possible, that all publicity be edited by us, before being released.

Some months ago, the Central Committee appointed Clarence Snyder as a committee to check all publicity. Due to his efforts, a number of items of publicity which were of questionable value, and more than likely, of definite harm to our plan, were suppressed. For the good of all, let us co-operate, and remember to never give interviews for publication without first consulting him on the matter. Publicity seeking persons can do much harm to our groups and members, through ignorance or mercenary motives. One piece of publicity may look helpful to one group, but may cause much embarrassment or harm to individuals in another. Obviously, if every one who gets an idea about publicity is permitted to scatter it to the four winds, pandemonium would result. On sober reflection, we cannot but agree that a "safety valve" is needed in connection with this phase of our work.

We have a Post Office Box, No. 1638, Station C, to which many requests for help are addressed. An effective plan to answer these requests and make equitable distribution of the names among the groups, must be worked out and maintained.

IV. Exchange of ideas and suggestions among groups: e.g.—

No two groups operate exactly alike. Why do some groups have more social times? Some have literature tables? Some have regulations regarding admittance of "slips" outsiders, guests, etc.? Why do some groups boast a better percentage of recoveries? Why are some more successful in putting the "slipper" back on his feet? Why are meetings conducted differently in different groups? How can one group help another in matters of overlapping and hospital visitations? What ideas does your group have, to help one another maintain sobriety?

Hundreds of such questions could conceivably arise, through association of our twenty-three groups.

St. Vincent's Charity Hospital in Cleveland

Chapter 6.4

First A.A. Newsletter, Cleveland Central Bulletin, Clarence's "brain-child"

Clarence was about to enter the army and felt that A.A. members in the service of their country were going to be without the benefit of A.A meetings and friends at home, part of the fellowship which had been so successful in keeping them all sober.

He suggested that a newspaper of sorts would be beneficial to himself as well as the other members in the armed forces. Harry D., who owned the D. Company, a printing company on 1104 Prospect Avenue, offered to be the printer for the newspaper.

Many believed that Harry D. was the founder and first editor of the Cleveland A.A. newspaper. But, in a letter to Clarence, dated November 14, 1942, Harry modestly wrote,

"See what God wrought! This letter accompanies the second issue of Central Bulletin, which was your brain-child, I believe."

Harry's letter continued:

Naturally I'm tickled pink with it, for it will do a tremendous amount of good in strengthening the localities as well as the men originally intended for—the boys in service.

We have a dandy editorial setup, with S. of course the finest contributor ... Mark H. and I are the lesser of the two co-editors and it sure is fun, in spite of the many extra hours it demands.

Volume 1, No. 1 was released in October 1942. It was printed on both sides of one 8 1/2 x 11 inch sheet of paper, promising that "If it is warranted, another page will be used." The size was recommended by the editors, so that, "all issues can be assembled in standard loose-leaf binders." The standard read in bold letters:

CENTRAL BULLETIN

UNSELFISHNESS—HONESTY—TRUTH— LOVE

The first page contained an editorial defining the purposes of the newspaper, a small piece on a dinner honoring Bill Wilson, a plea to secretaries to compile lists of all members who were in the service, and a call for a new name for the newspaper. It stated that "This name, *The Central Bulletin*, does not convey its purpose."

But only one other name was submitted, and the editors decided that the name, *Central Bulletin*, would remain.

The format for the second issue remained basically the same, except that it contained four pages, with the back page an ad reminding people to buy bonds "For Defense."

The editorial for the second issue dealt with the dinner honoring Bill Wilson. Harry D. wrote Clarence that the editorial, written by S., "was a masterpiece. Incidentally, Wilson's talk was one too." The letter continued to discuss a point which was meant to embarrass Bill Wilson. It seems that a certain, or certain Cleveland member(s), set out to "quiz" Bill on the "financial skullduggery he was purported to have engaged in."

Many in A.A. have blamed Clarence and pointed to him as the one questioning Bill's financial gains from the A.A. fellowship. But Clarence told the author this was far from the truth. Though Clarence didn't believe in making any money from this "avocation," he never wanted publicly to embarrass Bill.

At the time this situation concerning Bill surfaced, Clarence was in another state and in the Army. He had to hear about these concerns in the newsletter. The *Bulletin* also contained an article regarding gossip in the second issue of the newsletter. According to Harry's letter to Clarence, this gossip article "will sink home to the perpetrator." It seems that Harry and several other Cleveland members had an idea who this person was, but Clarence couldn't recall why they wouldn't mention his name.

The second issue also announced a 24-hour phone service and listing in the telephone directory. It contained a meeting list and "News from the Camps" letters from those in the service. In that issue, there was a short letter from Clarence stating, "If any of my friends wish to write me, address me as follows —."

The Third Edition came out in December of 1942. It had a new masthead. At its center, there was a sun design, with an A.A. in the center, surrounded by the Four Absolutes. On either side of this sun was the title CENTRAL BULLETIN. Also, this issue began a series of editorials on each of the Twelve Steps.

The May 1944 issue announced that the

> *Central Committee welcomed into A.A. this month, the Arcade Group, formed of alcoholics who had been handling their problems through the Oxford Group Movement (which includes non-alcoholics as well as alcoholics). The group announced its acceptance of the A.A. program based on the Twelve Steps and will limit its membership to confessed alcoholics.*

The *Central Bulletin* continued to bring news to A.A. members in Cleveland and to those who had moved on to other areas of the United States. The October 1944 issue announced the first Young People's Meeting, stating:

> *Age is no barrier if you wish to participate in the meetings of one of the newest groups, organized in October. The group calls itself the Young People's Group, and it was formed by several of the younger A.A.'s ... 20's-30's ... But they stress the fact that they do not exclude 'oldsters' from their meetings.*

The group met on Wednesdays at 8:30 P.M. in the West Side Evangelical Hall on West 38th Street and Bridge.

The bulletin also announced the deaths of members. One of these articles (in the March 1947 issue) stated "One of the founders of A.A. in Cleveland, Charley J___ passed away on the 3rd of March and was buried on the 6th .... He was one of the founders of the Corinthians and was the originator of the name of the group." The Corinthians was not a regular A.A. meeting, it was more of a social subsidiary, founded so that members could have a place to socialize and fellowship together.

The *Cleveland Central Bulletin*, which is still published today, contained probably the best articles and A.A. writings in the 1940's. To delve into these writings at depth would probably increase this volume twofold. A book on the *Cleveland Central Bulletin* and its importance in A.A. history is in the works.

The Cleveland Arcades—home of the Arcade Group

Chapter 6.5

Army life in Fort Knox

Every citizen [should] be a soldier. This was the case with the Greeks and the Romans, and must be that of every free state. [38]

In the summer of 1942, Clarence decided it was time to join the army. In August, he contacted the Selective Service board to apply for Volunteer Officers Candidate training. On August 8th, his application was approved.

Clarence at Ft. Knox

The earliest correspondence concerning Clarence and the army is a letter from Irwin M. wishing Clarence a "victorious return." Then on October 20th Clarence received this response from the Louisville, Kentucky, office of Alcoholics Anonymous—a response to one of his letters:

Pvt. Clarence H. Snyder,
U.S. Army, Co. B, 8th Bn. A.F.R.T.C.
Fork Knox, Ky.

Dear Pvt. Snyder:-

We are very glad indeed to have your letter and are looking forward to having you attend our meetings.

We meet at the Kentucky Dairies Auditorium, Third and Kentucky Streets, at 8:00 o'clock, and if you can possibly get away would like to have you with us next Friday. Jim McC. is our leader here.

(Mrs.) Mildred Z.

Clarence kept up with his meetings and, by mail, received news of what was going on with Cleveland A.A., and he received the Cleveland *Central Bulletin*. There were many Ohio members in the armed forces, and the newsletter was a means for these members to get A.A. news from home.

Clarence's second wife
Selma Gertrude Kitterer

By this time Clarence had married Selma Kitterer, who was living in Cleveland during Clarence's army service. Documents show they were married Friday, November 28, 1941, the day after Thanksgiving. Selma was related to Theodore A. Kitterer, Minister of the First Evangelical and Reformed Church on Arlington Avenue and Thornhill Drive. She was also related to Superintendent Rev. Armin A. Kitterer of Evangelical Deaconess Hospital. Evangelical Deaconess was one of the early hospitals to which A.A. members were taken for "drying out."

A.A. members at Deaconess hospital were paying $8.00 per day for private rooms plus medications and extras. Any A.A. member having a semi-private room could have another A.A. member stay there "without additional charge for room and attendance."

Clarence at Ft. Knox near Louisville, Kentucky

Clarence and Selma

Selma

In a letter to Dorothy, his ex-wife, Clarence described a typical night in the army as follows:

> *Last night I went to Elizabethtown to do a little shopping and relaxing and staying at the U.S.O. all night. I went to a picture show, with lots of blood spilled. A cowboy picture, vintage 1909 and a Sabotage picture without vintage. I ate lunch in E. Town today and had a fine meal. Our grub here at camp is, as a general rule, terrible. Poorly cooked, poorly served and many times not enough. They specialize in grease here, and I shouldn't be surprised to see the ice cream served in grease if we ever get ice cream.*

As part of his 14-16 hour daily routine, Clarence was receiving Officers Candidate training. He was made a squad leader, which he wrote Dorothy, was "in essence a corporal, with a squad of men to mother, teach, be accountable for and report on."

In his letter to Dorothy, Clarence also asked about the dinner that had been held for Bill Wilson. Clarence said:

> *I haven't heard much news on the Sunday party for Bill W. Next time you write, I will appreciate a sort of detailed report I do know that they had 450 for dinner and another 300 afterward .... what finally happened re: the matter of Bill and Doc's remuneration from the Foundation.*

Clarence and Dorothy kept up with their correspondence throughout Clarence's stint at Fort Knox. Dorothy relayed news about their son and about A.A. doings. Selma was not involved in any A.A. matters and knew little about A.A. news.

In the army, Clarence made plans to go into business with Hank P., who was Bill Wilson's partner in the office in Newark. Hank was married to Dorothy Snyder's sister. Bill and Hank had several arguments over what Hank said was Bill's leaving him out of the "glory" for writing the book. And there was also a lot of talk about

Hank's having an affair with someone at the office. In the end, Hank left A.A.

There is some possibility that it was Hank who convinced Clarence to join the army but there has been no documentation to that suggestion. After Clarence's tour in the army, he was classified 1A in the draft on July 17, 1943 and on August 30, 1943 the Selective Service finally responded regarding Clarence's application to be an Officer in the army. They referred it to another department.

Clarence worked with Hank selling porcelain mugs and figurines all throughout the 1940's. After Hank's divorce from Dorothy's sister, the business finally went under and Clarence's association with Hank dissolved. The last correspondence from Dorothy regarding the fiasco with Hank was in 1947. Hank never really stayed sober and died drunk and on pills.

After Clarence left the army, he returned to Selma and to Cleveland A.A. He continued his work there in helping to carry the message. Clarence always believed in doing his best, whether it was in the army or in business or in his avocation, which was working with alcoholics.

Chapter 7

Decentralization - Promises and Reality

"Power intoxicates men. When a man is intoxicated by alcohol, he can recover, but when intoxicated by power, he seldom recovers."

— James F. Byrnes

Chapter 7.1

Statement of 1948

"In the councils of Government we must guard against the acquisition of unwarranted influence, whether sought or unsought .... The potential for the disastrous rise of misplaced power exists and will persist."

— Dwight D. Eisenhower

In July of 1948, the Board of Trustees of the Alcoholic Foundation adopted a set of principles. According to Clarence, Dr. Bob approved that Statement of Principles. In that statement, the Board said, "The aim of the Foundation [would be to] limit its organization and activities to the bare essentials required to perform its important but limited duties." The Foundation apparently believed A.A. was becoming too organized. And this was something that Dr. Bob was totally against. Clarence told the author he believed that Dr. Bob had a feeling that, after his (Dr. Bob's) death, there would be changes within A.A. in which A.A. would be professionalized and no longer "kept simple." Clarence said this was the reason Doc endorsed the Statement of Principles.

Within its text, the statement contained a plan to inaugurate *"a program of gradual decentralization of headquarters activities to the end that the responsibility of 'carrying the message' may be gradually assumed by local groups and committees."*

It was important, the statement said, that

> *The A.A. Movement remains unshackled by the fetters of organization and is kept free from the corroding effect of political procedures which stem from over-organization.*

Over-organization was the thing that the original Ohio members feared the most, Clarence said to the author. They knew, he said, that with the passing of Dr. Bob, and the end to the influence Dr. Bob had with Bill Wilson, unless there was something in writing, the simplicity of the program might be forever lost.

According to Clarence, when Dr. Bob passed on, the Statement of 1948 was quickly replaced with the so-called Statement of 1950. Dr. Bob's influence and counsel were no longer a factor. Clarence believed the long-term members in Ohio were incensed as were other long-term members around the country.

The Board of Trustees of the Alcoholic Foundation never really made the original 1948 statement of policy available to the fellowship except, in a small way, through the *Grapevine*. But the *Grapevine* article was worded in such a way that the full impact of the statement was lost.

In a letter to Clarence, Royal S. (an attorney who wrote the incorporation papers for *The Grapevine Inc.*) stated:

> *"I enclose a copy of the Statement of 1948 which you may not have seen and which has been virtually suppressed by the Trustees."*

This supposed suppression has continued until this day. When the author asked to see a copy of the Statement, he was told that it probably didn't exist and if it did, its whereabouts were unknown.

The full Statement of 1948 and correspondence concerning it is contained in Appendix H.

One of the foundations of the Orthodox Movement was this Statement and its dissemination to the groups for their approval since the groups were never allowed to either see it nor pass on it.

Cleveland wanted to have a celebration for the fifteenth anniversary of the founding of A.A., the date of Dr. Bob's last drink, and the matter was discussed at length. The result was a decision to hold an international gathering to be sponsored by "The Pioneer Groups ... Akron, New York and Cleveland."

Bill Wilson came to Cleveland to attend a meeting of the Cleveland Central Committee on March 7, 1950. The purpose was to discuss the possibility of holding the International Conference in Cleveland. When Bill spoke, he stated that:

> ... *in his opinion and that of Dr. Smith, Cleveland was the logical place for an International Conference because of its geographical location and because of the contribution of the Cleveland Groups to the early growth of A.A., defining this as development of the sponsorship system thus proving that A.A. could work on a large scale instead of only through the original members.*

A tentative plan for financing such a conference proposed that each Cleveland Group be asked for $20.00 toward a goal of $2,000.00, and that there be a registration fee of $1.00 for each participant. The foundation was also asked to contribute.

A committee was formed to develop this conference. Dick S. was elected General Chairman of the First International Conference Committee. The committee had high hopes for the proposed conference.

A letter to group secretaries said: *"It's going to be one whale of a Conference—more A.A.s by far than have ever been gathered in one place before! At this point it looks like anywhere from 10,000 to 50,000!"*

When the Conference actually took place, July 28 to 30, there were about 7,000 participants. Three hotels were used for the Conference: the Carter Hotel, the Hollenden Hotel and the Cleveland Hotel. The Big Meeting was to be held on Sunday afternoon at the Cleveland Public Auditorium, which seated 10,000.

Hollenden Hotel.   Cleveland, Ohio.

Hollenden Hotel

The high spots for the 1950 Cleveland Conference were to be as follows:

FRIDAY, JULY 28

10:00 A.M. (Carter Hotel) Hospitalization. The benefits of co-operation between A.A.s and organized medicine. Doctors will explain the latest in hospital therapy and practice.
2:00 P.M. (Hollenden Hotel) A.A. in Industry. Development of cooperative programs among A.A.s and personnel directors in business and industry (duPont, Eastman Kodak and Thompson Products).

4:00 P.M. The Printed Word. A symposium on A.A. publications for their editors, writers and managers.
8:30 P.M. (Carter Hotel) The A.A. Family. A special meeting for non-alcoholics affiliated with the movement through family ties. The first A.A. wife will speak (Lois Wilson).

SATURDAY, JULY 29—MEETINGS INCLUDED:

1) A.A. in Corrective Institutions with Warden Clinton Duffy of San Quentin,
2) The Woman A.A. Meeting (for women only),
3) The A.A. Conference Meeting to discuss definition of the traditions of A.A. and other matters of policy, and a Banquet which was to be followed by entertainment and dancing (for $5.00 per person).

SUNDAY, JULY 30—TWO HIGHLIGHTS:

10:30 A.M., The Spiritual Significance of A.A. and
2:00 P.M., the Big Meeting with only two speakers, Dr. Bob and Bill.

The registration for the Conference was $1.50 per person payable at any time during the Conference in order to get the Official Button.

Also introduced at the Conference was the Proposal by the Trustees, Dr. Bob, and Bill for The General Service Conference of Alcoholics Anonymous.

Clarence stated that Dr. Bob was against the General Service Conference until Bill convinced him otherwise. But Dr. Bob knew that he was going to die, and was finally persuaded that the General Service Conference would be the best thing for A.A. He was also convinced that A.A. was not going to become over-organized due to the Statement of 1948 which promised decentralization. With the Statement of 1948 in place and with Bill's convincing, Dr. Bob agreed to put his approval to the General Service Conference.

The International Conference proved to be the last major public appearance for Dr. Bob. He died in November of that same year.

After Dr. Bob passed on, A.A. underwent many changes, which Clarence was sure would not have been acceptable to Dr. Bob.

Chapter 7.2

The First General Service Conference

"One uses one's principles to tyrannize or justify or honor or affront or conceal one's habits. Two men with similar principles may easily want totally different things with them."[39]

We here set forth in full the proposal:

**PROPOSAL BY THE TRUSTEES,
DR. BOB and BILL for
THE GENERAL SERVICE CONFERENCE
of ALCOHOLICS ANONYMOUS**

I. Purpose

    a. To become basic guardian of A.A. traditions and world-wide service.
    b. To perpetuate The Alcoholic Foundation and the A.A. General Headquarters at New York City.
    c. To be a service body only; never a government.

II. Composition

    a. The proposal will include A.A. State and Provincial Delegates, Trustees of the Foundation and Staff members of the General Service Office and Grapevine.
    b. Delegates to be in each State by Representatives from local Groups.
    c. Two State Panels to be chosen every two years alternately.

1. Panel #1 composed of Delegates from thickly populated States and Provinces, to meet every other year.

2. Panel #2 composed of Delegates from balance of States and Provinces, to meet in alternate years.

3. Relation of Conference to A.A.
    a. Vehicle for expression of views on matters vital to A.A.
    b. Vehicle to protect policy of A.A. and guard against hazardous deviations from original Traditions.
    c. A reliable guide to right thought and right action on serious matters pertaining to A.A.

4. Relation of Conference to General Headquarters
    a. A dependable guide to The Alcoholic Foundation, whose Trustees are the Custodian of A.A. general funds, the book, "Alcoholics Anonymous," the General Service Office and the *Grapevine*.
    b. To consult with Trustees in filling vacancies on the Foundation Board.
    c. To guide Trustees in their direction of A.A. Foundation work.
    d. Finally, after successful operation, to control final shape and form of the movement.

5. State and Provincial Delegates
    a. State and Provincial Delegates to be chosen for two years terms as indicated above (2 b and c)

6. Conference Rotation
    a. Overlapping of 2 panels of State and Provincial Delegates
    b. First Year Panel #1 to be composed by inviting one two-year Delegate from each of 28 States and Provinces having largest A.A. population, plus a few Delegates additional from States approaching 5,000 A.A. population
    c. Second Year Panel #2 to be composed by inviting one two year delegate from the balance of States and

Provinces, also including extra Delegates from States and Provinces approaching 2,000 A.A. population
d. Third Year Panel #1 areas will elect new Delegates
e. Fourth Year Panel #2 areas will do the same.

7. Conference Delegates

a. Selected from largest centers of A.A. population
b. Panel #2 to include Delegates from second largest centers of all States and Provinces

8. Method of selection of Delegates

a. To be chosen by Assemblies of A.A. Group Representatives, by at least, a two third vote.

9. Financial Structure

a. Each A.A. Group to make a $5.00 contribution to Alcoholic Foundation Conference Fund.
b. Groups, participating, to pay Delegates expenses up to $100.00
c. Conference Fund expects to pay expenses over $100.00

10. Meetings

a. Yearly, at New York
b. Extra meetings only in emergency
c. Two Thirds of Delegates registered considered a quorum

11. Procedure

a. Financial reports of the Foundation.
b. Financial reports of the Headquarters Services
c. Consideration of Finance and Policy matters of importance
d. Suggestions and resolutions
e. Consideration of any deviation from A.A. Traditions or misuse of "Alcoholics Anonymous"
f. Election of Conference Officers
g. Draw on by-laws

h. Committee to draft full report of proceedings and the state of A.A. generally, to be sent to groups throughout the world.

12. General Warranties of Conference

a. To observe the spirit of A.A. Traditions

b. To guard against any enforcement of wealth or power.

c. To assure adequate operating funds plus ample reserves

d. To assure that no member of the Conference shall ever have unqualified authority

e. To make all important decisions by discussion and vote

f. To guard against any resolution that will incite public or private controversy

g. To see that the Conference never attempts to govern Alcoholics Anonymous

h. To guarantee that the Conference shall always be democratic in thought and action.

About that Conference, Clarence wrote to Dorothy on March 9, 1951:

Fact of the matter is, that over 4 years ago, Bill had this idea of a gen. service conference, and he spoke to me about it in his office in N.Y. at that time. How can one suggest that this is some new development in A.A.?

The question is, WHY A CONFERENCE? Personally, I must go along with all the old-timers who feel that as A.A. grows larger and becomes more accessible, the need for any important control in N.Y. or any other place diminishes. Of what constructive use is the N.Y. office to Cleveland, Canton, Mansfield, Chicago, Los Angeles, or Podunk? We have our groups, and all anyone would have to do is take his choice of several ways of contacting A.A.

He would look in the Phone book in most any town, he could ask the first cop he would meet, he could talk to most any judge, he could ask most any clergyman, and most social workers, also he could inquire at any newspaper office and the editor could locate an A.A., since he probably is one himself. I am willing to bet, that if you stood on the corner of

E. 9th and Euclid, or Hollywood and Vine, and asked the first five people you see walking by, how you could get help for your drinking problem, or how to get in touch with A.A., you would get help .... If they want an office, surely they can operate an office to ship books, literature etc. and an occasional referral to a group, on a heluva lot less than 250,000.00 to 350,000.00 per year. Or am I and a lot of other guys nuts?

It would be unfair today to say that the New York office only handles an "occasional" referral. There are hundreds of requests, queries, and out-of-town visitors that come to New York. But Dr. Bob's and Bill's stated intent had been to lessen the organization and professionalizing of A.A.

Then there was the matter of control and element of "government." The proposed Conference, albeit a noble idea, was still a government, a supposed government comprised of representation from all of the groups.

There were "Twelve Suggested Principles" in the proposal for the General Service Conference, entitled, "Your Third Legacy—Will you accept it? by Dr. Bob and Bill," printed in October 1950 under Section Five (temporary Charter for the General Service Conference).

It was stated in Principle Twelve: General Warranties of the Conference, Q&A Section dealing with the Conference and Headquarters:

While it can publicly deplore misuse of the A.A. name or departures from Tradition, it ought never attempt punishment or legal restraint of non-conformists in A.A. or out. The Conference will give us an example and a guide, but not a government. A personal government is something, God willing, that Alcoholics Anonymous will never have.

It should be noted that AAWS for a while obtained registered trademark status for the circle and triangle emblem. Also the

initials "A.A." and the name "ALCOHOLICS ANONYMOUS" were registered, and Alcoholics Anonymous World Services Inc. in New York (A.A.W.S.) has threatened suit, and then beginning in 1985, brought suit against numerous people and companies who have either used the A.A. name or emblem, or reprinted literature even though in the public domain.

In January 1999, A.A.W.S. started to be involved in law suits against A.A. members and outside enterprises in foreign countries. Thus they have initiated "legal restraint" against those "non-conformists," both in A.A. and out.

Clarence remembered that, on several occasions, Bill came to Cleveland and Akron to "sell" the membership on the idea of the conference, and that many members were against the idea. They were afraid of the possibility of an A.A. "government" based in the New York office. The mid-west A.A.s had a program, both successful and continuously growing. Why did they need such a Conference, they felt?

Bill argued that the Conference was needed to ensure that such a government would never take place. Thus, on July 10, 1946, Bill had written to the Board of Trustees of the Foundation as follows:

> *It cannot be denied that the Alcoholic Foundation of today is quite undemocratic, and not enough responsible to the A.A. movement which supports it and depends upon it.*

Though Bill apparently had planned for the Conference to have authority over the Board of Trustees—"Our Trusted Servants"—Clarence felt that the Conference was merely a means to keep the Fellowship quiet, while the Board "did their own thing, apart from what A.A. really should be," as he put it.

CONFERENCE HIGHLIGHTS, "a Special Report for the Groups on the General Service Conference of A.A.," gave the following reasons for the establishment of the Conference:

Since the founding of A.A the many services and policy decisions required to "keep it going" at the national and international level have been handled by the founders and their friends through the Alcoholic Foundation. As A.A. has grown, the importance of sharing this responsibility with the membership has become increasingly clear. It has become clear that the "collective conscience" of A.A. should help insure the survival of the movement.

The General Service Conference is the means whereby that "collective conscience" can be expressed and can guide the Trustees of the Foundation on matters of policy affecting A.A. today and tomorrow.

There were thirty-seven delegates attending that first Conference. At the Conference, William I. D. (Bill D., A.A. #3) of Akron represented Cleveland, and Bert P. represented Columbus, Ohio.

Clarence always disliked the ideas of Conferences, whether International or General Service. Clarence was wary of the reasons for such affairs. In a letter to Dorothy, dated March 9th, 1951, he wrote:

So it is just another one of those cut and dried affairs cooked up, such as the conference last summer at Cleveland was [the International Conference]. Please don't let anyone around here get the idea that you don't know what a cooked up deal that was by Wilson and the S. brothers, the groups found out piece by piece of what took place. That was another fiasco. They were talking about 30 to 50,000 members in attendance at various times, and they wound up in the hole. Had about 4,000 members there not counting the wives and outsiders. Very few from Cleveland, I am proud to say. They came from all around where people were not in a position or inclined to know. Bill keeps talking dramatically about the million who do not yet know. Boy those are his hope. He sure don't want anyone to know either. When anyone around him gets to know anything, poof, off goes the head.

The first A.A. Conference appeared to be a success. The fellowship was supposed to now have a "participating responsibility in determining the future of A.A." However, Clarence still had difficulty obtaining any information from the Board of Trustees regarding policy and where the money went. The minutes and actions of the Board were "classified," and neither Clarence nor the Fellowship at large was allowed to know what actual facts took place behind its closed doors. Conference delegates were not privy to this information either. Clarence was for keeping things simple. He wrote:

> *As far as I am concerned, this is a Fellowship, and that it should remain. All we need is simplicity. The steps, the absolutes, and a couple of alkys who want to do something with themselves. Then we are in business .... Of course I feel I am right in this, and if I am in the wrong, a lot of smarter guys and gals than I are in the wrong with me. But based on pure principles, I can't see how they can be wrong, since they are enjoying a quality of life which is so distinguished in contrast to the miserable existence which once was. These persons also, I have noticed do not find it necessary to find refuge in sanitarium hideaways, nor comfort in psychiatrists.* [40] *I just string along with them on the basis of their happy experiences.*

Decentralization of power never came to pass.

Dr. Bob, Clarence, and many of the other early Ohio members envisioned A.A. as a simple fellowship, designed to help the still sick and suffering alcoholic "recover from a seemingly hopeless state of mind and body." But as the years passed, Clarence felt A.A. no longer resembled the A.A. he had attended back in the 1940's. Henrietta Seiberling's warning that "money will spoil this thing" had, in Clarence's mind, come to pass.

Chapter 8

The Orthodox Movement—Back to Basics

"My God, this is nothing like the Alcoholics Anonymous I once knew—this is more like 'A.A. light.'"

— an anonymous long-term member

Chapter 8.1

The Orthodox Movement

"We have left undone those things which we ought to have done; and we have done those things which we ought not to have done; and there is no health in us."

— Anglican/Episcopalian Book of Common Prayer

After Dr. Bob died, many changes took place in A.A., which were disturbing to the early members in Cleveland and Akron. Ideas and concepts to which Dr. Bob was opposed began to come to pass. Ideas which were believed to have been regulated before Dr. Bob died were suddenly resurrected from dusty shelves.

As Clarence saw it, Doc's calming effect and sane thinking was no longer there. Bill and the Board of Trustees in New York had free reign to do with A.A. as they pleased.

The Orthodox Movement was comprised of a small cadre of staunch, old time A.A. members and friends. Among them were Henrietta Seiberling, Bill Van H., Bert T., and Royal S. In most ways Clarence, though associated with this movement, was on its periphery. But Clarence did correspond with and make telephone calls to and receive thanks from members.

Royal S.—an attorney, AA member and Trustee—wrote several letters to the Board of Trustees. Royal had been instrumental in helping drawing up the incorporation of the *Grapevine* and in helping with other legal matters concerning Alcoholics Anonymous. The A.A. General Service Archives appeared to contain no responses to the Royal S. inquiries. In fact, though requested, none of the original letters from Royal or the other orthodox group people were made available to this writer. In fact this writer was told that there was nothing in the archives relating to any Orthodox Movement or the Statement of Principles of 1948. Copies, however, were given to the author by Clarence, as part of a collection of archival material saved by Clarence over the years.

Additional materials have been furnished by Royal F. Shepard, Jr., who was gracious enough to share his father's papers with this writer.

After the Statement of 1948 was replaced by the Statement of 1950, all references to the 1948 statement of policy, which was endorsed by Dr. Bob, were seemingly removed from the New York office.

The Orthodox Movement's goals were to keep the A.A. movement true to its original intent and purpose. Orthodox members felt that the new direction which A.A. was beginning to take would water down or dilute the effectiveness and success which the movement to that date had achieved. The members of the Orthodox Movement printed up copies of the Statement of 1948 to disseminate to the A.A. membership along with their correspondence to the Board of Trustees. They campaigned at meetings, asking other members to query the Board as to what was happening.

Henrietta Seiberling was attending meetings with Bill van H. and Bill D. (A.A. #3) and relating developments to the A.A. members. King School Group—A.A. Group #1, Dr. Bob's group—was one of the places that they went. However, except for the correspondence and copies (which are in Appendix H, little is known about the efforts of this short-lived burst of protest. All that is known is that they did not succeed in their attempts to keep A.A. true to what they believed was its original purpose.

Nevertheless, Bill Van H. wrote Clarence on January 8, 1951: *"Don't get too exercised about the big promotion"* by Bill Wilson and the Board of Trustees against the Orthodox Movement. *"Like the saying 'There will always be an England,' there will always be a few of us old steady heads."*

Chapter 8.2

Henrietta Seiberling Speaks Her Mind

"And the truth shall set you free"—John 8:32

Henrietta Seiberling was not an alcoholic. In 1933, she was a housewife with three children. But not just an ordinary housewife—she was the daughter-in-law of the founder and one-time president of the Goodyear Tire and Rubber Company. And she had much to do with the founding of A.A.

In January 1933, Harvey Sr. and his son, Russell "Bud" Firestone, sponsored an appearance by Dr. Frank N. D. Buchman and his "Oxford Group team" in Akron. And as part of the day's events, a big dinner was held at the Mayflower Hotel in Akron.

Henrietta and her son, John Seiberling, attended that first dinner and meeting as well as the balance of the meetings from January 14th through the 22nd; and when Frank Buchman shouted to those assembled, "Get right with God," Henrietta decided to get right with God through membership in the Oxford Group.

When Bill Wilson, an Oxford Group member from New York, had come to Akron in 1935, he had phoned Dr. Walter Tunks, a minister affiliated with the Oxford Group, and Tunks in turn gave him Henrietta's number. Through that phone call, which was supposedly made with Bill's last nickel, a meeting was set up at Henrietta's home, the Gate Lodge at 714 North Portage Path in Akron, Ohio, where she lived in the small two-story half-timbered house guarding the entrance to Stan Hywet Hall, her husband's family estate. That is where Bill and Dr. Bob Smith first met and Doc first got his indoctrination into the idea of "one alcoholic helping another." And in the ensuing years, Henrietta worked with both to help in A.A.'s founding.

But Henrietta became disenchanted with A.A.'s development as the years rolled on. According to John Seiberling, Jr., Bill and Bob told her, "Henrietta, I don't think we should talk too much about religion or God," but Henrietta responded:

> *Well, we're not out to please the alcoholics. They have been pleasing themselves all these years. We are out to please God. And if you don't talk about what God does, and your faith, and your guidance, then you might as well be the Rotary Club or something like that. Because God is your only source of Power.*

Throughout her association with A.A., Henrietta was always outspoken in her zeal for service to God. She had cautioned that "money will spoil this thing." She had complained to Bill that A.A. in later years was proceeding more on the level of psychology than through spirituality. Bill's response to her had been, "I know, but they think there are so many people that need this and they don't want to send them away" by talking about what God had done in their (the early members') lives. Henrietta felt A.A. people had forgotten their "source of Power," God.

In the early 1950's, when Henrietta was living in New York at 863 Park Avenue, she had become especially disturbed about the way A.A. was going and wrote Clarence:

> *"A lot of people up here are buffaloed into being 'W.W.s' (Wilson Worshipers) instead of 'A.A.s'.' Notice that A.A. is at the beginning and W.W. is at the end, even of the alphabet."*

She also wrote Clarence:

> *Bill will stand exposed for the show off that he is. He is so empty that as you know Anne [Smith] begged me to do a little "missionary work" on him. She [Anne Smith, Dr. Bob's wife] was sorry to have heard him at the last banquet she came to hear.*

In the same letter, Henrietta wrote Clarence, "I knew he [Bill] had petitioned the Foundation to give Dr. Silkworth and himself the royalties [that were] going to Bob [Smith]." Henrietta felt, as did Clarence, that there should be no royalties paid for what was supposed to have been an avocation.

At the time of Dr. Bob's death, Henrietta wrote Clarence about A.A.'s memorial *Grapevine* issue for Dr. Bob. She wrote:

> *[I] can't really read it through because the truth is so doctored up to suit Bill's claims—The telephone conversation involving me is utterly false and all of it so 'slanted'—I wish he would have left me in the anonymity I have kept.*

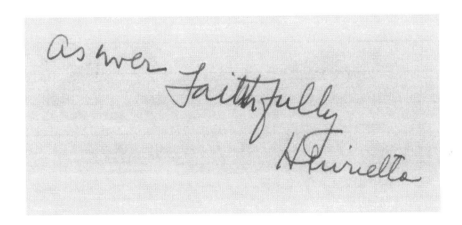

Several letters from Henrietta Seiberling to Clarence are transcribed and follow here. Last names of AA members contained in these letters have been omitted in respect for AA's Tradition of Anonymity.

863 Park Avenue
Thursday 2/9/51

Dear Clarence

Your letter arrived this morning & tho I am off to town, I am sending you this Statement which puts in very definite & concise form what those of us (who form a real "grapevine" to keep the work true to its original purpose & source of power) Have in mind, I meant to send it before this but my Mary Gertrude decided to marry a young man here after seeing him every evening after they first met, for 10 evenings. I think it probably happened in answer to a prayer that she find one who appreciated her unique qualities & inner fineness. God has been good to me & mine, as well as to all our seeking people. I find if I go about my Father's business.

He takes care of mine in a way beyond my imaginings. You are zealous, too, Clarence in keeping our trust & we will grow, I know in grace. If you have a few copies of this typed off she was probably referring to the Statement of 1948] & give around to those interested in being in our grapevine, I am sure it will be good.

I debunked a few of Bill's man made Traditions at meetings, the 12 steps are of God & no man can claim them, but this letter enclosed states 5 points we would like kept to.

If you can locate a copy of the Grapevine of about 3 years ago in which Bob wrote a piece in answer to a challenge I gave him about allowing Bill to always say "Dr. Bob & I," I said, "why do you let that fellow speak for you, why don't you speak for yourself." Next issue had an article by "Bob" himself in it, he said he "hoped that it would always be kept simple, the way it started"—That is better proof than any alleged death bed statements—however, our works is not based on the leadership or dictates of any man, no matter how well meaning he might be, as Bob was—He meant well & he let God use him. That is all one needs to say about Bob. The rest follows as day the night.

I will write you about the contacts I have gotten in other localities. Beware of Archie (T.) in Detroit, but Sarah Klein, Longwood Ave. might be open minded, I will write her. Her husband was changed in Akron & lived at Florence Griffith's. I noticed an article by Sylvia Kaufman in the Chicago bulletin. She is probably a close friend of Earl T_____ I may contact her at some time. She is a good worker I understand. How much for her Heavenly Father I don't know. More later.

Hurriedly, (signed) Henrietta

863 Parks Avenue — Thursday.

Dear Clarence

Your letter arrived this morning & this 'Jane' of to town, I am sending you this statement (which puts in very definite & concise form what (like) us (who form a real 'grapevine' to keep the work true to its original purpose & source of power) have in mind. I meant to send it before this but my Mary Gertrude decided to marry a young man here after seeing him every evening after they first met, for 10 evenings — I think it probably happened in answer to a prayer that she find one who appreciated her unique qualities & inner fineness — God has been good to me & mine, as well as to all our seeking people. I find if I go about my father's business, He takes care of mine in a way beyond my imaginings.

You are zealous, too, Clarence in keeping our trust & we will grow, I know in grace —

If you have a few copies of this typed off & give around to those interested in being in my grapevine, I am sure it will be good.

I described a few of Bill's May made productions of meeting the 12 steps are of God no May can claim them) but this letter enclosed states 5 points we would like kept to —

If you can locate a copy of the Grapevine of about 3 years ago in which Bob wrote a piece in answer to a challenge, I gave him about allowing Bill to always say "Dr Bob & I" I said" Why do you let that fellow speak for you, why don't you speak for yourself" Next issue had an article by "Bob" himself — In it, he said he "hoped that it would always be kept simple, the way it started" — That is better proof than any alleged death bed statements —

However, our work is not based on the leadership or dictates of any man, no matter how well meaning he might be, as Bob was — He meant well & he let God use him That is all one needs to say about Bob — The rest follows as day the night,

I will write you about the contacts I have gotten in other localities — Beware of a relative in Flatbush but Sarah Klein Longwood Ave might be of use — I will write her. Her husband was changed in Lehem & lived at Florence Griffith's I notice an article by Sylvia Kaufman in the Chicago paper She is probably a close friend of Earl Treat who may contact her some time. She is a good worker I understand — How much for her nearly together I am more later Hurried Hurrieder

863 Park Avenue
(Monday – September _, 1951)

Dear Clarence,

Believe it or not I started that heading to you in June! Since then I have been up in Michigan on the Seiberling Island in July, back here in August—my John's wife had a little son on Sept 6th. I am now a thrilled & happy grandmother, my little Dottie flew off to San Francisco this same week & returned last night. I prayed for her safety as I don't trust flying & got a real assurance that she was going to be all right, very suddenly, after she had left for the airport.

I have seen the top surgeon here 12th doctor about my foot & he just phoned that I should be ready for him to operate on it Thursday!

I just want to send you a little line to tell you that I would have written when up in Michigan but I didn't have your address & I have been so hectic since—Keep up your good work.

The June Grapevine gave Bill W. away. I should think—writing just "what the delegates would say" when they returned—also the first for Lois even tho the copyright is done away with. Some bird! I put his brother-in-law, Leonard Strong onto many a design of the "smoothie"—also that the Grapevine should not have Bill writing in it, his nauseating stuff & should return to letters & witnesses of people which it has somewhat. Some of the board told him, Bill, he'd better get some good writers on it or it would have to fold up, that they wouldn't subsidize it (after my complaints).

Some one wrote from Kansas City that his talk there was so "commercial" that he was ashamed to have outsiders hear it.

Bill Van H. seems to be going strong, thank God for him & you & all the other faithful "bleeding deacons."

Did I tell you I wrote D. [Henry D. – first editor and printer of the *Cleveland Central Bulletin*] a nice letter & told him that his paper could be a source of real power & that I hoped he would hold our people "to the Highest" when it meant ridicule loss of subscriptions— just so he was right in God's eyes—that was the important thing. So let me know how it is coming.

I hope you are over your operations. Being reliant on God helps us thru many an ordeal & we know we can trust Him—even tho at times it seems hard to take.

Tell Eddie his Irish man called me up & came to see me that afternoon. I will contact him again. A lot of people up here are buffaloed into being "W.W.'s" (Wilson Worshipers) instead of "A.A.'s" Notice AA is at the beginning & WW is at the end even of the alphabet.

My best to your lovely wife & my best to you.

Hurriedly (signed) Henrietta

863 Paris Avenue —

Dear Clarence —

Believe it or not I started that heading to you in June — Since then I have been up in Muskegan on the Seiberling Island in July; back here in August — my John's wife had a little son on Sept – 16th I am now a thrilled & happy grandmother. My little Lottie flew off to San Francisco this same week & returned last night. I prayed for her safety as I don't trust flying & got a reassurance that she was going to be all right, very suddenly, after she had left for the airport;

I have seen the tops surgeon here, the 12th doctor about my foot & he just phoned that I should be ready for him to operate on it Thursday —!

I just want to send you a little line to tell you that I would have written when up in Michigan but I didn't have your address & I have been so hectic since — Keep up your good work —

The June Grapevine gave Bill it away I should think — Writing just "what the delegates would say" when they returned — also the first thing on the agenda to sew the book projects up for Lois (even tho' the copyright is done away with — Some bird! — I put

his brother-in-law, Leonard's out so many a
design of the "smoothies" — also, that the Grapevine
should not have Bill routing in it, his nauseating
stuff, & "Relations to Letters & witnesses / people
which it has somewhat — Some of the board told
him he'd better get some good writers on it or
it would have to fold up, that they wouldn't subsidize it (after my complaints).

Some one wrote from Kansas City that his
lot's there was so "commercial" that he was a-
shamed to have outsiders hear it —

Bill van H seems to be going strong —
thanks God for him & you & all the other faithful
"Bleeding deacons" —

I'd tell you I wrote to
better & tell him that his paper could be a source
of real power, & that I hoped he would hold our
people "to the Highest" — even if it meant ridicule
Goes of subscriptions — just so he was right in God's
eyes — that was the important thing — He let me
know how it is coming.

I hope you are over your operations —
Being reliant on God helps us with many a

ideals & we know we can trust him — even tho'at times it seems hard to take —

Tell Eddie his Christ man called me up & came to see me that afternoon — I will contact him again — A lot of people up here are buffaloed into being "W, Wis" (Wilson Worshippers) instead of "A a". Notice A a is at the beginning & W W is the end, even of the alphabet —

My best love to your lovely wife & my best to you —

Hurriedly
Henrietta —

Monday —

863 Park Avenue
Tuesday (undated)

Dear Clarence,

I was glad to hear from you but sorry to hear that you had this throat trouble & I certainly hope that this will be your last operation. They are certainly not pleasant but I do think the scientific way everything is done in surgery now, is amazing. They make it as easy for us as possible.

I am going to be in Cleveland next Monday & Tuesday (12th & 13th) seeing the dentist & staying at the Carter.

I hadn't heard anything about the Silkworth Sanitarium scheme but wouldn't be surprised as I probably have said to you before "an idle brain is the devil's workshop" & poor Bill's brain has been so idle for so long, he is at his wit's end

what to do next. I knew he had petitioned the Foundation to give Dr. Silkworth & himself the royalties going to Bob. Perhaps this is a way to get some kind of control or any loose money, as Silkworth is old & frail & can't last too long. I will ask this evening, one of the men who ought to know about it.

But, Clarence, so long as we get before the Groups a statement of what our principles are & that idea that we are going to adhere to them, that is our main objective.

In the light of these principles, adopted by the Foundation, whatever Bill does will be shown up for the phoney stuff he is trying to pull.

Don't worry about him, personally—so long as we get over to the many sincerely seeking eager & devoted people, as most of our people are, just what we must follow. Bill will stand exposed for the show off that he is. He is so empty that as you know Anne (Smith—Dr. Bob's wife) begged me to do a little "missionary work" on him. She was sorry to have heard him at the last banquet she came to here.

I have lots to tell you, as I observe his delirious machinations in print everywhere—His accounts in the Memoriam Grapevine [the Memorial Edition of the *Grapevine* after Dr. Bob's passing] Telephone conversations, etc. Everything phoney—But God is in His Heaven & He is "not mocked"—all we can do is ask Him to use us for His service.

Suppose he gets his convention, it may boomerang in him, if enough good delegates come. The NY City groups, those that came, elected a darn good man—also, they have a fine new president of the Foundation & people are getting onto Bill, thanks to you & others.

I probably have told you some of my Bible guided reading but to have you see it all in line, this is how it went.

When Bill was thrashing around in his "devil's workshop," several years ago, he thought of having the annual banquet, with "old A.A. friends" at the dais—Sam Shoemaker, Mr. Chipman, me, Bob & Anne were coming etc.—I had a feeling when he asked me to come, that I was asked to be background for this fellow to dramatize himself & recoiled from it, but to be sure that I was not just following personal feelings, I asked God to show me the right attitude, & I would do what I should—I opened & read Luke XXII.

863 Park avenue   Tuesday —

Dear Clarence -

I was glad to hear from you but sorry to hear that you had this throat trouble - & certainly hope that this will be your last operation - they are certainly not pleasant but I do think the scientific way every-thing is done in surgery now is amazing - they make it as easy for us as possible -

I am going to be in Cleveland next Monday & Tuesday (12th + 13th) seeing the dentists staying at the Carter.

I hadn't heard anything about the Silsworth sanitarium scheme but wouldn't be surprised. As I probably have said to you before "An idle brain is the devil's workshop" & poor Bill's brain has been so idle for so long he is at his wits end what to do next. I knew he had petitioned the Foundation to give Dr Silsworth himself the royalties going to Bob. Perhaps this is a way to get some kind of control. Many loose money as Silsworth is old & ... many last too long. I will ask this evening ... of the men who ought to know about it.

But, Clarence, so long as we get before the Groups a statement of what our principles are, that idea that we are going to adhere to them that is our main objective —

In the light of these principles, adopted by the foundation, whatever Bill does will take skinny up for the phoney stuff he is trying to pull —

Don't worry about him, personally — So long as we get over to the many sincerely seeking, eager & devoted people, as most of your people are, just what we must follow, Bill will stand up piked for the show off that he is — He is so empty that psychiatrist Anne, begged me to do a little "missionary work" on him — She was sorry to have heard him at the last banquet she came to, here —

I have lots to tell you, as I observe his devious machinations, in print everywhere — His accounts in the "memoriam" Grapevine were made up — telephone conversations, etc — everything phoney — But God is in His Heaven, & He is "not mocked" — all we can do is to ask Him to use us for His service —

Suppose he gets his convention, it may boomerang on him, if enough good delegates come — the N.Y. City groups, those that came, elected a darn good man — also, they have a fine new president of the foundation — people are getting onto Bill, thanks to you & others —

I probably have told you some of my little

guided reading but to have you see it all in line, this
is how it went —

When Bill was thrashing around in his "devil's
workshop," several years ago, he thought of having
the Annual banquet, with "old A.A. friends" on the
dais — Jan Shoemaker, Mr Chipman, me, Bob & Anne
were coming etc — I had a feeling when he asked me
to come, that I was asked to be background for this
fellow to dramatize himself & recoiled from it —
but to be sure that I was not just harboring personal feelings, I asked God to show me the right
attitude, & I would do what I should — I opened
to read — Luke XXII to I hope you have a Moffatt Parallel
version — "A quarrel unreasoning them, etc. ... their ambition—
the late the name of "Benefactor" but not you —
He who is greatest among you must be like the
youngest — There goes Bill's playing on A.A.'s gratitude
as their "benefactor" — He who is chief, like a servant —
— "song may eat & drink at my table in my kingdom"
And so, as a "servant" I declined the dais & wrote
Bill that I could not accept any invitation
whatsoever for the banquet — & I had lunch with
Bob & Anne the next day — & as I say, the last words
time when she phoned me in alarm & said that
she did not want to seem distressed
lest it was —

I hope you have a Moffatt Parallel version—"a quarrel arose among them etc.... their authorities take the name of 'Benefactor's' but not so with you. He who is greatest among you must be like the youngest." There goes Bill's playing on AA's gratitude—"so ye may eat & drink at my table in my kingdom" and so, as a "servant," I declined as "guest" on the dais & wrote Bill that I could not accept any invitation whatsoever for the banquet & I had lunch with Bob & Anne the next day—& as I say, the last words she ever spoke to me were at the following Xmas time she phoned me in Akron & said although she did not want to seem disloyal that it was really guided that I didn't go to the banquet "that Bill was awful"— He is so completely empty spiritually it is really affecting his countenance, Clarence.

Well, in the next instance, when I began to read all his self promoting Propaganda stuff in the Grapevine, I was dismayed at the lengths to which his egotism was leading him & so again I asked to be shown, to understand how a man who had ever glimpsed any of our programme (which of course he really hadn't ever conceived of—He only appropriated & expanded on what we were developing in Akron, before he came & learned from us—just Oxford Group stuff) & how a man could go so far astray spiritually was hard for me to understand—so I took my Bible & opened up & there I found before my eyes Luke XVI— Read it, the "factor ... misapplying the property of his master," "What am I to do ... I am too weak to dig & ashamed to beg," so he planned how to have people 'welcome him into their homes"—He just lied—& so, he showed that he was a "child of this world" & "looking ahead for himself" & the master told him "if you are not faithful with mammon" (or this world's goods)," how can you be trusted with the Riches"—etc., etc.—"You are the people who get men to think you are good, but God knows what your hearts are! What is lofty in the eyes of men is loathsome in the sight of God."

So I can understand how Bill is driven with the urge to keep himself ingratiated with men & before the eyes of men, constantly, because he has lost completely the vision "true riches," with which our little group was entrusted. I turned in my questioning to another passage just aimlessly & this is what I read. "Fear not, little flocks, it pleases the Father to give you His Kingdom" so I felt that I had my answer.

Then, when Bill sent me a letter asking me to dilate on a long list of virtues Anne Smith was supposed to possess, so he could write an article, I told him that Anne had achieved the ability to keep herself in the background & would not want the pages of a magazine supposed to help men thru witnessing & sharing, taken up in praise of her—so he took my idea & wrote an article with that slant & gave me a dig about how she was "content to sit in the back of the meeting" & not in the "front seat."

Maybe you don't remember that I used to sit in front as leaders were timid then, & I used to try and fill up the front & be there to give them a feeling of some one to help them. Anne sat in the back so she could greet people & see them all—also before declining to expatiate on Anne's so called "virtues," I read my Bible again & I happened to read about the rich young man saying "Good Master" & Christ said "Why do you call me 'good?' No one is good but God." That was my guidance there.

And then, finally, when we sent out that Harrison letter of Roy's, I picked up the Bible & read Corinthians III which I enclosed with the letter to you—Who is Bill, who is Bob? say I—"They are simply used by God to give you faith. Each as the Lord assigns his task "so you must not boast about men—you belong to God." Did you read the Upper Room Feb. 22nd?

really guided that I didn't go to the banquet, that Bill was awful." He is so completely empty spiritually it is really affecting his countenance, Clarence.

Well, in the right instance, when I began to read all his self-promoting propaganda stuff in the "grapevine", I was dismayed at the lengths to which his egotism was leading him & so again I asked to be shown, to understand how a man who had never glimpsed any of our programme (which, of course he really hadn't ever conceived of - He only appropriated & expounded on what we were developing in Akron, before he came & learned from us - just Oxford Group stuff) - how a man could go so far astray spiritually was hard for me to understand - so I took my Bible & opened up & there I found before my eyes Luke XVI - Read it. "the factor" misapplying the property "of his master", "what am I to do... I am too weak to dig & ashamed to beg", so he planned how to have people "welcome him into their homes" - He just lied - & so, he showed that he was "a child of this world" - "Looking ahead for himself" & the master told him "if you are not faithful with mammon" for this world's goods, "how can I be trusted with true Riches" - the etc - "You are the people who get men to think you are good, but God knows what your hearts are! What is lofty in the eyes of men is abomination in the sight of God." So I can understand how Bill is driven with the urge to keep himself ingratiated with men & before the eyes of men, constantly, because he has lost completely the vision, "true riches" with which our little group was entrusted. I turned, in my questioning to another passage just aimlessly & this is what I read "Fear not, little flock, it pleases the father to give you his Kingdom—" so I felt that I had my answer.

Then, when Bill sent me a letter asking me to dilate on a long list of virtues Anne Smith was supposed to possess, so he could write an article, I told him that Anne had achieved the ability to keep herself in the background & would not want the pages of a magazine supposed to help men thru witnessing & sharing, taken up in praise of her—so he took my idea & wrote an article with that slant & gave me a dig at my how she was "content to sit in the back of the meeting" & not in the "front seat."

maybe you don't remember that I used to sit in front
as leaders were timid then, & I used to try to pull
up the front to be there to give them a feeling of some
one to help them. Anne sat in back so she loved
greet people & see them all—also I predicting
to expaliate on Anne's so called "virtues." I read
my Bible again & I happened to read about the
rich young man saying "Good master" & Christ
said "Why do you call me "good?" No one is good
but God." That was my guidance there—

And then, finally, when we sent out that
Harrison letter of Roy's, I picked up the Bible
& read I Corinthians III which I marked
with the letter, to you—"Who is Bill, who is Bob"
say I—They are simply used by God to give you faith
each as the Lord assigns his task—" So you must
not boast about men —— you belong to God."
Did you read the upper Room of Feb 22nd?

So, Clarence, there is the Way pointed out to
me—& to you & all of us—We need not worry—
When I went to Missouri & Kansas City I asked to
be shown what to say—When all my faith & here
said one word of disillusion ment of Bill—parallel

I told the couple I stayed with ... ...
spiritual enough to take it. because this was what
I read just after I asked what to talk about —
Romans ~~~~~ IV - 18 vers - "I will not make free to
speak of anything except what Christ has accomplished
by me; by my words, by my deeds, by the force of
miracles & marvels by the power of the Spirit of
God."
        These passages, I know, are really "guided"
I didn't seek them out — All the answers for us
all can be found if we just pray & work —
        Get well, & we'll forget about Bill & leave
him in God's hands — If there are delegates elected,
we will pray that they are men who seek to serve God
& not as sots for any man's aggrandizement — We
can keep our original purpose before people's
eyes by doing just what you are doing — splendidly — Leading meetings & remaining true to
our first principles — & vision & real power to
change lives — Bill

Bill   sent me a copy of the
Central Bulletin with the article headed "Where
are we headed" or something like that — I think
Hankwerth has his eyes opened but also remember
his paper has to represent all groups & can
reflect all sides & so

So. Clarence, there is the way pointed out to me—& to you & all of us—We need not worry—When I went to Missouri & Kansas City I asked to be shown what to say. In all my talks I never said one word of disillusion meant of Bill—privately I told the couple I stayed with & who I knew were spiritual enough to take it because this was what I read just after I asked what to talk about. Romans XV.18vrs—"I will not make free to speak of anything except what Christ has accomplished by me; by my words, by my deeds, by the force of miracles & marvels by the power of the Spirit of God."

These passages, I know, are really "guided." I didn't seek them out—all the answers for us all can be found, if we just pray & work.

Get well & we'll forget about Bill & leave him in God's hands. If there are delegates elected, we will pray that they are men who seek to serve God & not as tools for any man's aggrandizement. We can keep our original purpose before people's eyes by doing just what you are doing so splendidly. Leading meetings & remaining true to our first principles & vision & real power to change lives.

Bill Van H___ sent me a copy of the Central Bulletin with the article headed "Where are we headed" or something like that. I think D_____ has his eyes opened but also remember his paper has to represent all groups & can reflect all sides & so I imagine he doesn't feel that he can allow his attitude to be antagonistic in his paper. I will probably see him when I am in Cleveland—but I think that Roy & Horace C____ & Bert & I & all the different connections that have cropped up suddenly, like with you, & Roland & Bill B___ & all, we were all meant to be a spiritual underground to work together to keep this beautiful thing, the way we all (& I am sure) God, meant it to be.

Get yourself real well & enjoy that sweet wife & all the blessings that come to us who love the Lord.

We can pity Bill for he "knows not what he does"— Did you see the article on AA in Fortune? It was written by the AA who wrote "Mr. Blandings Builds His Dream House" Bill supplied to with misinformation of course.

My Mary Gertrude who marries this June will live in Chicago, so I will be going out there sometime & will contact the Groups.

I wrote Archie last fall a very mild letter but he never answered. You know he was brought by my friend to my house from Detroit—but he is still in need of strength I suppose. As the psychiatrists say still, "grandiose, infantile & self absorbed"

See you soon. My best as ever (signed) Henrietta

I imagine he doesn't feel that he can — I will probably see him
attitude to be antagonistic — *in his form*
when I am in Cleveland — but I think that Roy &
Horace   & Bert & I & all the different connections
that have cropped up suddenly, like with you, & Roland
& Bill   & All, we were all meant to be
a spiritual underground to work together to keep
this beautiful thing, the way we all (& I am sure)
God, meant it to be —

            Get yourself real well & enjoy that
sweet wife & all the blessings that come to us
who love the Lord — We can pity Bill, for he knows
"not what he does" — Did you see the article on AA
in Fortune? It was written by the ale who wrote
"Mr Blandings Builds His Dream House"
Bill supplied the misinformation of course —
            My Mary Gertrude who marries this June
will live in Chicago, so I will be going out there
sometime & will contact the Groups —
            I wrote Archie last fall a very nice letter
but he never answered. You know he was brought
by my friend to my house from Detroit — but he is still
in need of strength I suppose — As the psychiatrists say
still "grandiose, infantile & self absorbed." — As you know
my ideal as ever Henrietta

MRS. JOHN FREDERICK SEIBERLING
714 NORTH PORTAGE PATH
AKRON, OHIO

(Dated Friday July 31st, 1952)

Dear Clarence,

It was such a happy surprise to get your letter—I have wanted to answer it long before this but have just been "burning daylight" as the old saying goes.

My Dorothy & I drove here from New York July 4th & she had 3 weeks here only & I have been notified by the Seiberling brothers & sisters that they felt they should rent my house, as we are here so little, so John & his wife and baby came as soon as I could get it opened and ready, & Mary & her husband came from Chicago for a week; all to go over & collect their belongings, piling up for 29 years. So you can imagine that I've stayed away from pen & paper.

I drove back to New York Sunday with Dorothy—car loaded with things & Fred picked me up & drove me back Tuesday. I see John off next week & then, as usual, Henrietta really will tear into things—&—finish up—It was a terrific blow—the thought of not having this sweet little place to come to & enjoy the beauties of nature, trees, birds, sunshine & quiet & to be with so many good friends & at first, I didn't know how to take it. So I just surrendered it & asked to be shown what to say & what to do & put myself out of the picture entirely & let God show me—after a few days, I think I was guided to have the right attitude & wrote my brother-in-law a letter to which he responded the next day, with many thanks & much appreciation since we've been back I feel a warmth of affection from Fred's brothers & sisters, that in the end, means more than ever my haven of my own joy & tranquility & so God works things out for us always & I realize that we have to have things like that to make us turn to Him & rely completely on Him. "The branch that beareth not fruit, He cuts off but He purges the branch that beareth fruit" so "it will bear more fruit." I realized that it was just another challenge to meet, so that I would rely more completely on His direction, & I knew that relying on "His direction," I would "never be misled" I may work something out, renting the house furnished or move the furniture to the Big House & I can stay there when I want to, I know.

I was so interested to think of your being in Georgia & seeing Roland & Dorothy—they are such dear wonderful real people & I think we can be so grateful to our Maker for giving us a fellowship with so many all over   all with the same purpose in life & trying to live the same quality of life.

Last night, Bill Van H__ & Mickey came over & got me & we picked up Bill D___ [AA #3], who now lives near King School & we went out to Stow where I led the little group in a meeting. It was just like the old times at T. Henry's—every one felt they could get up & talk & you could feel that we were really gathered together in His name & we had the real fellowship of the "Holy Spirit" that was left in the world, so we would never "be comfortless"—Bill D___ said he had been to Albany, Georgia, to speak. I told them that I had your letter & they were so glad to get news of you & spoke of you in the meeting.

I feel very sure that God has His Guiding Hand on our work. It looked for a while as if Bill Wilson would like to crowd God out but we know that it is up to us to seek more &

more of God's power to help other people to know this way of life & our fellowship. You certainly are doing your part & thank God, all those who have glimpsed the real vision are doing theirs & the joy of it is, to me, that those who have only been offered " the stone," are so eager & grab at the "bread," that we know we have to offer—as you say it is appalling how little they have been offered by the would be "elder statesman"—but the 12 steps & the fact that, as Stanley Jones says, whenever man opens his mind to God, He reveals Himself. These have helped the groping AA's—who have been denied so much of the real "bread" & given the "stone" of Bill Wilson's designs.

But, Clarence, I made one big whale of a surrender of Bill & all his schemes & all thought of him & the possibilities of what harm he could do just left me in the most amazing way. I don't have to try to "not think of him" again, I just don't. He is completely consigned to God by me & I know He can handle him. We will be closely knit even with his taking the money & trying to take the book. I am sure he will need our pity & compassion because he has put himself apart from the real fellowship—more & more I see that the 16th Chapter of Luke that I read in answer to my asking to understand Bill & what he was doing, illuminated the situation. He has put himself with the "children of darkness"—he has his henchmen & ingratiates himself with those in the dark. Let us keep ourselves "children of the Light" & keep on serving God instead of "Mammon." Bill has made his choice—Read the chapter over.

I heard talk in Missouri 2 years ago about his connection with Sheen (Bishop Fulton Sheen) but I don't imagine it so. He imagines himself all kinds of things. His hand "writes" dictation from a Catholic priest, whose name I forget, from the 1600 period who was in Barcelona Spain—again, he told Horace C___, he was completing the work that Christ didn't finish, & according to Horace he said he was a reincarnation of Christ. Perhaps he got mixed up in whose reincarnation he was—It looks more like the works of the devil but I could be wrong. I don't know what is going on in the poor deluded fellow's mind. He asked Bill D___ if he knew where I was & Bill said "on Park Ave." & he said "Have you seen her."

I learned from a Texas friend that a chaplain in the prisons said the only way they really reached prisoners, was thru Alcoholics Anonymous, even for the non alcoholic—so besides such things as that, Bill & his schemes pale into insignificance for us—I am sure. We can stand by & see him claim the "glory" if we can keep the "power" to help transform lives— thank God, you & so many others are still doing that.

I imagine Selma will like the south. They are dear people & I hope you like them I realize that what may seem the "closed door" of my idyllic little place here, may be the opening of many more doors & vistas, so maybe it is a release for me to go around & see more people— any way we all know & I felt confidant of that, for which I am grateful that we are equal to anything in Him who strengthens us.

Bill Van H___ had his "purging" the other day. The little boy's "mother" had been taking a course at Kent (*corrected from 1st edition) Normal & little Billy was thru his school & Bill planned to go on a fishing trip with him & he came home one night & found she had taken off. He learned she went to California. The little boy was the apple of Bill's eye, but he will

Friday July 31st

Dear Clarence. MRS. JOHN FREDERICK SEIBERLING
714 NORTH PORTAGE PATH
AKRON, OHIO

It was such a happy surprise to get your
letter—I have wanted to answer it long before
this but have just been burning daylight!
as the old saying goes.

My Dorothy & I drove here from New
York July 4th & she had 3 weeks here only
& I had been notified by the Seiberling brothers
& sisters that they felt they should rent my
house, as we are here so little, so John & his
wife & baby came as soon as I could get it
opened & ready, & Mary & her husband came
from Chicago for a week; all to go over & collect their belongings, piling up for 29 years.
So you can imagine that I've slaved away
from pen & paper.

I drove back to New York Sunday with
Dorothy—car loaded with things & Fred picked
me up & drove me back Tuesday—I see
John off next week & then, as usual, Henrietta
really will tear into things—& finish up—

It was a terrific blow—the thought of
not having this sweet little place to come to
& enjoy the beauties of nature, trees, birds sunshine, & quiet & to be with .... You certainly
are doing your part & thank ....

so many good friends - & at first, I didn't know
how to take it - so I just surrendered it & asked to
be shown what to say & what to do & put myself out
of the picture entirely & let God show me - after
a few days, I think I was guided to have the
right attitude & wrote my brother-in-law a letter,
to which he responded the next day, with many
thanks & much appreciation - & since we've been
back, I feel a warmth of affection from Fred's
brothers & sisters, that, in the end, means more than
even my haven of my own joy & tranquillity -
& so God works things out for us always &
I realize that we have to have things like that
to make us turn to Him & rely completely on Him -
"The branch that beareth not fruit, He cuts off,
but He purges the branch that beareth fruit,"
so it "will bear more fruit." I realized that it was
just another challenge to meet, so that I would
rely more completely on His direction & I knew
that relying on "His direction, I would "never
be misled," & I may work something out, renting
the house furnished or move the furniture
to the Big House & I can stay there when I
want to, I know.
    I was so interested to think of your being
in Georgia & seeing Roland & Dorothy - they
are such dear wonderful

real people & I think we can be so grateful to our Maker for

giving us a fellowship with so many all over—all with the same purpose in life & trying to live the same quality of life.

Last night, Bill Van H. & Mickey came over & got me & we picked up Bill H., who now lives near King School, & we went out to Stow where I lead the little group in a meeting. It was just like old times at T Henry's—Every one felt they could get up & talk & you could feel that we were really gathered together in His name & we had the real fellowship of the "Holy Spirit" that was left in the world, so we would never "be comfortless"— Bill H. said he had been to Albany, Georgia to speak. I told them that I had your letter & they were so glad to get news of you & spoke of you in the meeting.

I feel very sure that God has His Guiding Hand on our work. It looked for a while as if Bill Wilson would like to crowd God out but we know that it is up to us to seek more of God's power to help other people to know this way of Life & our fellowship— You certainly are doing your part & thanks

...your friends & at first I did...

God, all those who have glimpsed the real vision are doing theirs- the joy of it is, to me, that those who have only been offered "the stone," are so eager, & grab at the "bread," that we know we have to offer - as you say. it is appalling how little they have been offered by the would be "Elder statesman"- but the R steps & the fact that, as Stanley Jones say, wherever man opens his mind to God, He reveals himself - these have helped the groping A's who have been denied so much of the real "bread"- & given the "stone") Bill Wilson's designs.

But, Clarence, I made one big whale of a surrender of Bill & all his schemes & all thought of him & the possibilities) what harm he could do just left me in the most amazing way - I don't have to try to "not think" of him" again, I just don't - He is completely consigned to God by me & I know He can handle him - We will be closely but knit. even with his taking the money & trying to take the books, I am sure he will need our pity & compassion because he has put himself apart from the real fellowship —

more & more I see that the 16th Chapter of Luke that I
read in answer to my asking to
understand Bill & what he was doing, illuminates
the situation – He has put himself with the
"children of darkness" – he has his henchmen &
ingratiates himself with those in the dark –
Let us keep ourselves "children of the Light."
& keep on serving God, instead of "Mammon."
Bill has made his choice – Read the Chapter over.

I heard talks in Missouri 2 years ago about
his connection with them but I don't imagine
it is so. He imagines himself all kinds of things
His hand "writes" dictation from a Catholic
priest, whose name I forget, from the "1600 period"
who was in Barcelona Spain – again, he told
Horace C   he was completely the work
that Christ didn't finish, & according to Horace
he said he was a "reincarnation of Christ –
Perhaps he got mixed in whose reincarnation
he was – It looks more like the work of the
devil but I could be wrong – I don't know what
is going on in the poor deluded fellow's mind
He must be wistful. He asked Bill if he
knew where I was & Bill said "in Paris are" & he
he said "Have you seen her?"

I learned from a Texas friend that a Chaplain in the prisons said the only way they really reached prisoners was thru Alcoholics Anonymous, even for the non alcoholic — so besides such things as that, Bill & his schemes pale into insignificant forms — I am sure —

We can stand by & see him claim the "glory" if we can keep the "power" to help transform lives — Thank God, you & so many others are still doing that —

I imagine Selma will like the South. They are dear people — & I hope you like the new situation —

I realize that what may seem the "closed door" of my idyllic little place here, may be the opening of many more doors & vistas, & maybe it is a release for me to go around & see more people — Any way we all know & I felt confidant of that; (for which I am grateful) that we are equal to anything, "in Him who strengtheneth" us —

Bill bau H had his purging the other day. The little boy's "mother" had been taking a course at Kent normal & Little "bear more fruit" for this last challenge to meet & he seems to know that "bearing fruit" is what we are here for.

He is going to take me up to Cleveland to their luncheon group some time. Maybe in the course of time, I'll meet Ed H___—But it's the "father who seeth in secret," that matters. Just so we keep His Guidance, which is so very real. I know, too.

So let me know what's going on with you, Clarence—I'll probably be here until the middle of September, at least.

It is unnecessary to say "keep up your good works"—You do that anyway, but I am very grateful for such true people as you & Selma, & Bill Van H___ & Roland & all—we'll have our own "Grapevine," "underground" but from "overhead"—God has been good to us to give us a glimpse of such a little "colony of Heaven" as St. Paul calls it.

Annabel & Wally go to the King School still—Ernie G_____ [the first Ernie G., Dr. Bob's son-in-law] was there & so many of the "faithful"—John C___ led; Marie B___ appeared (remember them?)

[Marie B. was Walter B.'s wife. Walter's story
The Back Slider was in the Big Book.]

Bob G_____ died & so did poor Ernie S____, if you remember him. I saw Henry S_____ in NY—Bill D____ brought him over—Bill W. wouldn't let him in the "convention."

Goodbye, Clarence—Your good work speaks always of you to so many. It is a great joy to think of, isn't it.

as ever Faithfully (signed) Henrietta

Billy was there his self too + Bill planned to go on a fishing trip with [Bernie] + he came home one night + found she had taken off – He learned she went to California The little boy was the apple of Bill's eye, but he will "bear more fruit" for this last challenge to meet + he seems to know that "bearing fruit" is what we are here for. He is going to take me up to Cleveland to their luncheon group some time. Maybe in the course of time, I'll meet Ed H — But it's the "father who seeth in secret", that matters – Just so we keep His Guidance, which is so very real, I know – nothing else really matters, as you know, too.

He let me know what's going on with you, Clarence – I'll probably be here until the middle of September, at least –

It is unnecessary to say "keep up your good work" – You do that any way, but I am very grateful for such true people as you – Selma + Bill van H + Roland self – We'll have our own "Grapevine", "underground" but from "overhead" – God has been good to us to give us a glimpse of such a little "colony of Heaven"

as St Paul calls it — Anneatel & Wally go to the King
School still — Ernie Galbraith was there — & so
many of the "faithful." John Cluffs led; Marie
Bray appeared (remember them?) Bob Graham
died & so did poor Ernie Springston, if you
remember him — I saw Henry Shivering in
N.Y. — Bill Holson brought him over — Bill W —
wouldn't let him in the "Convention."

Goodbye, Clarence — Your good work
speaks always of you to so many — It is a
great joy to think of, isn't it.

As ever —
Faithfully
Henrietta

**Stan Hywet Hall
H. Seiberling House
(Gate Lodge-Where Bill
& Bob met)
Akron, OH**

Seiberling Gate Lodge

Chapter 8.3

New York and Midwest A.A.—Coming of Age

"I explain this at some length because I want you to be successful with yourself and the people with whom you work. We used to pussyfoot on this spiritual business a great deal more out here (New York City) and the result was bad, for our record falls quite short of the performance of Akron and Cleveland, where there are now about 350 Alcoholics, many of them sober 2 or 3 years, with less than 20% ever having had any relapse. Out there they have always emphasized the spiritual way of life as the core of our procedure ....[41]

Clarence summarized to the author his view of the difference between New York and Mid-West A.A. Clarence felt that the approach in Ohio was, "Trust God, Clean House, and Help Others." He felt that the approach in New York was, "Don't Drink and Go To Meetings."

Clarence felt that the emphasis on spirituality was what had made Ohio A.A. so successful. He pointed out that New York A.A. had but a few members who were maintaining any sort of abstinence from alcohol, and that most Ohio members had achieved what was to become permanent sobriety, and had numerous, strong A.A. meetings in evidence.

Clarence felt that if the primary purpose of A.A. were only to stop drinking and, in order to maintain that abstinence, only go to meetings, A.A. was doomed to failure. Clarence remembered Dr. Bob once saying: "There is an easy way and a hard way to recovery from alcoholism. The hard way is by just going to meetings."

Clarence stated that nowhere in the Steps of A.A. does it say one has to stop drinking. He was speaking of the A.A. statement that the only REQUIREMENT for membership is "a desire to stop drinking."

If A.A. members put the steps into their lives, beginning with the first three steps, they have admitted that they were powerless over alcohol, that they could not manage their own lives, and they have made a decision to turn their lives and their wills over to the care of God. They were no longer in charge. A Power Greater than themselves had been asked to take over.

If an A.A. member is constantly, on a daily basis, fighting taking a drink, there is no one in charge but the A.A. member. There is no power present which is greater than oneself. The A.A. book states:

"And we have ceased fighting anything or anyone—even alcohol." [42]

Midwest A.A. puts the reliance on God, who is a Higher Power, and not on the A.A. meetings or other A.A. members. New York places reliance on a human power. The A.A. book clearly states:

"that probably no human power could have relieved our alcoholism." [43]

Bill Wilson made numerous trips to Ohio to try and find out what they had that worked so well. He spoke with Clarence and with Dr. Bob and attended meetings. He tried to bring back the program of recovery as it was in Ohio to the New York members, but they would not assimilate the spirituality into their brand of A.A.

Clarence felt that what Ohio had was special. He spent the rest of his life speaking around the country and the world, relating what A.A. and God had done for him. Many people seemed to find Clarence's personality abrasive, and he occasionally stated that he was the one who had started A.A. This might have been a reason that many refused to listen. They placed what Clarence said, and his way of saying things, before the importance of what A.A. had been. They were more concerned with the messenger's personality than with the principles of his message.

In the late 1940's and early 1950's, A.A. was beginning to come of age. Meetings were growing both in the number of meetings and in the number attending the meeting. Members were attaining sobriety and retaining it for long periods. Even today, A.A. continues to grow in numbers far beyond the dreams of the early members. However, at what cost?

Is the purpose of A.A. to have the greatest amount of membership, making A.A. available to all those who claim to want it by any means possible, including the watering down of the steps and the quality of recovery? Or is the purpose of A.A. to help others recover from "a seemingly hopeless state of mind and body" by following the "prescription for a miracle" as written down in the basic text?

Where is God in A.A. today? Is it only "Don't drink and go to meetings," or is it the promise of a changed life? Are A.A. members "going to know a new freedom" merely by not drinking? The promises in the A.A book are supposed to come to fruition "before we are halfway through" the ninth step. According to Clarence, simplistic abstinence could never call these promises into being.

There are vast differences in A.A. today. Tolerance demands that A.A. members allow other members to follow the path they have chosen for themselves. What type of recovery does the alcoholic wish to have? Which are his or her choices today? Are the alcoholic's choices limited by the location of meetings? All brands of A.A. should be offered to regular and prospective members.

The main difference between New York A.A. and Midwest A.A. is the emphasis which is placed on spirituality. The basic text and the Steps are completely identical.

"We stood at the turning point." [44] What kind of recovery is it, that the A.A. member wants to achieve?

A.A as a whole stands at that turning point. It is once again "Coming of Age," but coming to what end? Coming to the point of merely not drinking alcohol? Or developing a program of real recovery from a seemingly hopeless state of mind and body?

Should there be a New York A.A., a Midwest A.A., a California A.A.?—or just an Alcoholics Anonymous Fellowship, available not only to those who need it, but also to those who want to recover?

Growth and change are necessary parts of life. But to what end?

Chapter 9

Clarence's Life after the 1960's

A Prophet in His Own Town

"A prophet is not without honor, save in his own country."

—Matthew 13:57

After Clarence left Ohio to move to Florida, he continued to be active in the fellowship of Alcoholics Anonymous. He also continued on with "earning a living."

Clarence worked at several different positions, including many sales jobs, something to which he seemed best suited. He settled down with his wife, Selma (Kitterer), in St. Petersburg, Florida, and found a home group.

Clarence seemed to be the type of person you either loved or hated. There appeared to be no real middle ground. As the author saw it, Clarence was at times egotistical, and yet humble in his own way. He continued with the hardline A.A. his sponsor had taught him. Dr. Bob did not believe in half measures. Neither did Clarence.

In his later years, Clarence traveled around the country, speaking and carrying the message of a changed life to those who wanted to hear it. Local meetings had a difficult time with Clarence. For the most part they didn't seem to want to hear his particular brand of A.A. The saying that a prophet is without honor in his own town fit Clarence well.

There were those too, with whom Clarence found favor. These were usually people who found Clarence's interpretation of what

A.A. should be like, to be in their best interest. These, at first, were few. But their numbers grew.

Clarence became involved with the Masons in Florida. Like Dr. Bob, Clarence was a 32nd degree Mason.

He became involved in speaking at civic and other organizations about A.A. He became involved in church affairs; and he believed he tried to practice and live the principles of the A.A. program as best he could. He continued to sponsor numerous people, and there are many today in St. Petersburg who were sponsored by Clarence. Most still enjoy continuous sobriety.

Clarence and Selma were divorced (the filed date of the dissolution of their marriage was June 16, 1971). The author found that Clarence was reluctant to speak about any of his marriages, so details remain something of a mystery. After the divorce, Clarence continued on with his A.A. work as an avocation. He never required any one to pay for his speaking engagements. However, he did not turn down any "honorariums" offered that were paid, and he did request that those who invited him to speak outside of Florida pay for his travel, meals, and lodging.

He spoke throughout the United States, Canada and a few foreign countries. He constantly got into trouble with his statements concerning the founding of A.A. and his claim that he was the one who had founded the first A.A. meeting. Whatever the accuracy of his claim as a founder, there is ample evidence that the meeting he started in Cleveland, at 2345 Stillman Road in Cleveland Heights, was the first meeting to be called Alcoholics Anonymous. As we stated, Nell Wing (Bill's secretary) acknowledged to the author that Clarence was the first person to use the initials "A.A." in referring to Alcoholics Anonymous.

There were many firsts in A.A. which could be directly attributed to Clarence Snyder. But his method of making them known became a sore point with many. Clarence did not believe in the tradition of anonymity. He felt he came into A.A. before there were any traditions and that for the most part they didn't apply to him. He used his first and last name everywhere he went. He granted television, radio and newspaper interviews. He allowed his face to be photographed in connection with A.A.—a violation of Tradition Eleven.

When Bill Wilson died in 1971, Clarence offered his services to the New York office to help in any way he could. But that office politely declined the offer. Clarence said, looking back on that refusal, that he probably expected it.

In 1969, Clarence was introduced to Grace Snipes Moore. Clarence was still married to Selma at the time. Grace was an alcoholic who was attending meetings. Clarence said he was introduced to Grace as the oldest living member of A.A., "the oldest man in the world."

Grace and Clarence married in 1971 and they eventually moved to Casselberry, Florida, where they purchased a house at 142 Lake Triplet Drive South. They established their home there and began traveling around the country together speaking.

Grace was openly theistic, and Clarence began to express similar ideas. Though Clarence had always believed in God and did not shrink from expressing his belief, he began more open confession of his religious beliefs. He became more involved in church matters and spoke more openly about Jesus at meetings and at retreats.

As an elder statesman in A.A., and as the member with the longest period of continuous sobriety of any person living at that time, Clarence was respected by many. People flocked to his home to be "taken through their steps" by Clarence. They came from all over the country. There were people who had many years of abstinence, but who wanted sobriety. They learned that sobriety had little to do with not drinking but had a lot to do with living. Clarence liked to use the term "so-dry-ity" when referring to the state these people were in before they underwent a life change.

There were Roman Catholic priests, business executives, housewives, and many other folks. All these who sought out Clarence, were unhappy with the way their lives were going and were seeking something more. With Clarence, they read the Big Book and found that its principles were being ignored in what they had heard at meetings. There was a type of recovery, they found, that was exemplified in the Big Book but was not present in the rooms of A.A.

Clarence was awarded the prestigious Jefferson Award, both on the local level and the national level, for service to humanity. It was granted for A.A. work from 1938 forward. Clarence was also given many other honors for his A.A. work.

Though these awards brought great honor to Clarence, he did not feel as if they were nearly as much an honor as what was awarded him when he brought someone through the steps and led someone to a changed life in service to God. Clarence felt he was an instrument whom God used for God's glory and honor.

Clarence held retreats in Florida twice a year, carrying the message of recovery, and leading people to his Lord, Jesus Christ. He made commitments for similar retreats in Wisconsin, New York, New Jersey and other places. He went wherever he was asked.

At these retreats the A.A. message was stressed. The Christian message and Prayer and Praise sessions began after the official ending of the retreat as not to confuse the two, so that those in attendance would not be mistaken as to which was the A.A. part and which was the religious part.

In those later Florida years, Clarence's life was filled with joy and contentment. He was married to a woman who loved him and was sharing his life and helping in carrying the message. He was respected by many, although disliked probably by just as many. However, Clarence always believed that, in order to do God's will, there would be those who would scorn him and try to cause derision. "If God is for me, who can be against me," Clarence often said, quoting Romans 8:31 in the Bible.

Clarence's life appeared to be the fulfillment of the promises in the Big Book and his serenity was evident wherever he went. Clarence had a message to carry to those who wanted to hear it. He had a commitment to his sponsor to "fix rummies" as an avocation. He honored this commitment and carried the message until the day he died.

Clarence Snyder in 1983

Chapter 10

Clarence "Goes Home"

"His lord said unto him, Well done, thou good and faithful servant: thou hast been faithful over a few things, I will make thee ruler over many things: enter thou into the joy of thy lord."[45]

It was November of 1983, and Clarence was off on another of his many speaking engagements. This particular one was in British Columbia, in Canada.

He was feeling a little under the weather and thought that he was coming down with a bad cold. Being the trooper that he was, he felt that even though he was possibly sick, he must go on and speak. He felt he had a message to carry, and all those good people had taken the time and effort, not to mention the expense, to bring both Clarence and his wife Grace all the way up to Canada. He was the main speaker; and never before had he backed down from a speaking engagement.

He got progressively worse as the days passed. By the time the weekend of the conference arrived, he had gotten much worse. He was coughing, and his body was racked with pain. Both he and Grace spent much time in their room together, praying for a healing. Other Christians who were there had "laid hands" upon him and had anointed him with oil. The healing for which they had been praying had only partially transpired—just enough to enable Clarence to regain some strength, continue on, and speak.

It was Saturday, the day he was going to speak. Clarence had spent a restless night, and despite Grace's insistence that he rest, he decided to go on with the talk. He had a commitment to fulfill, and he was going to fulfill it, no matter what.

That night, after sitting through the introductions and opening remarks, Clarence began to make his way to the podium. He felt miserable and weak. His body ached all over.

Clarence began his talk; and at many points, he had to stop to catch his breath. Halfway through the talk, he lost his voice and could not continue. He was rushed to a local physician; and it was discovered, after a lengthy examination, that he had contracted laryngitis and some sort of bronchial infection.

Clarence and Grace were invited by one of the local A.A.s to stay at his home since Clarence was in too weakened a condition to make the arduous trip home, back to Florida.

Eventually, Clarence gained enough strength to make the long plane ride home.

He and Grace had both decided during the trip home to cancel the balance of his speaking engagements, until he was better and more able to give them his full attention and energy. His health improved slightly, except for the lingering congestion, which refused to abate.

A close friend offered Clarence and Grace the unlimited use of his beach-front condominium so that Clarence could rest and recuperate. The warm weather and the beach, especially the sunsets, cheered Clarence. However, the nagging congestion would not go away. Clarence and Grace continuously prayed, and believed for a miracle.

One night, Clarence all but collapsed, and had to be rushed to Orlando. He was admitted into Florida Hospital and stayed there from December 20th through January 23, 1984.

His condition worsened, and Grace stayed by his side day and night—this despite her doctor's admonition that her health would eventually deteriorate and that she too would probably become a patient. In the past, Grace had been plagued by a series of heart attacks, and the doctors were concerned that the arduous pace she was setting would bring on another attack.

But Grace refused to budge. She stayed by Clarence's side throughout his ordeal, constantly praying. Her prayers were echoed by these of hundreds of people whose lives had been touched by Clarence.

The attending physicians tried numerous medications and combinations of medications to effect a change in Clarence's condition. However, no improvement was forthcoming. Tests continued to be made, to enable the physicians to determine the origin of his illness and enable them to treat it with positive results.

These tests finally proved one thing conclusively: Clarence had developed a malignancy in his left lung. Due to the size of the malignancy, Clarence's weakened condition, and his advanced age (he was 82 at the time), the doctors decided not to operate. It would be too dangerous, they felt.

Instead they arranged for a series of low dosage radiation treatments followed by a period of rest. Then another series of radiation treatments would begin. The doctors felt that if Clarence showed some improvement after the first series of treatments, he could go home and complete the rest phase as an outpatient until he needed to undergo the next series of radiation treatments.

Clarence's condition did improve enough for him to go home to Casselberry, Florida, to his home at 142 Lake Triplet Drive South. Supplied with oxygen tanks, and a small suitcase containing the myriad of medications that he was given, Clarence was transported home by ambulance.

The second series of radiation treatments ended on February 9th, just two days before the 46th anniversary of his sobriety date. He had returned home with oxygen tanks which were, by this time, in constant use to relieve the difficulty he was having in breathing— these plus medications that were to be taken hourly, in order to stave off further infection due to his weakened condition and low white blood cell count.

Clarence had a visiting nurse who came three times a week to help out and to administer injections of a medication intended to rebuild his immune system, which had been weakened by the radiation and the cancer.

Aided by all this medical care, the short visits by close friends, Grace's prayers, and the prayers of others, Clarence began to show some signs of improvement.

It was during this period of improvement that the author was allowed to come to Florida and spend a week with Clarence and Grace. He realized that this time spent together would probably be the last while Clarence was alive. The author had the choice, due to financial limitations at the time, either to come down then, or to come to Clarence's funeral. Both possibilities were discussed; and it was decided that it would be more beneficial for the book project to choose the former. The author personally decided that it would be better for the author, as his friend and sponsee, to see Clarence while he was still alive, rather than attend his funeral. The author wanted to remember Clarence's smile and his sense of humor, not just the empty shell of his physical body in a casket.

Upon the author's arrival at their home, Clarence was asleep and Grace's face was showing the strain of her long and arduous ordeal. She kept believing that God would heal her beloved Clarence.

She was also well aware of the fact that God had but two ways of healing, at least of the kind she was praying for: a physical healing that would remove the cancer and restore Clarence to health, so that he could continue in doing His work amongst the "rummies," or as she believed, a final healing which would indicate that Clarence had finished God's work appointed for him here on earth. Both Clarence and Grace believed that if this work was indeed finished, Clarence would be welcomed home to be with his God. And all of us knew that there were enough people whom Clarence had taken through the steps who would be able to carry on and assume his mantel.

The author was put up in Clarence's study, amongst volumes of A.A. books, photographs of Clarence taken during various periods of his life, and souvenirs of the many world-wide trips he had taken during the previous forty-six years.

There were plaques containing awards and citing achievements. There were "thank-yous" and other mementos. The walls exuded a sense of history, and they portrayed a sense of humility, for nothing ostentatious appeared amongst the various items. Despite the absence of humility that seemed a part of Clarence's public appearances, this room was the antithesis of those outward appearances.

The author unpacked, washed up after the long trip, went into the living room, and saw that Clarence was now awake and sitting in his favorite chair. It was the recliner next to the fireplace, the very same fireplace in front of which he had sat over the years. Clarence began spinning tales, conversing about A.A.'s past history, and discussing what he felt were present problems.

The ever-present oxygen tanks stood by his side, reminding of the obvious infirmity of the man who had once been so proud and healthy. Despite his long ordeal, he did not appear to be drawn or down in spirit. He removed the tubing from his nose and smiled. He welcomed the author into his home and apologized for not being awake on the author's arrival.

Clarence said he could not speak for very long as it was arduous for him to do so. He said he would have to continue with his oxygen tanks. He apologized again and then returned the oxygen mask to his face and sank back into his chair. The strain of attempting to speak was taking its toll.

Grace was tinkering in the little kitchen, preparing herbal tea and snacks. She called out, asking the author to sit down and relax, saying, "You must be tired and hungry after your trip from New York."

Bob R., who had been a close friend of theirs for over twenty years, kept vigil constantly. He was doing whatever he could to make their lives more comfortable. We all sat and talked about the retreats already planned for May 11-13 and September 21-23 of that year.

We all knew that Clarence would probably not be there to speak or even to be in attendance. However, no one wanted to speak of that. These retreats were to be part of the annual retreats Clarence and Grace had put on for many years. At first, the retreats were called "Camp Florida Retreats." Later, when they were moved to a different location, they were (and still are), called the "Leesburg Life Enrichment Retreats." These retreats, as well as the ones in New York and Amery, Wisconsin, were a time-honored ritual for both Clarence and Grace.

Clarence sat in his chair and, when he could, he would take part in the conversation. He would tell a joke or two, or speak of special happenings during the retreats over the years. Sometimes he just nodded his head.

We spoke about the healings at the retreats, of the people who had taken their steps at these retreats, and of the motorcycle gang that had come down to the retreat one year. The "bikers" had frightened the older crowd. But after some of them had shared their experiences, they had become welcome as just another "bunch of rummies."

The oxygen tank remained by Clarence's side, and there was a blanket upon his lap to ward off any chill that might develop. And the stenciled "target" was visible on the left side of his chest. This enabled the doctors to focus their radiation treatments, and were constant reminders of the cancer which had invaded his body.

Seemingly most of the old-time A.A. members (the pioneers) had died as the result of the years of self-destructive behavior in which they had engaged—the smoking, the drinking, and the rough lives they had led. Bill Wilson had died of complications from emphysema. Doc had prostate cancer which spread eventually throughout his body and to his throat. Most had died as a result of the ravages of their youth. Through all his present cancer ordeal Clarence was holding on to a faith in that, whatever God wanted, he (Clarence) would get. After all, He (God) was Clarence's manager, Clarence believed.

We spoke often, whenever his strength would allow it. We laughed at the jokes and the stories he told. He retained his sense of humor despite his weakened condition and the obvious prognosis of imminent death.

Grace, when not tinkering around the house or waiting on the various special guests who dropped by from around the country and around the world, was always by his side. The love of her life needed her, and she was there.

Grace had met Clarence in July of 1969, and they were married for life on September 26, 1971 (or 1972—the marriage certificate was not available). Clarence had always insisted that whenever possible she accompany him on his speaking commitments, as he often relied upon her strength and prayers.

Once, as Grace was preparing to meet Clarence on one of these commitments, she wrote this letter to her soon-to-be husband. They both knew, from the day they met, that they would be married. Grace's letter shows the love she had for her beloved. The letter was written on Monday night, July 22, 1970, and said:

> *My precious Duke —*
>
> *I'm packed and ready to fly away to meet you tomorrow night. Praise the Lord —*
>
> *My darling should anything happen to me, Plane fall, etc.— Try to remember that you have made me happier than I even have any right to be. Should my time to die come before I am in your precious arms again I want you to know that, with all my heart I shall forever love you. Yes even in Heaven we shall eternally be together ....*

She signed the letter, "Your Amazing Grace." She added a P.S., "... I shall tear this letter up upon my return home Aug. 4th." She never did "tear this letter up," and Clarence kept it with his most important papers. Their relationship was the closest thing to perfection in a marriage that the author had ever seen. They were truly husband and wife to each other.

The time came for the author to return to New York. We tearfully said our "so longs"—never "good-bye," for that would be a lack of believing. Yet the author knew in his heart he would never see this man again. At least not upon this earthly plane.

The author packed his belongings. As he left, they could not see the tears which were running down his cheeks. The flight back to New York was a sad and lonely one. The author had grown to love this man and was about to lose him. Clarence was missed already. In the five short years of our relationship, as the author's sponsor and friend, with Clarence's help and guidance, he had begun to

understand his own recovery, true recovery from alcoholism in its spiritual sense. He had begun to learn, from the example of Clarence's life, what finding God was all about.

Clarence's widow, Amazing Grace Snyder, with a friend

The weeks passed and Clarence's condition worsened. He had to be placed back in the hospital. The author spoke almost daily with him while he was in the hospital, honored to be one of the few people with whom Clarence would speak in the last few weeks. These few were Bob R., Steve and Sue F., Grace, Marjorie H., and the author.

Marjorie was another New Yorker whom the author had met through Clarence. Clarence loved Marjorie dearly, and when he had heard she was coming down to Florida to be there with him, he hung on, despite his worsening condition. Marjorie helped out and was constantly in the hospital by his side.

It was about eleven-thirty at night on the twenty-second of March. The winds were blowing outside; and despite the insulated glass in the author's windows, the curtains were fluttering. The house was quiet, and the chill in the room hit as the phone began to ring. The author did not want to answer it for he knew what was about to be reported from the other end of the line.

The choked voice on the other end said, "Clarence has gone home to be with the Lord." It was Marjorie. The author asked how Grace and the rest of the family was. Marjorie replied that, despite the obvious loss, there was also an atmosphere of joy. They all felt they knew where Clarence had gone and with whom he now was.

After a brief conversation in which the author and Marjorie tried to console each other, the phone call ended. Tears once again began streaming down the author's cheeks. He had lost a true friend and sponsor.

At four P.M. on the twenty-fifth of March, 1984, in the First Presbyterian Church of Maitland, Florida, Clarence's last earthly A.A. meeting was held. First there was a full Masonic service. As stated, Clarence was a 32nd Degree Mason.

This Masonic service was followed by a few speakers who had known and loved Clarence. There were Steve F., Bob R., Fr. Joe E., and Marjorie. Clarence was also there. However, this was probably the only meeting he had ever attended in his honor at which he didn't speak. The author felt God was also there, and that He spoke through those who carried, and continue to carry, His message.

Clarence was buried at Cameron Cemetery in Cameron, North Carolina, in Grace's family plot. Though not too many people attended the actual burial, all were there in spirit. We all knew that Clarence's earthly remains were not important, only the message which he had imparted to us.

Clarence's spirit shall forever live in the tens of thousands of lives he touched and will continue to touch. His spirit will continue, as those whom he "fixed" go forth to carry this message of experience, strength, hope, and permanent sobriety.

We close:

Our Father who art in Heaven,
Hallowed be thy name ….

Epilogue: What It Is Like Now

You, your closest friend, and your father are on vacation together, hiking in a remote jungle. Your two companions stumble into a nest of poisonous vipers and are bitten repeatedly. You know neither will live without an immediate shot of anti-venom, yet there is only a single dose of anti-venom and it is in your pocket. What would you do? [46]

While I was listening to Joe, thinking of what he's become, all of a sudden it took me that I'd find God and get Him to make me like Joe. It took me like that. I just felt, all of a sudden, determined to find God.

Determined! he repeated, with energy astonishing in this broken and hopeless creature of alcoholism. "And," he went on, "while I was kneeling, while I was praying, I felt the spirit come upon me. I said, 'Oh, God, make me like Joe! and while I prayed, I felt the Spirit come upon me. I knew I could become like Joe. I know I'm saved.'" [47]

A.A. continues to grow with phenomenal numbers. A myriad of twelve-step self-help fellowships have branched off, copying the original fellowship.

However, is this rapidly expanding "self-help" fellowship conveying the original message? Was the original intent "self-help?" Or was it "God's Help?"

What of the original rate of recovery, as it was recorded in the beginning? What has become of the "Fellowship," not to mention Sponsorship?

It has been said that, in the beginnings of A.A., there were only "low bottom drunks." They were desperate for recovery; for they had lost, or almost lost, all of their worldly and spiritual values. In today's A.A., there are many who come into the rooms of A.A. as people who have lost virtually nothing. Or have they?

Most experts in the field of recovery agree that the first thing to leave an alcoholic or addict is his or her spirituality, also that the spiritual life is the last part of one's life to return.

Alcoholics entering A.A. today vary in both economic and social status. There are many who come into A.A., forced by the courts and treatment centers. They are required to do 90 meetings in 90 days.

Nowhere does it say in the A.A. literature that there is such a thing as "90 in 90." This concept was dreamed up by the treatment field. Many who come into A.A. are not, nor can they be, classified as alcoholics. Clarence always said that, "Every alcoholic is a drunk, but not every drunk is an alcoholic."

It was up to the prospective member and his or her sponsor to determine whether or not the prospect was indeed an alcoholic, or just someone who drank to excess.

Perhaps we know where A.A. has come from, and of its history and experiences. We know where it has been, through its literature, and through local, state, and national archivists. However, do we know where it is going? What does the future hold for this movement, born of the desperation of two men, who met one Mother's Day in Akron, Ohio?

In many ways, A.A. is expected to become all things to all people. And in its efforts to accommodate everyone, people with widely divergent ideas, has its original intent been watered down? Has the message of hope, healing, and recovery been diluted?

Many long-term A.A. members no longer attend meetings. The author has spoken with several dozen of them. They all appeared to be disgusted and disillusioned with the proliferation of drug stories, the discussion of co-dependency and of dysfunctional families, and with "psychobabble" heard at meetings.

These old-timers are tired of hearing participants discussing their counselors and their therapists, their "relationship sponsors," and their "inner child." The old-timers most desire to hear about sponsorship, recovery, and the hope for a permanent solution to the problem of alcoholism. Many long term members, people no longer found at A.A. meetings, have "retired" from the "new program." Where have they gone?

There was a growing movement in A.A. in the 1990's. There is what has become known as "underground" meetings. They have sprung up around the country. They exist in New York, Denver, California, Boston, Wisconsin, and Florida, just to name a few places. And we mention only the ones that have been discussed. Many others exist, but only their members, and those they choose to tell, know of their existence.

These "underground" meetings are not advertised; and attendance at them is by invitation only. One has to be "sponsored" into them, much the same as people had to be "sponsored" in the beginnings of A.A. These meetings are open for alcoholics and their families only.

The sharing that one hears at these meetings is related only to recovery from alcoholism. Speakers talk of the solution rather than of the problem. "War Stories" are usually not heard at these gatherings. Speakers tell how they got well and how they are staying on the path of recovery. Members talk to the newcomer with stories of experience, yes. But they also impart their strength and hope. For hope is what the still sick and suffering alcoholic needs to hear.

Participants in these meetings fellowship together and carry the message as it was given to them. Their numbers are growing, both in strength and in size. Their recovery rate is climbing to a point beyond that of the treatment centers and, unfortunately, that of A.A. meetings themselves.

A.A. has been in existence for more than eighty years. Yet where are the long-term members? Does one see them at meetings? Seldom are they to be found in and around the rooms of A.A.. Every so often, they are heard at conventions and conferences, on "Old Timer's" panels.

What is to become of A.A.? What is to become of the floors of headquarters office space with high rentals, expensive books and therapeutics? What of the high salaried employees, and of the "professionalism" in an organization of which it was said, it "shall remain forever nonprofessional"?

What of the message of recovery that one drunk carries to another as an avocation, a way of life? Has monetary gain become an evil necessity? Has selfishness replaced self-caring? Has the desire to help the greater number of people, led to lower expectations and to diluting of the message to make it more palatable to those sought to be "attracted"? Has A.A. focused on adding meeting rosters to show growth which, to some, equals success?

The A.A. preamble—read at almost every meeting—states:

> *Alcoholics Anonymous is a Fellowship of men and women who share their experience, strength and hope with each other, that they may solve their common problem and help others to recover from alcoholism .... Our primary purpose is to stay sober and help other alcoholics to achieve sobriety.*

This preamble states all that A.A. was supposed to have been. But A.A. has diverted itself from its primary purpose in the guise of "helping" as many people as possible and has all but forgotten the individual who still suffers.

There are plenty of groups in existence which care about, and care for, the needs of narcotics addicts, cocaine addicts, sex and relationship addicts, overeaters, bulimics, pathological gamblers, those with emotional disorders, families, agnostics, atheists, rational thinkers, women, men, gays and lesbians, doctors, lawyers, air line pilots, musicians, etc., etc.

The author believes there is a cry in the wilderness for a different approach—one that worked in the past for thousands upon thousands of alcoholics, drunks, dipsomaniacs and inebriates.

That approach meant and means, *Alcoholics Anonymous* meetings—meetings in fellowship *for* alcoholics and *by* alcoholics—groups of people meeting together to deal with recovery from the disease of alcoholism.

Clarence H. Snyder believed in the premise that recovery from alcoholism can be permanent, and that the primary purpose of A.A.

was not to keep the alcoholic away from a drink, "a day-at-a-time." He believed in an A.A. which was a bridge into a new life for the alcoholic, in order that they might **LIVE** a "day-at-a-time."

Bill Wilson once stated, in a letter to Clarence dated November 9, 1955, "After all, A.A. is a sort of kindergarten—it's something we pass through to a better way of life and a wider usefulness." Bill often repeated this statement.

It has been the purpose of this book to help the reader, both member and non-member of Alcoholics Anonymous, to have a better understanding of how people can "pass through to a better way of life and a wider usefulness."

This book has also been written to provide the general reader, no matter what his or her problems, an understanding of a life-changing program of recovery, a program which can be utilized for all of life's concerns and afflictions, to the betterment of humanity.

Hopefully, those who have read this book will now have a better understanding of the A.A. program, its history, its growth and of —

HOW IT WORKED

Author's Addendum

The retreats which Clarence started are still held today. Though somewhat changed in format from the original retreats, Clarence's message of permanent sobriety is still carried by those who knew him.

These retreats are being held in New Jersey, Florida, Wisconsin, California, Alaska and England. (Note: the author is unaware of any of the current locations of these retreats.)

Clarence's recorded talks are available through many independent recovery recording companies.

As the so-called "official" A.A. Archival repositories are closing their holdings to continued research by both A.A. members and historians alike, new archival repositories are opening their collections to study the history of Alcoholics Anonymous. One of these is the Chester H. Kirk Collection on Alcoholism and Alcoholics Anonymous at the Brown University Center for Alcohol and Addiction Studies in Providence, Rhode Island.

The Internet also contains numerous sites relating to the history of A.A. There are also several books on the market including Mel B.'s biography of Ebby T. and several biographies of Bill Wilson by other authors.

As was stated in the tagline of a once popular American television show (*The X-Files*, which aired from 1993 to 2002):

"THE TRUTH IS OUT THERE"

A note on sources: the sources for many of the contents of the appendixes were part of a personal collection of A.A. memorabilia that was given to the author by Clarence H. Snyder. Other sources are noted in each appendix.

Appendix A

What was the Oxford Group?

In the autumn of 1922, the Lutheran minister, Rev. Frank N. D. Buchman, and a few of his friends, formed what they called "A First Century Christian Fellowship."

Frank Buchman had resigned his connection with the Hartford Theological Seminary around 1921 and had begun his evangelical work of carrying a message of life-changing by "getting right with God."

Around 1927, Buchman began working in England. Several of his followers were connected with Oxford University; and when they began to tour South Africa, the press called the evangelical team "The Oxford Group." Although most of the team was from Oxford University, Frank Buchman was never officially connected in any way with the university.

This name stuck. By 1932, A. J. Russell's book *For Sinners Only* was published, and made frequent reference to the Oxford Group. In 1937, the group was officially incorporated in Great Britain as a not-for-profit entity, known as The Oxford Group.

The fellowship held small group meetings, prayer meetings and what were called "house parties," at which its adherents spent "quiet time" in meditation, seeking "guidance" from God. Part of these meetings involved "witnessing," or giving testimony regarding prior sins, and what God had done in their lives to remove these sins (or defects in character or shortcomings).

Frank Buchman and his followers held certain theological beliefs, including the following: [48]

    1) Sovereignty and Power of God.
    2) The reality of sin.
    3) The need for complete surrender to the will of God.
    4) Christ's atoning sacrifice and transforming power.
    5) The sustenance of prayer.
    6) The duty to witness to others.

Its beliefs included other elements added as the movement grew and became more popular. Examples are: The belief that an experience of Christ would transform a believer, IF he truly believed, beyond anything he had dreamed possible. The belief that an adherent could and should make prompt restitution for personal wrongs revealed to him by his life-changing experience. And the belief that adherents should be part of a sort of "chain-reaction" of life changing experiences by sharing the experience of what Christ had done for them with others.

The Oxford Group believed one must surrender to God, not only to be "converted" from sin, but to have one's entire life controlled by God. They believed in "Quiet Time," or meditation, during which a believer would get guidance of what to do, or what direction one should take. They believed in open confession of sin, one-to-another, following James 5:16 in the scriptures. They believed in the healing of the soul and in carrying the message of personal and world-wide redemption through the sharing of members' testimony by witnessing.

Frank Buchman and his followers believed that people had sick souls, most of which was caused by "self-centeredness." Oxford Group members believed that people were powerless over this human condition, this defect of the soul. To recover, people had to admit they were separated from God and their fellow human beings, and that God could manage their lives. Then they made a decision to turn their lives over to the care and direction of God. They had to make an inventory of their lives and of their sins, and to make full restitution to others—those they had hurt by their sins or shortcomings. They also had to witness to others as to their own conversion from sin, and be available to convert others from sin. Oxford group members believed and were taught that the only way you could keep what you had been given by God, was to give it away to another. They did not try to force anyone into their path. They were to live their lives as an example, which would inspire others to want to follow.

The Oxford Group called its conversion process "soul-surgery." Its so-called surgical procedure boiled down to what were called the FIVE C'S: CONFIDENCE, CONFESSION, CONVICTION, CONVERSION, and CONSERVATION.

Oxford Group people also believed that their followers should have a formula for checking their motives in following this path. Part of the checking procedure involved the FOUR ABSOLUTES: HONESTY, UNSELFISHNESS, PURITY and LOVE. Oxford Group people believed these were the four absolute standards of Jesus. We mention the absolutes in the text of our book. A.A. members knew that no one could ever hope to attain the perfection of absolute anything. They instead were told to strive for perfection, as their guide for progress, knowing that they would never fully attain it.

Bill Wilson was visited by Ebby T., an Oxford Group follower. Bill was told by Ebby, "I got religion." Bill went to Calvary Mission in New York City with Ebby and later surrendered to Christ, making open confession of his alcoholism at the mission, which was run by Calvary Episcopal Church. Bill soon had his "white light" spiritual experience at Towns Hospital and after this surrender, never drank alcohol again. [49]

Bill reportedly knew when he was going to have a binge. Prior to his spiritual experience, Bill had been a patient at Towns Hospital and knew that he had to make reservations at Towns Hospital. He would call up two weeks in advance of the binge and tell Towns when he was going to be there. His binges were planned. After his spiritual experience, he never found the need to call for reservations again.

Dr. Bob, too, had had experience with the Oxford Group. After Frank Buchman's series of Oxford Group meetings at the Mayflower Hotel in Akron in January 1933, Henrietta Seiberling and Dr. Bob's wife, Anne Smith, convinced Dr. Bob to attend the meetings which were, by now, being held at the home of T. Henry and Clarace Williams.

Dr. Bob, though he had confessed his drinking and had been a devotee of the Oxford Group and of its writings and teachings, had not been able to stop drinking. It was not until he had met with Bill Wilson, another Oxford Group member, and was relating, one-drunk-to-another, that he eventually surrendered. Dr. Bob met Bill on Mother's Day in May of 1935, and later drank while going to and attending a medical convention in Atlantic City, New Jersey in June 1935. Bill Wilson gave Bob his last drink of beer and possibly a pill or two just prior to Dr. Bob's performing surgery, on June 10th, 1935, according to the traditional dating. This had been Dr. Bob's last "slip."

Recent documentation however has proven that the June 10th date could not have been the day of Dr. Bob's last drink. The medical convention Dr. Bob went to in Atlantic City, New Jersey started on June 10th and lasted until June 14th. Given what was reported—Dr. Bob getting drunk and leaving the convention, and returning by train to Akron, and Doc then being helped by his nurse at her home for several days, and afterwards returning to Akron to perform surgery—the 10th would be impossible. It was also reported that Doc wouldn't let his daughter Sue go to a school dance the night of his surgery and the documentation shows that the dance was held on June 17th, most probably the actual date of Dr. Bob's last drink.

Bill Wilson was once quoted as saying that even though he didn't want the connection to the Oxford Group and its religious teachings associated with Alcoholics Anonymous, he had incorporated most of their ideals and precepts in the Steps and in the writing of what was to become the A.A. recovery program.

Appendix B

The Evolution of the Twelve Steps of A.A.

When Bill Wilson sat down to write ideas for what were to be the Twelve Steps of A.A, he didn't just get them out of thin air. He had a basis for the Steps, founded on spiritual principles already in place. They come from the precepts of the Oxford Group, the Washington Temperance Movement (The Washingtonians), Biblical principles, and literature such as *The Common Sense of Drinking,* by Richard Peabody, *For Sinners Only,* by A.J. Russell, *I Was A Pagan,* by V.C Kitchen, *The Varieties of Religious Experience,* by William James, and others.

When Bill wrote the Twelve Steps the official story states that six were already in place in one form or another. Bill, it was reported, felt that the six steps had some loopholes through which an alcoholic could slip. It was written that he was not satisfied with the six already in place and decided to expand upon them so alcoholics could have a program of recovery, separate from the Oxford Group and separate from association with them.

Any references to the so-called Six Steps were made from 1953 onward. There is absolutely no documentation in Oxford Group literature or practices or early AA and AA related documents mentioning this so-called Six Step program. Bill's handwritten list of the Six Steps is dated in 1953, and Earl T.'s reference to them in his Big Book story ("He Sold Himself Short") is dated just prior to the Second Edition being published in 1955.

When he put the Twelve Steps in their original form, Bill felt at ease with them. They numbered twelve, and this, as has been reported, was a significant number for Bill. Bill noted that Jesus had twelve disciples, and the as-yet-unnamed movement now had Twelve Steps to recovery.

The author believes the following is a simple account of the evolution of the Steps:

I. In 1933, the Oxford Group had Four Practical Spiritual Activities:[50]

1. The sharing of our sins and temptations with another Christian life given to God, and using sharing as witness to help others, still unchanged, to recognize and acknowledge their sins.
2. Surrender of our life, past, present and future, into God's keeping and direction.
3. Restitution to all we have wronged directly or indirectly.
4. Listening to, accepting, relying on God's guidance and carrying it out in everything we do or say, great or small.

II) It is officially reported but does not have any substantiation that there were six steps of recovery that had been adapted by the Alcoholic Squadron of the Oxford Group in Akron, in part from the Practical Spiritual Activities as were used in Akron, Ohio. [51]

1. We admitted that we were licked, that we were powerless over alcohol.
2. We made a moral inventory of our defects or sins.
3. We confessed or shared our shortcomings with another person in confidence.
4. We made restitution to all those we had harmed by our drinking.
5. We tried to help other alcoholics, with no thought of reward in money or prestige.
6. We prayed to whatever God we thought there was for the power to practice these precepts.

These so-called original six steps are first referred to when Bill W. spoke in Texas in 1953. He wrote them on a napkin. There is no documentation that I have either heard of or have seen prior to 1953.

Even the reference to these so-called six steps in the Big Book (Earl T.'s story) dates from after 1953. There are many references to these steps in the literature after 1953, but to my knowledge, no one has ever seen a piece of correspondence or document mentioning them before the 1953 date.

III) The next phase comes from the pre-publication multilith edition of the book, which was sent to early members and those interested in the movement.

People were asked to purchase the multilith for $3.50 and told that when the hard copy came out it would be sent to those who purchased the manuscript at no additional charge. There were reportedly only 400 of these printed by the office owned by Bill Wilson and Hank P. on 17 Williams Street in Newark, New Jersey. Ruth Hock was the secretary who did all of the typing.

(The complete "Multilith" copy used to be available and could be ordered from the A.A. Archives at P.O. Box 459, Grand Central Station, New York, N.Y. 10163.)

The beginning of the fifth chapter, entitled "How It Works," is quoted here in its original form:

HOW IT WORKS

> Rarely have we seen a person fail who has thoroughly followed our directions. Those who do not recover are people who cannot or will not completely give themselves to this simple program, usually men and women who are constitutionally incapable of being honest with themselves. There are such unfortunates. They are not at fault; they seem to have been born that way. They are naturally incapable of grasping and developing a way of life which demands rigorous honesty. Their chances are less than average. There are those, too, who suffer from grave emotional and mental disorders, but many of them do recover if they have the capacity to be honest.

Our stories disclose in a general way what we used to be like, what happened, and what we are like now. If you have decided you want what we have and are willing to go to any length to get it—then you are ready to follow directions.

At some of these you may balk. You may think you can find an easier softer way. We doubt if you can. With all the earnestness at our command, we beg of you to be fearless and thorough from the very start. Some of us have tried to hold on to our old ideas and the result was nil until we let go absolutely.

Remember that you are dealing with alcohol—cunning, baffling, powerful: Without help it is too much for you. But there is One who has all power—that One is God. You must find Him now!

Half measures will avail you nothing. You stand at the turning point. Throw yourself under His protection and care with complete abandon.

Now we think you can take it! Here are the steps we took, which are suggested as your Program of Recovery.

1. Admitted we were powerless over alcohol—that our lives had become unmanageable.
2. Came to believe that a Power greater than ourselves could restore us to sanity.
3. Made a decision to turn our will and our lives over to the care and direction of God—as we understood Him.
4. Made a searching and fearless moral inventory of ourselves.
5. Admitted to God, to ourselves, and to another human being the exact nature of our wrongs.
6. Were entirely willing that God remove all these defects of character.
7. Humbly, on our knees, asked Him to remove our shortcomings—holding nothing back.
8. Made a list of all persons we had harmed, and became willing to make complete amends to them all.
9. Made direct amends to such people wherever possible, except when to do so would injure them or others.

10. Continued to take personal inventory and when we were wrong promptly admitted it.

11. Sought through prayer and meditation to improve our contact with God, praying only for knowledge of His will for us and the power to carry that out.

12. Having had a spiritual experience as the result of this course of action, we tried to carry this message to others, especially alcoholics, and to practice these principles in all our affairs.

You may exclaim, "What an order! I can't go through with it." But do not be discouraged. No one among us has been able to maintain anything like perfect adherence to these principles. We are not saints. The point is, that we are willing to grow along spiritual lines. The principles we have set down are guides to progress. We claim spiritual progress rather than spiritual perfection.

Our description of the alcoholic, the chapter to the agnostic, and our personal adventures before and after, have been designed to sell you three pertinent ideas:

(a) That you are alcoholic and cannot manage your own life.

(b) That probably no human power can relieve your alcoholism.

(c) That God can and will.

If you are not convinced on these vital issues, you ought to re-read the book to this point or else throw it away!

IV) "… as we understand Him" was not in the eleventh step of the multilith version of the steps. It already was in the third step.

Jimmy B., an atheist, insisted along with Hank P. and other atheists and agnostics, that there be a change and that "God" be deleted at this step. Most members in Ohio felt that the spiritual program should be kept and emphasized; and most of the New York members felt that it should be completely removed. This "God—as we understand Him" phrase was a compromise to keep everybody happy. Since there were more members in Ohio, and they had the longest amount of sobriety, the spiritual flavor was retained.

V) The Twelve Steps as they have been printed in the Big Book of Alcoholics Anonymous from 1939 to the present, except Step 12, where "experience" was replaced by "awakening":

1. We admitted we were powerless over alcohol—that our lives had become unmanageable.
2. Came to believe that a Power greater than ourselves could restore us to sanity.
3. Made a decision to turn our will and our lives over to the care of God *as we understood Him*.
4. Made a searching and fearless moral inventory of ourselves.
5. Admitted to God, to ourselves, and to another human being the exact nature of our wrongs.
6. Were entirely ready to have God remove all these defects of character.
7. Humbly asked Him to remove our shortcomings.
8. Made a list of all persons we had harmed, and became willing to make amends to them all.
9. Made direct amends to such people wherever possible, except when to do so would injure them or others.
10. Continued to take personal inventory and when we were wrong promptly admitted it.
11. Sought through prayer and meditation to improve our conscious contact with God *as we understood Him*, praying only for knowledge of His will for us and the power to carry that out.
12. Having had a spiritual experience as the result of these[52] steps, we tried to carry this message to alcoholics, and to practice these principles in all our affairs.

The first edition was copyrighted by Works Publishing Co., April 10th, 1939. In recent investigations it was discovered, that this might have been an invalid registration, because "Works Publishing Co." was not in existence on that date, and because the entire manuscript was sold prior to this date for $3.50 without mandatory copyright registration.

The second edition was copyrighted by the A.A. Publishing Company in 1955.

The copyrights for the first and second editions of the book *Alcoholics Anonymous*, including the Steps and Traditions, were allowed to lapse and are entirely in the public domain.

The third edition was copyrighted by A.A. World Services, Inc., 1976. This copyright applies only to the stories "Too Young?" and "Unto the Second Generation."

Appendix C

The following sermon was preached on November 26, 1939 by Dilworth Lupton at the First Unitarian Church at Euclid Avenue and East 82nd Street, in Cleveland, Ohio. Mr. X was Clarence H. Snyder. This was one of the first pamphlets concerning A.A., and was used by A.A. members in Cleveland from the end of 1939 into the early 1940's.

Mr. X and Alcoholics Anonymous

by Rev. Dilworth Lupton

My friend, Mr. X, is a young man with a family. For five years, to use his own words, Mr. X did not "draw a sober breath." His over-patient wife was about to sue him for divorce. Now for over two years, he has not had a single drink. He maintains that his "cure" is due to the efforts of a group of "ex-drunks" (their own term) who call themselves Alcoholics Anonymous.

I have had several opportunities to meet members of Alcoholics Anonymous.

Not long ago I accepted an invitation from Mr. X to attend one of their meetings, held in a private home. They are simple affairs: First a brief prayer, then four or five give public testimony to their experiences, refreshments are served, and there is general fellowship. They call themselves religious, but I find no sign of excessive piety, sensationalism, or fanaticism. Furthermore they have a sense of humor, somewhat of a rarity in religious circles. They are not trying to make other people or the country into "dries." They merely say, "We are the type that can't take it, and we have found a way of leaving it alone."

In my own home recently nine members of this group submitted themselves to questions for four hours from a prominent physician and a psychiatrist. Both were impressed by the trim appearance, sincerity, manliness of the ex-victims, and by the seeming efficacy of their methods. As the physician said to me privately, "These boys have got something!"

Thank God someone is throwing light on the problem of the chronic alcoholic, a problem that has perplexed men for centuries. There may be a million victims in the United States. Chronic alcoholism is not a vice but a disease. Its victims know that the habit is exceedingly harmful—as one of them graphically expressed it to me, "I was staring into a pine box"—but they are driven toward drink by an uncontrollable desire, by what psychologists call a compulsive psychosis.

Complete abstinence appears the only way out, but except in rare cases that has been impossible of attainment. Religion, psychiatry, and medicine have been tried, but with only sporadic success. The members of Alcoholics Anonymous, however, appear to have found an answer, for they claim that at least fifty per cent of those they interest have stopped drinking completely.

From conversations with my friend, Mr. X, and with members of the Cleveland group, I am convinced that this success comes through the application of four religious principles that are as old as the Ten Commandments.

1. The principle of spiritual dependence

Mr. X, who had been drinking excessively for years, found that he couldn't summon enough will power to stop even for a single day. Finally, in desperation he consented to a week of hospital treatment. During this time, he received frequent visits from members of Alcoholics Anonymous. They told him that he must stop trying to use his will and trust in a Power greater than himself. Such trust had saved them from the abyss and could save him. Believe or perish! Mr. X chose to believe. Within a few days he lost all desire for alcohol.

Trust in God seems to be the heart of the whole movement. Religion must be more than a mere set of beliefs; it must be a profound inner experience, faith in a Presence to which one may go for strength in time of weakness.

This fact is made quite clear in the book *Alcoholics Anonymous*, which gives the philosophy behind the movement and also the testimony of thirty of those who have benefited. Although written by laymen it contains more psychological and religious common-sense than one often reads in volumes by religious professionals. The book is free from cant, from archaic phraseology. It gives with skill and intelligence an inside view of the alcohol problem and the technique through which these men have found their freedom.

I will let "Bill," one of the contributors to *Alcoholics Anonymous*, describe his own experience. He had been drinking in his kitchen— there was enough gin in the house to carry him through that night and the next day. An old friend came to see him. They had often been drunk together, but now he refused to drink! He had "got religion." He talked for hours … it all seemed impossible, and yet there he was, sober. But let me quote from the book:

> God had done for him what he could not do for himself. His human will had failed. Doctors had pronounced him incurable. Society was about to lock him up. Like myself, he had admitted complete defeat. Then he had, in effect, been raised from the dead, suddenly taken from the scrap heap to a level of life better than the best he had ever known!
>
> Had this power originated in him? Obviously it had not. There had been no more power in him than there was in me at that moment, and this was none at all.
>
> That floored me. It began to look as though religious people were right after all. Here was something at work in a human heart which had done the impossible. My ideas about miracles were drastically revised right then. Never mind the musty past; here sat a miracle directly across the kitchen table. He shouted great tidings.

How hard is it for us moderns to concede—much less express it as our deep conviction—that our inner lives ultimately are dependent upon a power-not ourselves. Such an attitude seems weak and cowardly. But we go even farther; we suspect that faith in a spiritual Presence outside ourselves is absurd.

Why absurd? Our bodies are dependent ultimately upon the physical cosmos, upon air and sunlight, and upon this strange planet that bears us up. Why is it absurd then, to think of our spiritual selves—our souls, psyches, call them what you will—as being dependent upon a spiritual cosmos? Is it not absurd, rather to conceive that the material side of us is part of a material universe, but that our nature is isolated, alone, independent? Is not such an attitude a kind of megalomania?

At any rate these ex-alcoholics declare that only when they recognized their spiritual dependence was their obsession broken.

2. The principle of universality

In our great museums one usually finds paintings covering several ages of art, often brought together from widely separated localities—the primitive, medieval and modern periods; products of French, American, English, and Dutch masters; treasures from China, Japan, and India. Yet as one looks at these productions he instinctively feels that a universal beauty runs through them all. Beauty knows no particular age or school. Beauty is never exclusive and provincial; it is inclusive and universal.

So, too, in the field of religion. We are beginning to recognize the substantial unity of all religious faiths. Back of all religions is religion itself. Religion appears in differing types, but they are all expressions of one great impulse to live nobly and to adore the highest.

This universality of religion is recognized by the Alcoholics Anonymous. Their meetings are attended by Catholics, Protestants, Jews, near-agnostics, and near atheists.

There is the utmost tolerance. It seems of no concern to the group with what religious bodies non-church-going members eventually identify themselves; indeed there is no pressure to join any church whatever. What particularly impresses me is the fact that each individual can conceive of the Power-not-himself in whatever terms he pleases.

"Bill"—the writer already quoted in *Alcoholics Anonymous* — makes this tolerance clear when he further narrates his conversation with his ex-alcoholic friend:

> My friend suggested what then seemed a novel idea. He said, *"Why don't you choose your own conception of God?"*
>
> That statement hit me hard. It melted the icy intellectual mountain in whose shadow I had lived and shivered many years. I stood in the sunlight at last.
>
> *It was only a matter of being willing to believe in a Power greater than myself. Nothing more was required of me to make my beginning.* I saw that growth could start from that point. Upon a foundation of complete willingness I might build what I saw in my friend. Would I have it? Of course I would!

Perhaps these laymen in Alcoholics Anonymous are laying foundations for a new universal movement in religion. Surely the conventional conceptions of religion have been too narrow. Religion, itself, is far bigger and broader than we thought. It is something we can no more capture through rigid dogmas than we can squeeze all the sunshine in the world through one window.

3. The principle of mutual aid

Consider again the case of Mr. X. When he was being hospitalized eighteen laymen visitors called on him within the brief space of five days. These men were willing to give their valuable time in trying to help a man they had never seen before. To Mr. X they related their own dramatic experiences in being saved from slavery to alcohol, and offered their assistance. Upon leaving the hospital Mr. X began attending the weekly meetings of Alcoholics Anonymous [*editor's note: these were actually meetings of the*

Oxford Group as Alcoholics Anonymous was not officially named in 1938].

Before long he was following the example of the men who had so generously given him of their help. From what I know of the practices of these members of Alcoholics Anonymous, I feel quite confident that Mr. X this very day is using virtually every hour of his spare time to assist other victims in getting on their feet.

As he said to me recently, "Only an alcoholic can help an alcoholic. If a victim of chronic alcoholism goes to a doctor, psychiatrist, or a minister, he feels the listener cannot possibly understand what it means to be afflicted with a compulsion psychosis. But when he talks with an ex-alcoholic, who has probably been in a worse fix than himself and has found the way out, he immediately gains a confidence in himself that he hasn't had in years. He says to himself in substance, 'If this fellow has been saved from disaster I can be too!"

The weekly meetings of the Alcoholics Anonymous operate on this same principal of mutual aid. The ex-victims bolster up each other's morale through comradeship.

Like ship-wrecked sailors on a raft headed for the shore, the bond that holds them together is the same that they have escaped from a common peril.

Upon each newcomer is impressed the necessity of helping other alcoholics obtain the freedom he has attained. They believe they gain strength from expenditure—not expenditure of money, of which most of them have but little, but of themselves. Said one of them to me, "What I have is no good unless I give it away." There are no dues, no fees, just the sheer pleasure and, in this case, moral profit, that comes from helping the other fellow. This mutual aid acts as a sort of endless chain. Mr. A, Mr. B, and Mr. C help Mr. X out of the frightful mess he is in; then Mr. X turns around and helps Mr. Y and Mr. Z. These in turn help other victims.

As "Bill" writes in *Alcoholics Anonymous*:

My wife and I abandoned ourselves with enthusiasm to the idea of helping other alcoholics to a solution of their problems. It was fortunate, for my old business associates remained skeptical for a year and a half, during which I found little work. I was not too well at the time, and was plagued by waves of self-pity and resentment. This sometimes nearly drove me back to drink. I soon found that when all other measures failed, work with another alcoholic would save the day. Many times I have gone to my old hospital in despair. On talking to a man there, I would be amazingly uplifted and set on my feet. It is a design for living that works in rough going.

4. The principle of transformation

During the last half century many able psychologists have turned the searchlight of their investigations on "religious experience." It seems quite clear from these studies that religion consists not primarily in the intellectual acceptance of certain beliefs. It involves even more the transformation of human character.

Such transformations have taken place not only in the lives of saints and religious leaders, but in the souls of multitudes of common folk as well. It is a scientific fact that through religious faith people are sometimes suddenly, and sometimes gradually aroused to a new set of interests, are raised from lower to higher levels of existence. Life and its duties take on new meaning, and selfishness (half-conscious often) is displaced by the conscious desire to help other people.

If any human being needs such a transformation, it is the chronic alcoholic. He may not be at the point where he is willing to admit that, but his family and friends are! Alcoholism is a sickness, to be sure, but it is unlike any other malady in certain fundamental aspects. Compare for example, the case of the alcoholic with that of a tubercular patient. Everybody is sorry for the "T.B." and wants to help. He is surrounded by friendliness and love. But in all likelihood, the alcoholic has made a perfect hell of his home and has destroyed his friendships one by one. He has drawn to himself not compassion and love, but misunderstanding, resentment, and hate.

There seems to be every evidence that the Alcoholics Anonymous group has been amazingly successful in bringing about religious transformation. Note how a doctor describes the effect of this technique on one of his patients:

> He had lost everything worth while in his life and was only living, one might say, to drink. He frankly admitted and believed that for him there was no hope. Following the elimination of alcohol, there was found to be no permanent brain injury. He accepted the plan outlined in this book (*Alcoholics Anonymous*). One year later he called to see me, and I experienced a very strange sensation. I knew this man by name, and partly recognized his features, but there all resemblance ended. From a trembling, despairing, nervous wreck, had emerged a man brimming over with self-reliance and contentment. I talked with him for some time, but was not able to bring myself to feel that I had known him before. To me he was a stranger, and so he left me. More than three years have now passed with no return to alcohol.

Every member of this movement declares that since he has come to believe in a Power-greater-than-himself a revolutionary change has taken place in his life; even his acquaintances note a marked change. He has radically altered his attitudes and outlooks, his habits of thought. In the face of despair and impending collapse, he has gained a new sense of direction, new power.

I have seen these things with my own eyes. They are convincing, dramatic, moving.

* * *

One final word to the members of Alcoholics Anonymous. Go back to your synagogues and churches; they need you and you need them. Preserve your principle of Universality, your faith that all religion is one. Never allow yourselves to be absorbed by any single church or sect. Keep your movement what you call it now, a "layman's outfit." Avoid over-organization for religious organizations always tend to follow the letter rather than the spirit, finally crushing the spirit. Remember that early Christianity was promoted not by highly involved organization, but by the contagion of souls fired with enthusiasm for their cause. And keep your sense of humor! So far you do not seem afflicted with the curse of over-seriousness.

To doctors and psychiatrists I would say: Be skeptical, investigate this movement with an open mind. If you become convinced of their sincerity and the efficacy of their methods, give these men your approval and open support.

Alcoholics Anonymous ought to have a wide reading by the general public. For one thing the public ought to learn first hand that the chronic alcoholic is suffering not from a vice, but from a disease; that it is impossible for him to "drink like a gentleman." Moderation for him is out of the question. For him there is no such thing as the single drink. It is one taste, and then the deluge.

Certainly every victim of alcoholism and every friend of victims ought to buy or borrow and read this book, then seek to get in touch with some member of the movement. The writer of this article will be glad to furnish addresses of the Cleveland leaders. Or communicate with Alcoholics Anonymous, Box 658, Church Street Annex, New York City.

Appendix D

A.A. Sponsorship Pamphlet

by Clarence H. Snyder

This is the first pamphlet ever written concerning sponsorship. It was written by Clarence H. Snyder in early 1944. It was printed by the Cleveland Central Committee under the title: "A.A. Sponsorship ... Its Opportunities and Its Responsibilities."

*The headings marked with an asterisk were not in the original draft for this pamphlet. They were added for the first and subsequent printings.

PREFACE

Each member of Alcoholics Anonymous is a potential sponsor of a new member and should clearly recognize the obligations and duties of such responsibility.

The acceptance of an opportunity to take the A.A. plan to a sufferer of alcoholism entails very real and critically important responsibilities. Each member, undertaking the sponsorship of a fellow alcoholic, must remember that he is offering what is frequently the last chance of rehabilitation, sanity or maybe life itself.

Happiness, Health, Security, Sanity and Life of human beings are the things we hold in balance when we sponsor an alcoholic.

No member among us is wise enough to develop a sponsorship program that can be successfully applied in every case. In the following pages, however, we have outlined a suggested procedure, which supplemented by the member's own experience, has proven successful.

PERSONAL GAINS OF BEING A SPONSOR

No one reaps full benefit from any fellowship he is connected with unless he whole-heartedly engages in its important activities. The expansion of Alcoholics Anonymous to wider fields of greater benefit to more people results directly from the addition of new, worth-while members or associates.

Any A.A. who has not experienced the joys and satisfaction of helping another alcoholic regain his place in life has not yet fully realized the complete benefits of this fellowship.

On the other hand, it must be clearly kept in mind that the only possible reason for bringing an alcoholic into A.A. is for that person's gain.

Sponsorship should never be undertaken to —

1. Increase the size of the group
2. For personal satisfaction and glory
3. Because the sponsor feels it his duty to re-make the world

Until an individual has assumed the responsibility of setting a shaking, helpless human being back on the path toward becoming a healthy, useful, happy member of society, he has not enjoyed the complete thrill of being an A.A.

SOURCE OF NAMES

Most people have among their own friends and acquaintances someone who would benefit from our teachings. Others have names given to them by their church, by their doctor, by their employer, or by some other member, who cannot make a direct contact.

Because of the wide range of the A.A. activities, the names often come from unusual and unexpected places.

These cases should be contacted as soon as all facts such as: marital status, domestic relations, financial status, drink habits, employment status and others readily obtainable are at hand.

IS THE PROSPECT A CANDIDATE?

Much time and effort can be saved by learning as soon as possible if—

1. The man[53] really has a drinking problem?
2. Does he know he has a problem?
3. Does he want to do something about his drinking?
4. Does he want help?

Sometimes the answers to these questions cannot be made until the prospect has had some A.A. instruction, and an opportunity to think. Often we are given names, which upon investigation, show the prospect is in no sense an alcoholic, or is satisfied with his present plan of living. We should not hesitate to drop these names from our lists. Be sure, however, to let the man know where he can reach us at a later date.

WHO SHOULD BECOME MEMBERS?

A.A. is a fellowship of men and women bound together by their inability to use alcohol in any form sensibly, or with profit or pleasure. Obviously, any new members introduced should be the same kind of people, suffering from the same disease.

Most people can drink reasonably, but we are only interested in those who cannot. Party drinkers, social drinkers, celebrators, and others who continue to have more pleasure than pain from their drinking, are of no interest to us.

In some instances an individual might believe himself to be a social drinker when he definitely is an alcoholic. In many such cases more time must pass before that person is ready to accept our program. Rushing such a man before he is ready might ruin his chances of ever becoming a successful A.A. Do not ever deny future help by pushing too hard in the beginning.

Some people, although definitely alcoholic, have no desire or ambition to better their way of living, and until they do …. A.A. has nothing to offer them.

Experience has shown that age, intelligence, education, background, or the amount of liquor drunk, has little, if any, bearing on whether or not the person is an alcoholic.

PRESENTING THE PLAN

In many cases a man's physical condition is such that he should be placed in a hospital, if at all possible. Many A.A. members believe hospitalization, with ample time for the prospect to think and plan his future, free from domestic and business worries, offers distinct advantage. In many cases the hospitalization period marks the beginning of a new life. Other members are equally confident that any man who desires to learn the A.A. plan for living can do it in his own home or while engaged in normal occupation. Thousands of cases are treated in each manner and have proved satisfactory.

SUGGESTED STEPS*

The following paragraphs outline a suggested procedure for presenting the A.A. plan to the prospect, at home or in the hospital.

QUALIFY AS AN ALCOHOLIC*

1. In calling upon a new prospect, it has been found best to qualify oneself as an ordinary person who has found happiness, contentment, and peace of mind through A.A.

Immediately make it clear to the prospect that you are a person engaged in the routine business of earning a living. Tell him your only reason for believing yourself able to help him is because you yourself are an alcoholic and have had experiences and problems that might be similar to his.

TELL YOUR STORY*

2. Many members have found it desirable to launch immediately into their personal drinking story, as a means of getting the confidence and whole-hearted co-operation of the prospect.

It is important in telling the story of your drinking life to tell it in a manner that will describe an alcoholic, rather than a series of humorous drunken parties. This will enable the man to get a clear picture of an alcoholic which should help him to more definitely decide whether he is an alcoholic.

INSPIRE CONFIDENCE IN A.A.*

3. In many instances the prospect will have tried various means of controlling his drinking, including hobbies, church, changes of residence, change of associations, and various control plans. These will, of course, have been unsuccessful.

Point out your series of unsuccessful efforts to control drinking … their absolute fruitless results and yet that you were able to stop drinking through application of A.A. principles. This will encourage the prospect to look forward with confidence to sobriety in A.A. in spite of the many past failures he might have had with other plans.

TALK ABOUT "PLUS" VALUES*

4. Tell the prospect frankly that he can not quickly understand all the benefits that are coming to him through A.A. Tell him of the happiness, peace of mind, health, and in many cases, material benefits which are possible through understanding and application of the A.A. way of life.

SHOW IMPORTANCE OF READING BOOK*

5. Explain the necessity of reading and re-reading the A.A. book. Point out that this book gives a detailed description of the A.A. tools

and the suggested methods of application of these tools to build a foundation of rehabilitation for living.

This is a good time to emphasize the importance of the twelve steps and the four absolutes.

QUALITIES REQUIRED FOR SUCCESS IN A.A.*

6. Convey to the prospect that the objectives of A.A. are to provide the ways and means for an alcoholic to regain his normal place in life. Desire, patience, faith, study and application are most important in determining each individual's plan of action in gaining full benefits of A.A.

INTRODUCE FAITH*

7. Since the belief of a Power greater than oneself is the heart of the A.A. plan, and since this idea is very often difficult for a new man, the sponsor should attempt to introduce the beginnings of an understanding of this all-important feature.

Frequently this can be done by the sponsor relating his own difficulty in grasping a spiritual understanding and the methods he used to overcome his difficulties.

LISTEN TO HIS STORY*

8. While talking to the newcomer, take time to listen and study his reactions in order that you can present your information in a more effective manner. Let him talk too. Remember ... Easy Does It.

TAKE TO SEVERAL MEETINGS*

9. To give the new member a broad and complete picture of A.A., the sponsor should take him to various meetings within convenient distance of his home.

Attending several meetings gives a new man a chance to select a group in which he will be most happy and comfortable, and it is extremely important to let the prospect make his own decision as to which group he will join. Impress upon him that he is always welcome at any meeting and can change his home group if he so wishes.

EXPLAIN A.A. TO PROSPECT'S FAMILY*

10. A successful sponsor takes pains and makes any required effort to make certain that those people closest and with the greatest interest in their prospect (mother, father, wife, etc.) are fully informed of A.A., its principles and its objectives.

The sponsor sees that these people are invited to meetings, and keeps them in touch with the current situation regarding the prospect at all times.

HELP PROSPECT ANTICIPATE
HOSPITAL EXPERIENCE*

11. A prospect will gain more benefit from a hospitalization period if the sponsor describes the experience and helps him anticipate it, paving the way for those members who will call on him.

CONSULT OLDER MEMBERS IN A.A.*

These suggestions for sponsoring a new man in A.A. teachings are by no means complete. They are intended only for a framework and general guide. Each individual case is different and should be treated as such. Additional information for sponsoring a new man can be obtained from the experience of older men in the work. A co-sponsor, with an experienced and newer member working on a prospect, has proven very satisfactory.

Before undertaking the responsibility of sponsoring, a member should make certain that he is able and prepared to give the time, effort, and thought such an obligation entails. It might be that he will want to select a co-sponsor to share the responsibility, or he might feel it necessary to ask another to assume the responsibility for the man he has located.

IF YOU ARE GOING TO BE A SPONSOR ... BE A GOOD ONE!

The headings marked with an asterisk were not in the original draft for this pamphlet. They were added for the first and subsequent printings.

Appendix E

The Steps of A.A.—An Interpretation

Written by Clarence H. Snyder
January 1972

Alcoholics Anonymous is not a "booze cure" or a psychological means of controlling one's excessive or obsessive drinking. A.A. is a program, a life changing program, and, in a great part, we owe our inception as a fellowship to our origin in the Oxford Group movement during the mid-1930's.

The Oxford Group was designed as a Life Changing program and we in A.A. have for our own uses and affiliation, modified their program, chiefly by designing our twelve step program in a manner that the alcoholic who feels he needs and wants a change from what they are experiencing, can comfortably accept and apply the program and thereby change their life.

To do so, requires certain attitudes, willingness, and acts on our parts. We have simplified the program, in the feeling that any alcoholic with an alcohol problem, can live a life free of the obsession to drink.

Our program of the twelve steps is really accepted in four distinct **PHASES**, as follows:

1) Need (admission)
2) Surrender (submission)
3) Restitution
4) Construction and Maintenance

PHASE #1—Is covered in Step 1—"We admitted we were powerless over alcohol, that our lives had become unmanageable"—this step points out phase 1—or our own need—there is a need for a change!

PHASE #2—Includes the 2nd through the 7th steps which constitutes the phase of submission.

Step #2—"We came to believe that a power greater than ourselves could restore us to sanity."

Since we could not manage our own lives, of ourselves, we found ourselves to be powerless over alcohol, we were encouraged by the power of example of someone or some others to believe that a power greater than ourselves could restore us to sanity. In this step, we have the "proof of the pudding" before we are asked to eat it!! Others tell us of their experiences and share their deepest feelings with us and those members are alcoholics such as we are, and there they stand, sober, clean-eyed, useful, confident and with a certain radiance we envy and really want for ourselves. So, we *WANT* to believe it! Of course, some persons could conceivably be a bit more startled at first by the reference to "being restored to sanity," but most of us finally conclude that in hearing of some of the experiences our new friends had during their drinking careers were anything but the actions of a rational person, and when we reflect upon our own actions and deeds prior to our own introduction to A.A., it is not difficult to recognize that we too, were pretty well out in left field also! In fact, most of us are happy in the feeling that we were not really responsible for many of our past unpleasant and embarrassing situations and frankly, this step does much to relieve our feelings of guilt and self-condemnation.

Step #3—"We made a decision to turn our *will* and our *lives* over to the care of God ..."

Now here is the step which separates the men from the boys (or the women from the girls)—this is the step which tells the story as to whether we are going to be *in* A.A., or *around* A.A. Yes, we can attend meetings, visit the clubs, attend the social functions, but, unless we really take step #3, we are continuing to make up our own program. Since our entire program is based upon dependence upon God and our lives are to be directed by Him! So, here we are, making a *decision* which in itself is quite an accomplishment for the alcoholic, since they are one of the most indecisive creatures in society, due to their incapacity to manage their own life due to their obsession—But—to make a decision to turn our life and our will over to the care of God—this creature in the far blue yonder, whom we have little acquaintance with and probably much fear of, this is really asking very, very much of an alcoholic! Rest assured, that if they are not ready, if they have not reached their "bottom" or extremity, and if they are not really "hurting more than they ever have," they are not about to take step #3. So—they go pretty much on their own as usual, except that they do have the advantage of better company than they had been associating with and this in time, could really foul up any type of drinking life they may have in the future! Another important feature enters here, in that they *know* now that there is a way out of their dilemma and this is bound to "work" on them as time goes on, if they have any pride at all in themselves! At this point—their biggest problem is to overcome *FEAR* and "Let go and let God."

Step #4—"Made a searching and fearless *Moral* inventory of ourselves."

This is a step which should be taken with the assistance of a sponsor, or counselor who is well experienced in this changed life—due to the capacity of the alcoholic to find justification for about anything—a sponsor can bring up through sharing—many various moral weaknesses which need attention in their life and can smooth the way for the alcoholic to examine them in a frank fashion.

The next step suggests that someone is helping with step #4—since it reads as follows:

Step #5—"Admitted to God, to ourselves, and to *another human being*, the exact *NATURE* of our wrongs."

We put ourselves on record and leave no options nor reservations! Note that it states, *NATURE* of our wrongs—not the wrongs themselves! We are not required to narrate details of our many indiscretions. Many of them we don't even remember, nor are conscious of. This is not a laundry for dirty linen, this is recognition of character defects which need elimination or adjustments!

Step #6—"Were *entirely* ready to have God remove *ALL* these defects of character."

This step allows for no reservations. The alcoholic, being an extremist must go the whole route. We are not a bit ready, or about to be ready, but *entirely* ready to have God, not us, remove *ALL* these defects of character, (the interesting ones as well as the more damnable ones!).

Step #7—"Humbly asked Him to remove our shortcomings."

We tried to make no deal, as we did in the past when situations would overwhelm us. It was common to say—"Dear God, get me out of this mess and I will be a good boy (or girl), I will not do thus and such, etc., etc., etc., ..." NONE OF THAT! We humbly asked Him to remove our shortcomings. The Good Book assures us that anything we ask believing, we shall receive!

Step #8—Begins our **PHASE #3**—that of restitution. So now we have admission in Step #1, Submission, Steps #2 through #7. Now for the Restitution in Steps #8 and #9.

Step #8—"Made a list of *all persons* we had harmed and *became willing* to make *amends to them all*."

Steps 8 and 9 should also be taken with the assistance of a knowledgeable sponsor or a counselor, since in our present state of impatience with almost complete lack of judgment, we could conceivably cause much harm in executing this phase of the program.

Most of us probably have persons on that list whom we just do not want to have any contact with. The step states plainly—*ALL* persons we had harmed! Obviously some of these persons are not available, having passed on, or disappeared etc., so we must ask God to handle those details.

But step #9 states—"Made direct amends   *Wherever   Possible* except when to do so would injure them or others."

We cannot and should not try to clear our slate or conscience at the expense of any others. This phase is very important and it eliminates the possibility of carrying over some details into our new life that could consciously come back to haunt or harm us in our new life. We are going into a new life, and we should "Let the dead bury the dead."

Now that we have taken 9 steps !!! we have concluded 3 phases of our program. These 9 steps we have accomplished—so—FORGET THEM!!! They have required action and you have taken the action, so there is no need of repeating it!

There are only two occasions when one must refer back to the first nine steps, #1—is in the event that the person "resigns and resumes," obviously they must start all over again! The other occasion when we may refer to the first nine steps is when we are trying to explain them to a new member and helping them with them.

So, now we have our **LAST PHASE**, that of *construction*—Steps 10-11- and 12. With these steps, we construct our life, these are our living steps. We no longer must be concerned with 12 steps—ONLY 3 STEPS!! How simple, how wonderful!!

Step #10—"Continued to take *personal* inventory, and when we were wrong, promptly admitted it."

This step has absolutely no connection with step #4. Note, in step #4, it calls for a searching and fearless *Moral* inventory. This step calls for a *personal* inventory.

This step is our daily check on ourselves. This is our check on the small and large and otherwise details of my life *TODAY*. My simple way of handling step 10 may help someone, since I find that it is most adequate for me, and I prefer to keep things simple and uncomplicated.

At night, after I am in bed, my day is over, I find this is one of my most important prayer times. I think about my day, what have I done, whom I have been with, what has transpired. Sometimes I find that I am not proud of something I have done today, and I owe someone an apology, I do not permit these things to go unattended.

I have found that it is not the so-called "big" things which seriously affect the alcoholic in their new life, but the "little" things. They can go on and on and add up and become a real burden and eventually have drastic effects upon our new life. This is the reason for step 10, keep things "cleaned up," keep the walk swept! Maintain a good healthy attitude.

Step #11—"Sought through Prayer and Meditation, to improve our conscious contact with God, praying *only* for knowledge of His will for us and the power to carry that out."

This is a great step, first, because it brings us into a prayer life. Back in step #3, we made a decision to turn our life and will over to the care of God. In step #11, we receive our orders!! Let us break this step down and discover how it is both simple and profound. We are seeking something, seeking to improve our conscious contact with God. What does that mean? To me it means He is not in the far blue yonder, beyond reach, but right here, close where I can talk to Him and listen to Him (the Bible states that He is closer than hands and feet, and that is most close!). So, I am seeking to make this contact through Prayer and Meditation.

What does this mean? To me, Prayer is talking to God, and Meditation is listening to Him! The good Lord endowed us with one mouth and two ears, which should suggest something to us!! We are enjoined—"Be Still"—and that is how we should be while listening! The answers surely will come if we but listen.

Now, the step tells us what to pray for. "Only for knowledge of His will for us and the power to carry that out." Since we submitted ourselves and turned our will and life over to the care of God in phase #2—now we ask for His orders and strength to carry them out. We are promised that He will never expect anything from us that He won't give us the power to execute.

Now then, do you see any place in the step thus far to suggest we pray for sobriety? Of course not, and it is absolutely unnecessary— you *HAVE* sobriety. Thank Him for it—but it is pointless to pray for what you already have. The 11th step states very plainly *how to pray* and *what to pray for!!*

Step #12—We have experienced 11 steps and something has happened to us. In fact, something happened at the end of step 9! Step 12 states very plainly—"Having had a Spiritual Experience as *the* result of these steps, we tried to carry this message to other Alcoholics and to practice these principles in *ALL* of our affairs."

What is a Spiritual Experience? That is the changed life we have been referring to. That is the change that comes to a person who has turned their will over to the care of God and continues to try and improve themselves, mentally, morally and spiritually. It states that we try to carry this message (not the alcoholic) to alcoholics.

We practice these principles of love and service in all our affairs. Not just in A.A. meetings and associations, at home, at business, everywhere! What a blessing this fellowship is. What a great opportunity to love and be loved. Why cheat yourself? We have the prescription, the means of getting well, staying well, growing and best of all, *SERVING*. Come on in, the water's fine!! Friends are wonderful, the fellowship is distinct and GOD IS GREAT!!

(This was transcribed from Clarence's handwritten copy.)

Appendix F

Clarence's Story: The Home Brewmeister
(as it appeared in the first edition)

HOME BREWMEISTER

Strangely enough, or by some queer quirk, I became acquainted with the "hilarious life just at the time in my life when I was beginning to really settle down to a common-sense, sane, domestic life. My wife became pregnant and the doctor recommended the use of Porter Ale . . . so . . . I bought a six gallon crock and a few bottles, listened to advice from amateur brewmeisters, and was off on my beer manufacturing career on a small scale (for the time being). Somehow or other, I must have misunderstood the doctor's instructions, for I not only made the beer for my wife, I also drank it for her.

As time went on, I found that it was customary to open a few bottles whenever visitors dropped in. That being the case, it didn't take me long to figure out that my meager manufacturing facilities were entirely inadequate to the manufacture of beer for social and domestic consumption. From that point on, I secured crocks of ten gallon capacity and really took quite an active interest in the manufacture of home brew.

We were having card parties with limburger and beer quite regularly. Eventually, of course, what with all the hilarity that could be provoked with a few gallons of beer, there seemed to be no need of bridge or poker playing for entertainment. Well . . . we all know how those things go. The parties waxed more liquid

274

and hilarious as time went on, and eventually I discovered that a little shot of liquor now and then between beers had the tendency to put me in a whacky mood much quicker than having to down several quarts of beer to obtain the same results. The inevitable result of this discovery was that I soon learned that beer made a very good wash for whiskey. That discovery so intrigued me, that I stayed on that diet almost entirely for the balance of my extended drinking career. Yes sir, the old Boilermaker and his Helper. The last day of my drinking career, I drank 22 of them between 10 and 12 A.M. and I shall never know how many more followed them until I was poured into bed that night.

I was getting along fairly well with my party drinking for quite some time however, but eventually I began to visit beer joints in between parties. A night or so a week in a joint, and a party or so a week at home or with friends, along with a little lone drinking, soon had me preparing for the existence of a top flight drunkard.

Three years after I started on my drinking career, I lost my first job. At that time, I was living out of town, so I moved back to the home town and made a connection in a responsible position with one of the larger companies in the finance business. Up to this point I had spent six years in the business and had enjoyed the reputation of being very successful.

My new duties were extremely confining and my liquor consumption began to increase at this time. Upon leaving the office in the evening, my first stop would be a saloon about a block from the office. However, as there happened to be several saloons within that dis-

276 ALCOHOLICS ANONYMOUS

tance, I didn't find it necessary to patronize the same place each evening. It doesn't pay to be seen in the same place at the same hour every day, you know.

The general procedure was to take 4 or 5 shots in the first place I stopped at. This would get me feeling fit, and then I would start for home and fireside, thirteen miles away. Well . . . on the way home numerous places must be passed. If I were alone I would stop at four or five of them, but only one or two in the event I had my mistrusting wife with me.

Eventually I would arrive home for a late supper, for which, of course, I had absolutely no relish. I would make a feeble attempt at eating supper but never met with any howling success. I never enjoyed any meal, but I ate my lunch at noon for two reasons: first, to help get me out of the fog of the night before, and second, to furnish some measure of nourishment. (My enjoyment of meals now is an added feature to the Seven Wonders of the World to me. I can still hardly believe it). Eventually, the noon meal was also dispensed with.

I cannot remember just when I became the victim of insomnia, but I do know that the last year and a half I never went to bed sober a single night. I couldn't sleep. I had a mortal fear of going to bed and tossing all night. Evenings at home were an ordeal. As a result, I would fall off in a drunken stupor every night.

How I was able to discharge my duties at the office during those horrible mornings, I will never be able to explain. Handling customers, dealers, insurance people, dictation, telephoning, directing new employees, answering to superiors, etc. However, it finally caught up with me, and when it did, I was a mental, physical, and nervous wreck.

I arrived at the stage where I couldn't quite make it to the office some mornings. Then I would send an excuse of illness. But the firm became violently ill with my drunkenness and their course of treatment was to remove their ulcer in the form of me from their payroll, amid much fanfare and very personal and slighting remarks and insinuations.

During this time, I had been threatened, beaten, kissed, praised and damned alternately by relatives, family, friends and strangers, but of course it all went for naught. How many times I swore off in the morning and got drunk before sunset I don't know. I was on the toboggan and really making time.

After being fired, I lined up with a new finance company that was just starting in business, and took the position of business promotion man, contacting automobile dealers. WOW . . . was that something??? While working in an office, there was some semblance of restraint, but, oh boy, when I got on the outside with this new company without supervision, did I go to town???

I really worked for several weeks, and having had a fairly wide acquaintance with the dealer trade, it was not difficult for me to line enough of them up to give me a very substantial volume of business with a minimum of effort.

Now I was getting drunk all the time. It wasn't necessary to report to the office in person every day, and when I did go in, it was just to make an appearance

278   ALCOHOLICS ANONYMOUS

and bounce right out again. Was that a merry-go-round for the eight months that it lasted???

Finally this company also became ill and I was once more looking for a job. Then I learned something else. I learned that a person just can't find a job hanging in a dive or barroom all day and all night, as jobs don't seem to turn up in those places. I became convinced of that because I spent most of my time there and nary a job turned up. By this time, my chances of getting lined up in my chosen business were shot. Everyone had my number and wouldn't hire me at any price.

I have omitted details of transgressions that I made when drunk for several reasons. One is that I don't remember too many of them, as I was one of those drunks who could be on his feet and attend a meeting or a party, engage in a conversation with people and do things that any nearly normal person would do, and the next day, not remember a thing about where I was, what I did, who I saw, or how I got home. (That condition was a distinct handicap to me in trying to vindicate myself with the not so patient wife).

I also committed other indiscretions of which I see no particular point in relating. Anyone who is a rummy or is close to rummies knows what all those things amount to without having to be told about them.

Things eventually came to the point where I had no friends. I didn't care to go visiting unless the parties we might visit had plenty of liquor on hand and I could get stinking drunk. Fact is, that I was always well on my way before I would undertake to go visiting at all.

(Naturally, this condition was also a source of great delight to my wife).

After holding good positions, making better than average income for over ten years, I was in debt, had no clothes to speak of, no money, no friends, and no one any longer tolerating me but my wife. My son had absolutely no use for me. Even some of the saloon-keepers where I had spent so much time and money, requested that I stay away from their places. Finally, an old business acquaintance of mine, whom I hadn't seen for several years offered me a job. I was on that job a month and drunk most of the time.

Just at this time my wife heard of a doctor in another city who had been very successful with drunks. She offered me the alternative of going to see him or her leaving me for good and all. Well . . . I had a job, and I really wanted desperately to stop drinking, but couldn't, so I readily agreed to visit the doctor she recommended.

That was the turning point of my life. My wife accompanied me on my visit and the doctor really told me some things that in my state of jitters nearly knocked me out of the chair. He talked about himself, but I was sure it was me. He mentioned lies, deceptions, etc. in the course of his story in the presence of the one person in the world I wouldn't want to know such things. How did he know all this? I had never seen him before, and at the time hoped to hell I would never see him again. However, he explained to me that he had been just such a rummy as I, only for a much longer period of time.

He advised me to enter the particular hospital to which staff he was connected and I readily agreed. In all honesty though, I was skeptical, but I wanted so definitely to quit drinking that I would have welcomed any sort of physical torture or pain to accomplish the result.

I made arrangements to enter the hospital three days later and promptly went out and got stiff for three days. It was with grim foreboding and advanced jitters that I checked in at the hospital. Of course, I had no hint or intimation as to what the treatment was to consist of. Was I to be surprised!

After being in the hospital for several days, a plan of living was outlined to me. A very simple plan that I find much joy and happiness in following. It is impossible to put on paper all the benefits I have derived . . . physical, mental, domestic, spiritual, and monetary.

This is no idle talk. It is the truth.

From a physical standpoint, I gained 16 pounds in the first two months I was off liquor. I eat three good meals a day now, and really enjoy them. I sleep like a baby, and never give a thought to such a thing as insomnia. I feel as I did when I was fifteen years younger.

Mentally . . . I know where I was last night, the night before, and the nights before that. Also, I have no fear of anything. I have self confidence and assurance that cannot be confused with the cockeyness or noise-making I once possessed. I can think clearly and am helped much in my thinking and judgment by my spiritual development which grows daily.

From a domestic standpoint, we really have a home

now. I am anxious to get home after dark. My wife is ever glad to see me come in. My youngster has adopted me. Our home is always full of friends and visitors (No home brew as an inducement).

Spiritually . . . I have found a Friend who never lets me down and is ever eager to help. I can actually take my problems to Him and He does give me comfort, peace, and radiant happiness.

From a monetary standpoint . . . in the past four years, I have reduced my reckless debts to almost nothing, and have had money to get along comfortably. I still have my job, and just prior to the writing of this narrative, I received an advancement.

For all of these blessings, I thank Him.

Appendix G

Hospital Rules

At a meeting of the Hospital Committee, consisting of representatives from each group, held at 12214 Detroit Avenue on Tuesday, October 21st, 1941, the following rules and regulations were adopted for general use by the Hospitals and the Sanitariums accepting A.A. patients.

Report of Central and Group Hospital Committee meeting held at the Women's Hospital October 21st, 1941

The following Group Hospital Committees were present:

> Lee Monday Lake Shore
> Lee Thursday Brooklyn
> Lee Friday Orchard Grove
> Windemere Women's
> Crawford Berea
> Miles Lorain Avenue
> Collinwood Men's
> Absent:
> Avon
> Parma

The rules were unanimously adopted by all groups represented which a copy is enclosed. It was suggested that the hospital be notified by members of the Central Hospital Committee and necessary printing be furnished by the Central Committee.

It was also suggested that the Hospital Committee of the various groups meet at least once a month to work out better hospitalization for A.A. patients. The next meeting will be

held at 8920 Euclid Avenue, Tuesday, November 18th, 1941,
at 8:30 P.M.

Signed,

THE CENTRAL HOSPITAL COMMITTEE

H. L. M_____

Chairman

PROCEDURE FOR ENTERING NEW PATIENTS

1. The sponsor's first action shall be to notify a group hospital committee and to obtain their sanction, before entering a patient, giving full particulars as to the identity and financial responsibility of said patient, and who is to be responsible for payment of bill.

2. It shall be the duty of the sponsor to see that the person who is to be responsible for the payment of the hospital bill has made satisfactory arrangements with them directly or prior to the admittance of the patient.

INSTRUCTIONS TO HOSPITALS

1. Call a physician immediately.

2. The hospital will make out a complete case history.

3. The hospital will be furnished official A.A. Visitation Record, which must be kept for each patient.

4. No one excepting A.A. members will be permitted to visit patients, except at the discretion of attending physician.

5. No visitors will be permitted after 11:00 P.M.

6. Patient will not be given his street clothes until the last day, except on occasions when sponsor brings him to a meeting. Upon returning from the meeting, clothes are to be taken from the patient.

7. All packages for the patient must be inspected by the person in charge.

8. Hospitals and Sanitariums will not permit more than two men to talk with any one patient at any one time.

9. Patients will not be permitted any outside contact, such as, mail or telephone calls, except through his sponsor.

10. Hospitals will have patients available to visitors at all times, up to 11:00 P.M., except where it conflicts with the Hospital rules.

11. Hospitals and Sanitariums will be used for the purpose for which they are intended, and not as meeting places or club rooms, except at the Women's Hospital.

12. Under no circumstances may a patient in Hospital or Sanitarium be taken to a meeting, without the approval of his sponsor.

13. Wives or husbands of A.A. members will not be permitted to be present, when a patient is being contacted.

14. No hospitals or sanitariums are to make any reference to A.A. in its promotional or publicity programs.

DEFINITION OF RETROVERT—OR "SLIPPER"

A man or woman who has been sponsored, and has attended at least one A.A. meeting, and then takes a drink, is considered a retrovert, or slipper.

RULES GOVERNING RETROVERTS

1. When a retro is placed in a hospital, the procedure followed shall be the same as that for the new patients.

2. Retroverts may not be placed in a hospital unless arrangements can be made for their complete isolation from new patients.

3. Except for visitation by sponsor, retroverts will be left completely alone for two days and two nights.

Appendix H

Preparative Material for
the Formulation of a Plan for
Headquarters Activities

(Dated April 17, 1948)

The time has come, after more than two years of preparation and discussion, to reach an accord upon a plan for the reorganization of Headquarters activities, assuming that the continuance of a Headquarters is necessary to the general welfare. The motives which should animate and the principles that should govern such activities are settled and beyond debate. Our task is the adoption of a mechanism and a plan for its governance which will translate our purpose into action.

Purpose

The function of the individual as a member, the office of the group and the objective of headquarters is, at their respective levels, in their own spheres and in their own ways, precisely the same, namely, to carry or facilitate the carrying of the message to alcoholics (Twelfth Step of Recovery). This restatement of purpose should serve as the frame of reference within which any Headquarters activities should be centered.

Principles

The Twelve Points of Tradition purport "to portray that Group Ideal toward which we have assuredly been led by a Higher Power." The principles implicit in the Twelve Points are also those which will support a Headquarters Ideal and assure its future. Let us refresh our recollection of the Twelve Points and paraphrase a little:

1. Headquarters ought to be a spiritual entity <u>having but one primary purpose</u>—that of carrying its message to the alcoholic who still suffers.

2. Problems of money, property and authority may easily divert Headquarters from its primary spiritual aim. Therefore, in recognition of human fallibility and the tendency to follow the primrose path of worldliness and bureaucracy, activities involving money, property and authority should be carried on, if they have to be carried on at all, subject to appropriate limitations and restrictions.

3. Headquarters should have the least possible organization. "The Trustees of The Alcoholic Foundation are, in effect, our General Service Committee. They are the custodians of our A.A. tradition and the receivers of voluntary A.A. contributions by which they maintain General headquarters and our General Secretary at New York. They are authorized by the Groups to handle our over-all public relations and they guarantee the integrity of our principle newspaper 'The A.A. Grapevine'."

4. We believe that the principle of anonymity has an immense spiritual significance. It reminds us that we are to place principles before personalities; that we are actually to practice a truly humble modesty. This principle is just as important, if not more so, in the case of individuals or representatives functioning at Headquarters level as it is at lower echelons.

The foregoing principles after formulation, with the concurrence of the Trustees and of individual members of ripe experience and sound judgment, have been widely promulgated and are universally accepted by the general membership. Most of us also believe with the famous political philosopher, Lord Acton, that "power tends to corrupt and absolute power corrupts absolutely." And with William James who said: "I am done with great things and big things and great organizations. I am for those tiny, invisible, molecular, moral forces which work from individual to individual creeping through the crevices of the world like so many wattles."

So, we approach the problem of organization somewhat as if it were a necessary evil realizing its potential dangers but confident that adherence to the motivation and principles which permeate the body of the Movement will at least minimize the prospect of the head getting out of order.

History

A.

Before considering the current proposals for the reorganization of Headquarters activities, it might be well to review what has previously been suggested and discussed.

In July of 1946 there was proposed a "Suggested Code of Tradition for A.A. General headquarters" embodying in summary the following principles:

> 1. The Board of Trustees of the Foundation should continue practically as presently constituted, a self-perpetuating body, the alcoholic members rotating and filling their own vacancies, the vacancies in the non-alcoholic membership being filled by majority vote of the whole Board.
> 2. The Trustees should preserve the A.A. tradition, supervise public relations, keep the general funds, and bear a general responsibility for the Grapevine and the Central Office.
> 3. The allotment of responsibility should be as follows:

I. To the Trustees—control of funds and final discretion in large matters of contract and policy.

II. To the Central Office Secretary—active administration of Foundation policies and broad executive discretion to manage ordinary services, business, public relations and publishing activities.

III.To the Grapevine Editor—full discretion in editorial policy and business engagements of the paper.

4. The above three functions should be welded into a working whole on a quasi-partnership basis through the medium of a General Policy Committee, composed of three Trustees, the Secretary and the Editor. The Committee is to investigate new or important policy commitments and report the same to a regular or special meeting of the Trustees. Similarly, the Secretary and Editor, as administrators for the Foundation of general policy, report all questions of medium or large importance to the General Policy Committee but such Committee by unanimous consent may decide such matters, subject to review by the Trustees.

5. Works Publishing Inc., wholly owned by the Foundation, has five directors and it is recommended that three of them be Trustees and two be selected from members of the Central Office staff. This corporation conducts the business of the Central Office and publishes the Book and the pamphlets. It is suggested that the Secretary should be the company's chief executive.

6. The Trustees are to select the Secretary and participate in the selection of the Editor, both of whom should report at the regular meetings of the Foundation.

7. It is contemplated that the Foundation should be primarily financed by contributions from the Groups and the sale of literature and that the Grapevine should be self-supporting.

B.

Following the presentation of the above Code and as a result of various comment thereon, the author thereof on July 10, 1946 issued a supplementary statement from which the following propositions may be gathered as representative of his views:

1. The Foundation should be the keystone of the Movement, bound to the Tradition and dedicated solely to A. A. service.

2. There should not be, however, complete centralization of everything in the Foundation through subsidiary corporations and committees to which would be delegated the minimum powers needed to transact Foundation business and to carry out its policy.

3. The alternative is to adopt the principle or partnership among the Foundation and the Central Office and Grapevine, this to be accomplished by the adoption of the above mentioned Code subject to relatively minor changes. While the Foundation will be the senior partner in this scheme of "democratic informality," it is unequivocally recognized that the Secretary and Editor will inevitably exert a broader scale leadership than the Trustees, that they will have to be of Trustee caliber, that they are primary figures and cannot be relegated to subordinate roles and that they will be the chief source of policy suggestions. However, "the Trustees must see to it that these two people never stray off on serious tangents."

C.

The response to the foregoing by the President of the Foundation may be summarized as follows:

1. To integrate the Foundation into the Movement as a co-partner with other instrumentalities of the Movement or as part of a tripartite head would plunge it into the maelstrom of group struggles, difficulties, pressures, politics and

turbulences, the determination of policies, and to impose upon the Trustees the supervision of activities and the exercise of powers for which it has no qualifications or democratic mandate. It would destroy the identity of the Trustees and their ability to discharge their true function as custodians of Policy and Tradition, as an appellate body rather than Executive Authority and their freedom to act as an impartial, stabilizing influence.

2. The extreme sensitivity concerning the status of the Secretary and Editor is not justified. Their "broad leadership" and authority among the groups are self-evident, the Secretariat having even lost its anonymity. Their activities are subject only to such curbs and checks as the Trustees in the exercise of their Trusteeship (which perhaps ought more clearly to be defined) impose.

3. It is recommended that thought be given to the creation of safeguards democratically arrived at within the Movement itself, perhaps by the organization of a General Council, leaving the Trustees to serve the Cause by staying on the side lines and performing the sort of chores which have previously occupied them.

D.

Under date of July 30, 1946, rejoinder was made to the President's statement of July 23 in which it was pointed out that (I) neither personal recovery nor group behavior any longer depended on R. S. and W. W. but that (2) such is not yet true in the area of General Headquarters which is still sustained by the presence and influence of these two men. Hence, the problem is to determine the structure upon which their final responsibilities will descend. After discarding a number of choices, including that of doing nothing, it is again suggested that there be published a binding Code of Structure that will draw the Foundation and the Groups together and guarantee democratic relations among the Trustees, Secretaries and Editors permanently. The following propositions were stated:

1. That there must be some central point in the Movement where interpretations can be made and decisions taken and these duties need to be definitely authorized.

2. The Trustees should have final decision on all large matters of contract and policy interpretation at which levels "we dare not leave full discretion with the General Secretary." Yet the Secretary, Editor and Policy Committee at lower levels must be given appropriate authorization.

3. While the totality of Headquarters activities would be entrusted to all three instrumentalities, the Foundation would be a relatively inactive but nevertheless senior partner—the court of final decision, including, if necessary or advisable, the ultimate determination of the succession of Secretaries and Editors.

4. Self-perpetuation is recognized as dangerous but elections being obviously impracticable, the only effective restraint is the fullest publicity about Headquarters.

5. As earlier suggested, there should be an Advisory Council of the older leadership among the groups.

Current Proposals

A central structure for the future is outlined in a comprehensive statement issued by W. W. on April 8,1947 and supplemented by letters dated October 30, 1947 and March 12, 1948. It embodies and envisions the following:

1. The structure consists of one principal "committee" and three related ones, each being incorporated.

2. The principal a membership corporation, "committee" is the Foundation, constituted as at present except that the General Service Conference below mentioned shall have a veto power in respect of nominations for vacancies. It is also suggested that the name or the Foundation be changed to one less suggestive of authority and formalism.

3. The three related "committees" are:

I. The General Office Committee incorporated as A.A. General Services, Inc., its stock being wholly owned by the Foundation. The Board of Directors will include three Trustees and two members of the Central Office. This group is responsible for the policy of the Central Office and the General Secretary will be charged with its management.

II. The General Policy and Publications Committee incorporated as Works Publishing, Inc., its stock being wholly owned by the Foundation. Its Board will include three Trustees, the Editor and the General Secretary. This group is to settle questions of "medium" policy which neither the Secretary nor Editor can settle alone (matters of large policy being reserved for the Trustees) and to publish all books and pamphlets (but not The Grapevine).

III. The Grapevine Committee incorporated as The A. A. Grapevine, Inc., the beneficial ownership being in the Foundation. Its Board includes two Trustees, the Editor and two staff members. The Group will publish the Grapevine.

4. To "close the gap" between the Foundation and the Groups and to act purely in an advisory and service Capacity, a General Service Conference is to be created consisting of individual members of groups (about 50) and Headquarters people. Various methods of selecting the members of the Conference are mentioned.

5. It is concluded that the Foundation must undergo marked alteration and no longer remain "off side" and autonomous. To conform to the pattern of the Movement it will have to become, in effect, an incorporated service arm of the General Service Conference, losing some of its independence and devoted to custody rather than management, a miniature or "Interim Conference." Like the General Office people and the Grapevine, the Foundation, although incorporated and to some degree autonomous, will basically be only a sub-committee of the Conference, thus conforming in general principle to the practice of the Movement everywhere.

CONCLUSION

I.

We revert to our original premise that the sole purpose of individual (once he has recovered), group and Headquarters activity is to bring the message to others.

Of course, one way to dispose of Headquarters problems is to get rid of Headquarters. This is not an entirely unthinkable, unlikely or necessarily unsound solution. It may come to that. It will come to that, or virtually that, if a substantial number of individuals or groups reach the conclusion that Headquarters no longer performs an essential function or perverts its legitimate function. History is replete with instances of religious and quasi-religious groups and movements which, rended by schism, heresy or by those claiming to be more orthodox than the custodians of orthodoxy, have given up to dissenters and objectants who have gone their several ways, sometimes to disappear or die, sometimes to survive and flourish.

Individuals and groups are not dependent on Headquarters. They can and do function autonomously, often in virtual ignorance of anything approaching an official Center. Unlike other movements and organisms, religious and otherwise, they need no Vatican or Hierarchy. They do need and do have the principles of recovery which nobody can take away from them.

To paraphrase, where two or more are gathered together in the name of AA, that is AA.

Therefore, Headquarters is dependent upon the Groups and their members. If they get the notion that Headquarters serves no proper purpose or is detrimental to the spirit of the Movement they may readily put an end to Headquarters activities by withholding contributions to the Central Office and by cancelling their subscription to the Grapevine.

They may also insist that the Book be thrown into the public domain, where some think it ought to be, in default of which another book may be written. There can be no proprietary interest or legal monopoly in the principles of recovery or the Sermon on the Mount. Likewise, as is the present case, papers and magazines may be published in consequence of local individual and group enterprise and attain such circulation as their merit and promotion may bring them.

Nor would the newcomer or inquirer encounter much difficulty in making contact with a group or individual without Headquarters aid. The nation is so studded with members, groups and regional committees (with their presence and activity known to practically every public and semi-public agency) that one can hardly cast a stone without striking an A.A. Moreover, the nuclear, cellular development and expansion of groups so that they cover the national scene is now a matter of natural growth without the benefit of Headquarters rather than a cultivated process stimulated by external fertilization.

There is also the consideration that if Headquarters gets out of hand the entire Movement suffers whereas, absent a Headquarters, if a group or section violates a tradition (as they have done and do) its action may be disavowed and the effect localized.

The foregoing preliminary observations are submitted not in discouragement of the idea that Headquarters should be continued in some form but as considerations pertinent to the long view—which is, paradox though it may seem, that as A.A. grows Headquarters activities should diminish to the vanishing point.

II.

We have before us the views of the proponent of certain changes and the expression of those who wish to maintain the status quo, or at least, proffer no counter proposals. It will be seen from the foregoing resume that there are points of agreement on certain basic and vital issues and it would seem the proper subject of inquiry to ascertain whether, this being so, a modus operandi may be attained without doing violence to the principles held by each.

We perceive at once that there is virtual accord on the <u>function</u> of the respective instrumentalities involved. Thus it is agreed on all hands that:

1. The Trustees are primarily custodians of policy and tradition. They are not initiators, executors or administrators. They are not particularly concerned with routine, day to day matters or, with questions of "medium" gravity. But they do have original jurisdiction over matters of large contract and important policy. And in all matters they are a tribunal of final decision, including the selection, or approval of the selection, of the General Secretary and Grapevine Editor. Finally, like any body charged with duties they should have the benefit of specific authorization.

2. Subject to the foregoing, the Secretariat should operate the Central Office and publish and distribute the Book and other literature.

3. Subject to the foregoing, the Grapevine staff should edit, publish and attend to the commercial operations of the paper.

4. To establish better liaison between Groups and Headquarters, to introduce an element of democracy and to obtain the benefit of approval and ratification that flows from full disclosure of plans and activities, an Advisory Council or General Conference of members should be formed to meet periodically with Headquarters people in a consultative basis.

In addition to the foregoing points there are certain elements in the situation that nobody suggests should be disturbed. Thus, The Grapevine is an incorporated body the beneficial ownership of which is (and perhaps the full ownership ought to be) in the Foundation. The stock of Works Publishing, Inc. (General Policy and Publications Committee) is entirely owned by the Foundation. And if the General Office Committee is to be incorporated as A. A. General Services, Inc., its stock will presumably be held by the Foundation. It may be noted that this seems to be a plethora of corporations. Perhaps, one stock corporation, other than the Foundation which is a membership corporation, with appropriate functional divisions would be sufficient. Or, all of the publications, including The Grapevine, might be placed with Works Publishing, Inc.

We come finally to the area where there seems to be confusion and lack of clarity rather than lack of agreement on fundamentals and that is in the matter of interrelation of the various Headquarters units. Aside from certain points to be touched upon later, most of the tumult seems to be due to the use in an unprecise manner of undefined expressions such as "integration," off-center," "on center" and so on.

It is submitted that, if in this paper, we have with reasonable accuracy set forth the proposals, the matters upon which there is agreement and the status of certain elements which are to be left as they are—the various parts of the Headquarters Whole fall naturally and logically into their ordained positions. Their relation to one another may be graphically charted and no characterization, however loose and indefinite, of the scheme as a whole or any or its segments can becloud the substance of the arrangement. Such is our conclusion and our feeling is that the use of too many words, slogans and labels has diverted us from reality.

Recommendations

III.

We view the Headquarters structure without reference to specific personalities or incumbents of present positions. The safeguards we are about to suggest are designed to effectuate so far as humanly possible the principles restated at the beginning of this paper. If they appear to be strict, it is because we are trying to protect the sanctity of principles against the errors of human fallibility. If they seem to be severe, it is because we feel that there should be an element of dedication in every person serving the Movement (in contrast with a business enterprise) in any capacity. If they appear to repose too little trust in the individual, it is because we have learned that power and authority, too long and widely exercised, change those that become accustomed to its exercise. As in the case of the principles of recovery and the Points of Tradition, these have been the lessons of experience. It is, therefore, recommended that the following policies and procedures be applied to the respective units of the Headquarters structure and be appropriately incorporated in their by-laws or other regulations:

1. The General Secretary and Editor should not be members of the Board of Trustees of the Foundation nor attend meetings thereof except to report.

2. The heads of each of the corporate entities such as the Central Office, Publications and the Grapevine may be members of the respective Boards of Directors.

3. The business and affairs of each of the organizations related to the Foundation should be carried on by the respective managements in the conventional way in so far as practicable.

4. Paid workers, especially those in executive positions, should be selected in view of their altruistic interest in the Movement as a humanitarian project and their principal compensation above a subsistence level, in so far as practicable, should be reflected in the satisfaction resulting from their labors. They should be people who are willing to live dedicated lives in a limited sense. The Movement is no place for "career" persons and should not compete with business, the arts and the professions for its help. Our own experience has shown it to be possible (if not necessary) to function on this idealistic level and this is confirmed by the experience of the American Friends Service Committee (Quakers) and other organizations.

5. The tenure of paid executive workers should be limited. This would be heresy in a business organization but the loss in efficiency and perhaps continuity of service is as nothing compared with the potential evil to be avoided. It is unnecessary to elaborate upon the dangers involved in the possible creation of a bureaucracy through the use of money,

power, authority, contacts and publicity from a central point. The peril in political life is recognized and should not be risked here. If rotation in office is essential in group life it is even more important at Headquarters level. For examples "outside" cf. limited rectorships in the church and rotation of office in certain educational institutions.

6. Consistent with the preceding suggestions and our Tradition, the principle of anonymity should also prevail in so far as practicable in conducting business through Headquarters.

7. The Foundation should not participate in "outside" enterprises nor accept funds from "outside" sources but neither the Foundation nor any related corporation need amend its charter so as to restrict its legally permissible activities. The actual functions of all units have been sufficiently set forth hereinabove.

8. Change of name of the Foundation is left open There should be no difficulty about this. In this connection some thought might be given to the protection of the A. A. designation in the several states of the Union.

9. The convening of a General Service or Advisory Conference to function as above outlined is not disapproved and the method of its selection is left open.

There are undoubtedly many errors of omission and commission in the foregoing resume due to carelessness and in part due to the record itself which is not always clear, consistent and complete but, subject to such correction as may be necessary, it may serve the purpose, indicated in the title. - 4/17/48

A Statement of Principles Governing the Policies and Activities of the Board of Trustees of the Alcoholic Foundation

(Dated May 12, 1948 and submitted to Members of The Board of Trustees by Leonard V. Harrison, President of The Foundation and adopted by Board of Trustees July quarterly meeting 1948)

During the past months the Trustees of the Alcoholic Foundation have made a critical review of problems arising from the phenomenal growth of the A.A. Movement and from the swelling routine activities of the Foundation. In connection with that review the Trustees reached certain conclusions which are set forth below.

Basically the Trustees regard themselves as servants of A.A., first, in performing these secondary tasks which are necessary to support the principal objectives of the individual members of A.A., and secondly, in preserving the stability and integrity of the A.A. Movement. They affirm the aim of the Foundation to limit its organization and activities to the bare essentials required to perform its important but limited duties. The Trustees were also guided by their desire that the Foundation grow as little as possible while the Movement expands boundlessly in its healing mission to all who seek recovery from the ravages of alcohol.

The unanimous conclusion reached by the Trustees is that they can discharge their duties and avoid confusion as to the lines of responsibility affecting the Trustee function and the administrative function in matters of policy and execution by continuing to perform their services as they have heretofore done.

The discussions referred to were likewise fruitful in that they involved a reexamination of first principles, an emergence of a common understanding concerning them and a resolution to adhere to them.

These discussions also indicated that the rapid growth of the A.A. Movement with its attendant problems makes highly desirable a periodic evaluation of ideals and examination of practices lest its spiritual birthright be impaired. The Trustees, therefore, believe it would be of value to older members, and informative to newer members, to set forth at this time the principles which they have reviewed, by which they are guided, and which require repeated reaffirmation; and to restate the function of the Alcoholic Foundation in its relation to the A.A. Movement and its members.

At the outset we must distinguish between the A.A. Movement which is not an organized body and the activities of the Foundation which is an incorporated body dedicated to serving the members of A.A. individually and collectively through its subsidiary facilities.

The Movement is exclusively a spiritual endeavor whose only aim is to attain personal recovery and to carry the message of the way to recovery to others. The Movement is the all-important thing. It is in no sense governed by the Foundation which, in truth, is entirely guided by the Movement.

The Movement is a spiritual entity, comprising in substance the individual members of A.A. and the Groups, in the local activities of which most, but not all, members participate. The precepts of A.A. grew out of experience, the experience of individuals and the experience of Groups. So far, the basic principles of A.A. are reflected, as to personal rehabilitation, in the Twelve Steps to Recovery; as to its relations, in the Twelve Points to Secure Our Future, sometimes called the Twelve Points of Tradition.

The Movement represents a spiritual ideal in process of growth. It can be imperiled by secular problems of money, property and authority. These problems are involved with organization. Development of organizational structure is inimical to A.A. as a Movement. Organization, therefore, has been and should continue to be kept to a minimum. As the Movement grows the need for Organization diminishes. Most of the problems of relations are coming to be handled by local and regional groups and committees, functioning autonomously, which is as it should be.

The Twelve Points of Tradition developed out of concern for the common welfare of A.A. They are applicable at all levels: individual, group, regional and central. Among other things the Twelve Points reaffirm out of experience that God alone is our ultimate authority; that we have but one primary purpose—to carry the message to the alcoholic who still suffers; that the principle of Anonymity has primarily a spiritual significance—to practice a truly humble modesty; that A.A. should remain forever non-professional and that only special services in extraordinary circumstances should be paid for; that the least possible organization is required; that all contributions are to be purely voluntary and the accumulation of excess funds discouraged; and that matters of business, policy, money and property should be separated from the spiritual concerns of A.A. to the extent of delegating such affairs to appropriate instrumentality.

The Alcoholic Foundation is such an instrumentality at the national level. The Trustees (Directors) comprise five non-alcoholics and four alcoholics. The Trustees are subordinate to the Movement; they do not initiate activities nor administer them, nor, in the first instance, deal with questions of "medium" gravity. They do have jurisdiction over matters of large contract and important policy and in all matters they constitute a tribunal of final decision.

The Trustees are primarily custodians of money, policy and tradition. More concretely, they have custody of the funds contributed by Groups and derived from the sale of the book *Alcoholics Anonymous* and the monthly publication *The A.A. Grapevine*, although the latter is not yet self-supporting; they maintain a general headquarters office to deal with inquiries from individuals and Groups; they conduct certain necessary business and legal affairs; they endeavor to protect the Movement from objectionable publicity where the problem cannot feasibly be handled at a local level; in general, they strive to safeguard the established tradition and policies derived from the thoughts and experiences of members everywhere.

Again, more concretely, the Trustees feel that they will best safeguard the established tradition of A.A. by seeing to the application of the Twelve Points of Tradition to A.A. activities at their central point, insofar as practicable, in the following respects; compliance in spirit and letter with the principle of Anonymity; rotation in office or position; observance of appropriate standards in compensation of paid workers; limitation of volume and scope of activities at the general headquarters office; and inauguration of a program of gradual decentralization of headquarters activities to the end that the responsibility of "carrying the message" may be gradually assumed by local groups and committees.

Finally, the Trustees feel that in order fully to carry on the duties with which they are charged the independence of the Foundation must be observed in respect of its constituency and its proceedings.

It is the considered judgement of your Trustees that if the A.A. Movement remains unshackled by the fetters of organization and is kept free from the corroding effect of political procedures which stem from over-organization, it will grow in vast numbers and beneficent influence among those who are open to its message.

(This Statement of Principles was transcribed from a copy that was sent to Clarence by Royal S. who was a member of the "Orthodox Movement.")

Appendix I

Who wrote what in the Big Book

Hank Parkhurst (outline for draft ms., The Unbeliever)—NYC/NJ
Dr. Silkworth (The Doctor's Opinion)
Bill Wilson (Chapter 1 Bill's Story, Chapter 8 To Wives)—NYC
Team work (Chapters 2-7, 9 and 11)—NYC, Akron, Cleveland
Robert H. Smith (Dr. Bob's Nightmare)—Akron
Hank Parkhurst (The Unbeliever)—NYC/NJ
Fitz M. (Our Southern Friend)—Washington, DC/Maryland
Clarence Snyder (Home Brewmeister)—Cleveland
Ernie G. (The Seven Month Slip)—Akron
Charlie S. (Riding The Rods)—Akron
Bob O. (The Salesman)—Akron
Arch T. (The Fearful One)—Detroit/Grosse Point
Dick S. (The Car Smasher)—Akron
Joe D. (The European Drinker)—Akron
Florence R. (A Feminine Victory)—NYC
Bill R. (A Business Man's Recovery)—NYC
Harry B. (A Different Slant)—probably NYC
Jim S. (Traveler, Editor, Scholar)—Akron
Walter B. (The Back-Slider)—Akron
Tom and Maybell L. (My Wife and I)—Akron
Bill Van H. (A Ward of the Probate Court)—Akron
Wally G. (Fired Again)—Akron
Paul S. (Truth Freed Me!)—Akron
Harold S. (Smile With Me, At Me)—NYC
Harry Z. (A Close Shave) – Akron (later moved to NY)
Norman H. (Educated Agnostic) – Akron
Ralph F. (Another Prodigal Story) – NYC
Myron W. (Hindsight) – NYC
Horace M. (On His Way) – NYC
Marie B. (An Alcoholic's Wife) – Akron
Ray C. (An Artist's Concept) – NYC/Carmel NY
Lloyd T. (The Rolling Stone) – Akron/Cleveland
Ethel M. (From Farm To City) – Ohio
Bill D. (Alcoholics Anonymous Number Three) – Akron
Sylvia K. (The Keys of the Kingdom) – Chicago
Earl T. (He Sold Himself Short) – Chicago
Esther E. (A Flower of the South) – Texas
Abby G. (He Thought He Could Drink Like A Gentleman) – Cleveland
Marty M. (Women Suffer Too) – NYC

Appendix J

Part of Bill's original story, page 30

935.   Nevertheless here I was sitting opposite a

936. man who talked about a personal God who told me

937. how hw had found Him, who described to me how I

938. might do the same thing and who convinced me

939. utterly that something had come into his life

940. which had accomplished a miracle. The man was

941. trasformed ; there was no denying he had been re-

942. born. He was radiant of something which soothed

943. my troubled spirit as tho the fresh clean wind of a

944. mountain top blowing thru and thru me _ I saw and

945. felt and in a great surge of joy I realized

946. that the great presence which had made itself felt

947. to me that war time day in Winchester Cathedral

948. had again returned.

949.   As he continued I commenced to see myself as in

950. as in an unearthly mirror. I saw how ridiculous and

951. futile the whole basis of my life had been. Standing in

952. the middle of the stage of my lifes setting I had been

953. feverishly trying to arrange ideas and things and people

954. and even God, to my own liking, to my own ends and to

955. promote what I had thought to be true happiness. It was

956. truly a sudden and breath taking illumination. Then the

957. idea came - " the tragic thing about you is, that you

958. have been playing God." That was it. Playing God. Then

NOTES

1. Richard R. Peabody, *The Common Sense of Drinking* (1930), pp. 185-186.
2. Proverbs 23:29-35, from the King James Version of the Bible.
3. Viktor E. Frankl, *Man's Search for Meaning: An Introduction to Logotherapy* (Boston: Beacon Press, 1959, 1963).
4. Jack London, *John Barleycorn* (New York: Century, 1913) p. 15.
5. Ibid. p. 14.
6. Robert V. Seliger, M.D., *Alcoholics Are Sick People* (Baltimore: Alcoholism Publications, 1945), p. 47.
7. Sigmund Freud, *Beyond the Pl*
8. Author's note: There has been some questioning regarding the actual events relating to these phone calls Bill had made to the Rev. Tunks and to Henrietta Seiberling. Oxford Group members were known to have been very close. They even worked together in teams. It seems unlikely that the Rev. Shoemaker would have allowed Bill to go out to Akron without at least one or two phone numbers of Group members. Henrietta Seiberling, in a letter to Clarence, stated that the stories about the *Pleasure Principle* (New York: Bantam Books, 1959) p. 72.
9. Charles L. Allen, *God's Psychiatry* (New York: Fleming H. Revell, 1953), p. 158.
10. A[rthur] J[ames] Russell, *For Sinners Only* (New York: Harper & Brothers, 1932), p. 62.
11. The Layman With A Notebook, *What Is The Oxford Group?* (London: Oxford University Press, 1933), p. 3. phone calls and conversations were "all made up," and "phony." The date of Dr. Bob's last drink is also in question. Officially, it has been regarded as June 10, 1935. Recent discoveries have shown however that the convention of the American Medical Association held in Atlantic City did not start until June 10, 1935. It would have been difficult for Dr. Bob to be at the convention on Monday, June 10th and also have gotten his

last drink from Bill on that same date. Though the June 10 date might be only symbolic, the actual date of Dr. Bob's last drink would have probably been on or around June 17, 1935.

12. The Layman With A Notebook, *What Is The Oxford Group?* (London: Oxford University Press, 1933).

13. *Twelve Steps and Twelve Traditions* (New York: Alcoholics Anonymous World Services, 1953), pp. 191-192.

14. *Alcoholics Anonymous* (New York: Works Publishing Company, 1939), p. 146. [Pages 132-133 in the present 4th edition]

15. This pamphlet, *The Four Absolutes*, may be ordered from the Cleveland Central Committee of Alcoholics Anonymous.

16. See the story of the first century *tzaddik* Honi Ha-Ma'agel (Honi the Circle Drawer) and the Carob Tree in Talmud Bavli, Masekhet Ta'anit 23a.

17. Peter Howard, *Ideas Have Legs* (New York: Coward, McCann, 1946).

18. *Alcoholics Anonymous* (New York: Works Publishing, Inc., 1939), Foreword, p. vii.

19. Milton A. Maxwell, Ph.D., Assistant Professor of Sociology at the State College of Washington in Pullman, Washington, "The Washingtonian Movement," *Quarterly Journal of Studies on Alcohol*, Vol. 11, 410-452, 1950.

20. Irving Harris, *The Breeze of the Spirit: Sam Shoemaker and the Story of Faith-at-Work* (New York: Seabury Press, 1978).

21. William James, *The Varieties of Religious Experience: A Study in Human Nature*, being the Gifford Lecture on Natural Religion delivered at Edinburgh 1901-1902 (London: Longmans, Green, 1902).

22. Kate Barklay, ed., *The Temperance Token: or Crystal Drops From the Old Oaken Bucket* (Geneva, New York: George H. Derby and Co., 1846).

23. James Allen, *As A Man Thinketh* (Toronto: Musson Book Company, 1902), p. 57.

24. Ibid., p. 58.

25. Cleveland's *Central Bulletin*, Volume 1, Number 11, August 1943.

26. Bill Wilson's secretary from 1947 to Bill's death in 1971, and A.A.'s first Archivist.

27. Letter to Ruth Hock from Clarence dated December 2, 1939.

28. Ernest Kurtz, *Not-God: A History of Alcoholics Anonymous* (Center City, Minnesota: Hazelden, 1979), p. 83.

29. [Bill Wilson], *Twelve Steps and Twelve Traditions* (New York: Alcoholics Anonymous World Services, 1952, 1953, 1981), p. 9.

30. Ibid., p. 189.

31. 1 Corinthians 12:12 and 12:24-25 in the King James Version of the Bible.

32. See Appendix C.

33. Two Listeners, *God Calling*, ed. by the Oxford Group author Arthur James Russell (London: R. J. James, 1935), p. 10.

34. From a letter dated Oct. 17th to Margaret "Bobbie" B. at the Foundation in New York City written by T. Frank B. of Cleveland Heights, Ohio (probably in 1942).

35. Bill Wilson, "After Twenty-Five Years," AA *Grapevine*, March 1960.

36. Jack Alexander, "Alcoholics Anonymous: Freed Slaves of Drink, Now They Free Others," *Saturday Evening Post*, vol. 213, no. 35 (March 1, 1941): 92.

37. From *Construction News*, issued weekly by the Kiwanis Club of East Cleveland, Ohio.

38. Thomas Jefferson, letter to James Monroe, 1813.

39. Friedrich Wilhelm Nietzsche, *Beyond Good and Evil* (Chicago, Illinois: Henry Regnery, 1955) p. 75.

40. Clarence may here have been referring to Bill Wilson's bouts with depression and pills which Clarence stated happened several times during Bill's "sobriety."

41. Ernest Kurtz and Katherine Ketcham, *The Spirituality of Imperfection: Modern Wisdom from Classic Stories* (Bantam Books, 1992), p. 109f.

42. *Alcoholics Anonymous* (New York: Works Publishing Company, 1939), p. 84.

43. Ibid., p. 60.

44. Ibid., p. 60.

45. Matthew 25:21 (King James Version of the Bible).

46. Gregory Stock, Ph.D., *The Book of Questions* (New York: Workman Publishing, 1987), p. 79.

47. Harold Begbie, *Twice Born Men: A Clinic in Regeneration* (New York: Fleming H. Revell, 1909), pp. 99f.

48. Garth Lean, *On the Tail of a Comet*, p. 73.

49. According to Mel B.'s biography—*Ebby: The Man Who Sponsored Bill W.*, Hazelden Pittman Archives (Center City, Minnesota: Hazelden, 1998)—Ebby "had two years and seven months of continuous sobriety in the beginning, a long period of about seven years' sobriety in Texas in the 1950's, and about 2 1/2 years' sobriety just before he died" in 1966. Mel B. states that in a letter from Bill Wilson to an A.A. member in Texas, it says that Ebby was paying for his own care at McPike's Farm (a treatment facility in Ballston Spa, New York) with his Social Security and with "financing of $200 a month that comes out of the A.A. book money at headquarters." Ebby died at a hospital near Ballston Spa and McPike's Farm, where he had been living under the care of Margaret McPike.

50. The Layman With A Notebook, *What Is the Oxford Group?* (London: Oxford University Press, 1933).

51. The steps are taken from the book *Alcoholics Anonymous Comes of Age* (New York: A.A. Publishing, 1957), pp. 160 ff.

52. In the first edition on page 72, the word "these" is used. In the second through sixteenth printings of the first edition, the word "those" is used. In all sixteen printings of the second edition and all of the following printings of the third edition, the word "these" is used on page 60.

53. The masculine form is used throughout for simplicity, although it is intended to include women as well.

Disclaimer

The Publication of this volume does not imply, nor does it suggest any affiliation with, nor approval of or endorsement from, Alcoholics Anonymous World Services, Inc. Alcoholics Anonymous is a registered trademark of Alcoholics Anonymous World Services, Inc., and the Twelve Steps are copyrighted and used with permission. All quotes from the book Alcoholics Anonymous are from the first and second edition, which are in the public domain. This writing of this book was at the direct request of, and authorized by, Clarence H. Snyder. The author was sponsored by Clarence and is himself a member of Alcoholics Anonymous. In deference to A.A.'s Tradition of Anonymity, members of Alcoholics Anonymous are identified only with their first name and last initial. Any members of Alcoholics Anonymous who are identified with their full names have given permission to be identified as such. This is the only biography of Clarence H. Snyder authorized by him. Any other biography relating to Clarence H. Snyder has no affiliation with this authorized and commissioned version.

When Alcoholics Anonymous published its Fourth Edition of their Basic Text, ALCOHOLICS ANONYMOUS, they chose to remove Clarence Snyder's story "Home Brewmeister".

When A.A. co-founder Bill W. wrote *ALCOHOLICS* ANONYMOUS COMES OF AGE, he wrote:

"Yes, Cleveland's results were of the best. Their results were in fact so good, and A.A.'s membership elsewhere was so small, that many a Clevelander really thought A.A.'s membership had started there in the first place. The Cleveland pioneers had proved three essential things: the value of personal sponsorship, the worth of the A.A.'s Big Book in indoctrinating newcomers, and finally the tremendous fact that A.A., when the word really got around, could now soundly grow to great size."

The explanation the author has heard removing stories from the Big Book was to better reflect the current membership of Alcoholics Anonymous. If anyone studies A.A. history and compares the rates of continuous sobriety between those in early Cleveland A.A. and the rate which reflects the current Fellowship, Bill W. said it best – *"Yes, Cleveland's results were of the best"*.

Clarence Snyder said that A.A. is "Not a stop drinking club". The A.A. BIG BOOK says on page 82 that "We feel a man is unthinking when he says that sobriety is enough." The A.A. Basic Text also says that its pages outline a "Way of life" and a "Design for living". Its pages don't show us how to stop drinking alcohol. They show us how to develop a new way of living not based on just stopping drinking.

If you, the reader, feel that you want the best results, please talk and/or write to your General Service Delegates and the A.A. World Service Trustees about restoring Clarence's story into the Basic Text of Alcoholics Anonymous. Compare what reflects the makeup of the current Fellowship with what is described within the pages of this volume and you want the best results and the best results for future generations of potential members of A.A., maybe we can restore A.A. to its design for living and way of life.

Think about it!!

Mitchell K.

PO Box 459
Grand Central Station
New York, NY 10163

www.aa.org
Attn: General Manager

If you have any questions or comments, please send them to Mitchell K. at howitworkedbook@gmail.com.

We will attempt to get back to you at our earliest convenience. We also hope that this volume raises more questions than it gives answers. We hope that it prompts the reader to learn more about AA history through their own research and studies and not just rely upon what this or any one writer says.

This writer claims progress, not perfection. He is just another member of the Fellowship of Alcoholics Anonymous. Nothing more and nothing less.

68149404R00236

Made in the USA
Middletown, DE
14 September 2019